Google Books

Google Books
Google Book Search and Its Critics

Peter Batke

ISBN: 978-0-557-32528-3

To Susanne

TABLE OF CONTENTS

INTRODUCTION

**PART ONE: A CLOSE READING OF DARNTON, GRAFTON ET AL.
ON BOOK DIGITIZATION.**

Background: Printed Words and Electronic Text	15
Early WP	17
Beyond WP: The Undiscovered Country	18
The Digitization of C. S. Peirce	20
Perspective on the Current Discussion	26
What is a Close Reading?	33

SECTION ONE: DARNTON

The Professor of the History of Books	36
The Historical Librarian	46
Exit the Historian, Enter the Librarian	49
Darnton's Final Arguments: Eight Points	57
Enter the Paladin: 2009	77
Spinning Google For the Europeans	89
Hold the Presses: "Google and the New Digital Future"	96

SECTION TWO: GRAFTON

Another Humanist Weighs In	99
Preamble	100
"Adventures in Wonderland"	103
The Dissent	106
"Future Reading"	108
The 1960s	111
Electronic Texts Demand Informed Users	118
Wrapping Up "Future Reading"	123
Reading a Positive Future	124
Worlds Made by Words	128
2007 Rewritten in 2009	130
Fine Bindings	133
"Codex in Crisis" is Divided Into Three Parts	136

**NOW, FOR SOMETHING ENTIRELY DIFFERENT:
OTHER VOICES**

The Libraries	143
A Voice from Paris	144
Books of Europe Unite	151
Wrap Up	153
Brin in the New York Times	154

MEANWHILE, BACK AT THE TRESTLE:
THE CODEX HANGS...

The Google Empire   157
e-Publishing   162
Cultural Pessimism   166
Grafton Live   171
The Blog   174
If and When   180
Time for Some Ripe Tomatoes   182
The Phoenix Rises   184

PART TWO: THERE IS SOMETHING ABOUT
GOOGLE BOOK SEARCH

Jump right in!   190
The Judgment of a Founding Father, Declined.   191
[Digression on Public Discourse]   193
Why Old Books?   197
The Moving Target   198
Setting the Stage   202

THE ARCHIVES

Archive Example No. 1. [http://archive.com]   204
Archive Example No. 2. [http://www.literature.at]   205
Archive Example No. 3. [http://gallica.bnf.fr]   207
[Three Digressions: Privacy, the Non-material, the Text Search]   208
Archive Example No. 4. [http://www.gutenberg.org]   213

A GOOGLE RHAPSODY

A Brief Discussion of Nuts and Bolts   218
Volume Sets vs. Pages   224
Rethinking Editorial Practice   229
Reprise and Theory: The Field of Play   235
Information, Then and Now and To Come.   245
Books, Read and Unread   254
Old Books   261
The Match   281
Where is Google Taking Antiquarian Books?   293

e-BIBLIOGRAPHY WITH COMMENTS:

Links to the Darnton Essays: 297
Links to the Grafton Essays: 298
Other Links: 300

Five years ago Google started scanning library books. To date some ten million books have been scanned. Introductory materials, history, future plans and tutorials are to be found at http://books.google.com.

A good deal of controversy is swirling about the project. There has been an ongoing suit by publishers and authors and a proposed settlement of the suit that has stirred up more controversy than it proposes to settle. Everyone is taking sides. February 2010 was the last milestone in the legal donnybrook. A judgment is awaited ....

This presentation will concentrate on the intellectual controversy the scanning has aroused and the great potential for benefit to the humanities. The legal issues will drift into the background.

The world of books will never be the same ....

The Fight about Old Library Books

The issues between Google and various interested parties making public statements or filing briefs in the US District Court in New York is nothing if not a fight. I am not in a position to comment on the legal aspects of the fight; the clocks run differently in that world. The "final" hearing in the review of the settlement by the District Court of New York was February 2010.

I am, however, interested in following some of the public discussion of the issues over the last few years, leading up to the fight. I also propose to shed some light on how to navigate all the new possibilities of working with electronic texts of really new and really old books. The really new benefit from electronic marketing and delivery, the really old are available free to all. Alas, the centenarian out of print orphans, old, but not old enough to be free, will have to wait till their fate has been decided in court.

There is nothing like watching a fight, that is, if there are no knives and guns involved. Before gangs and guns and drugs, in an earlier time, fights were very rare, at least in my zip code. I can only remember one fight in my long three years in high school and none in College. Granted it was a different time. Once every three years, two guys would simply get in each other's way, neither would back down, and some issue would now be settled by wrestling on asphalt. For all the historical remoteness of my own youth and for all the reflexive violence among young people today, the notion of "the fight" is embedded in the human psyche.

Issues can be resolved through analysis, or they can be resolved through a fight. The conflict of will in a fight, if it is a John Wayne, Hollywood, fifties kind of "fair fight," will establish some sort of principle of the triumph of the good in which both parties in the fight can eventually partake; that is the aesthetic of the fight. That is also the aesthetic of the court approved settlement. The belletristic equivalent of a fight is the philippic, the tirade, the obloquy, the diatribe, stricture, vituperation, the fulminating fustian, where words are no longer used for analysis but to attack, to attempt to remove something from existence, or at least diminish it, because existence cannot be shared happily with that something in the fantasy world of written thought. We get a lot of that these days with no settlement in sight.

The fight going on in the parking lot between Google and all comers about millions of library books has gone beyond analysis. Clearly, the crowd does not want a settlement, they want the fight to continue, in hope of part of the action. I prefer to limit myself to analysis. In my analysis, the more books that have been scanned and the easier they are for me to download and to look through, the better is the world. I am not averse to paying a reasonable fee for copyrighted materials. I have e-books on all my various electronic devices, on both the US and International Kindle, the Sony Reader, the Nook, the netbook, on several laptops of various weights and screen size, and on the last remaining desktop in my office. I am considering an iPhone. Amazon is keeping tabs on my growing library of e-books.

Let me sketch one aspect of the world of electronic texts, to get a toe in the water. The "Kindle Experience," if I may be so bold as to use a marketing concept, clearly shows the way. Within two minutes of taking my brand new Kindle out of the box I had purchased in electronic form, several books that I had ordered in hard, heavy copy the previous month from Amazon and had delivered by mail. The books were there to read within seconds, literally. The experience of ordering a book online from Amazon and having it show up at my door step two or three days later is already pretty good. To have that self-same book in front of my eyeballs in electronic ink on the Kindle within literally seconds of having the desire or the impulse to buy that book all the while sitting at my desk simply amazes me. I purchased the electronic copies only to be able to compare the reading experience on which I will elaborate below. The Kindle interface is available for Windows, the iPhone and soon on other devices and Macs.

It is so obvious to me that this is a good thing. I can see things only getting better; today I can buy many currently published books in electronic form and have them sitting on my Kindle in ten seconds through a gratis international G3 connection ($1.99 surcharge per delivery in Europe with a gratis USB workaround around that silliness). Since it is possible to download purchases for free over the Internet and transfer the file in seconds to the Kindle I have concluded that only silly people would pay the surcharge and only badly informed telecom companies would negotiate such an absurd deal. Let us try not to think about what went on when that deal was struck.

Thanks to Google's work in the last five years, I can have books published in the eighteenth and nineteenth centuries going up to 1923 in PDF form on my laptop in ninety seconds. The PDFs can also be read on the Kindle. If this trend continues, if the pace of scanning is maintained and if the quality of scans improves over time, I would consider many of my logistical problems as a digital humanities researcher solved. Given that many publications or data streams outside these two channels are also available via networked computer, I can only say, from my balcony, it seems that some good work has been done. Thank you, thank you, thank you all, this one is pleased. [Wave to the crowd.]

That leaves only the out of print books published after 1923 which are owned by the estates of writers for seventy years after the author's death, according to a relatively recent Act of Congress (no workaround here). This act of Congress was the latest in a series of modifications [read: extensions] of copyright that has swept away the long established fourteen-year copyright with one fourteen-year extension. This had been the balance between the rights of authors and the rights of the public. In every case, even under the fourteen-fourteen rule, the rights of the author were suspended through exemptions for materials provided for students in educational settings.

The questions are myriad, the problems are intractable, the perceptions of the public interest is clouded, and, alas, books are the last and the least on the list of copyright holders. There are, of course literary estates that do cultivate the work of their authors with new editions and research. Yet there are vast numbers, high percentages of out of print books that neither deserve nor ever expected to renew a revenue stream. It is only through the technical breakthroughs in digital photography and the huge investment by Google that appetites for renewed revenue from unused and largely useless artifacts have been whetted.

Personally I find the spectacle unseemly. I have been able to find areas of research in the nineteenth century where rare and expensive antiquarian sources have been digitized. Especially in Ottoman History, (from the perspectives of the neighbors of the Ottoman Empire), these sources still represent some of the best work extant. The fall of the Old Order after the First World War has put that bit of historiography on the back burner, where it has remained at a slow simmer. The entire beginning history of European studies of the Orient can now be examined from Google Book Search. There must be innumerable other fields that have had their origins revived in electronic form. I much prefer to spend my own time exploring these new electronic avenues than become embroiled in the questionable entitlements abridging the public weal. Nor do I have the confidence that some judge will immerse in the history and intention of copyright to the point of restoring the interests of the public and the ideals of the Founding Fathers in the free exchange of printed words, sentences and ideas. I fully expect some technical ruling to set the stage for more suits.

But that is analysis; it ignores the psychology of the "fight." No one listens to analysis while the fight is going on. The classrooms are empty; everybody is in the parking lot watching the fight. The typical reaction to a hundred pages of how to benefit from Google Books is: "But there is a fight going on." Instead of watching the fight we should be thinking about Google Books: 1) what is wrong with it, 2) what is right with it, 3) what one can do with it, 4) what should we do now that over ten million books have been scanned? Alas, I fear those questions will have to be postponed for some time, this fight promises to go extra innings.

In the meanwhile there are several safe areas, for the analysis of book digitization, parts of the parking lot where there will be no errant round-house blows striking an innocent eye, or no stray bullets should it get out of hand, lonely areas far from the madding crowd. We shall hang out here for analysis, undisturbed. The safe areas are "really new books" and "really old books," ironically.

Really New Books

For the really new books, those in print, the incentives for digitization are largely economic and are clearly understood by the people making big money to understand these things. There is no controversy here; no stranger's purses to be cut. It is cheaper to make, sell and deliver electronic books. The whole logistical area of printing and shipping and inventory falls away. For the buyer, the advantages are also in economy since the savings in production costs are generally passed on in a roughly 30 percent price reduction; for a three–pound, fifty-dollar textbook on data mining that is a considerable advantage.

For texts that are to be read in their entirety, the Kindle experience is superb. The font can be adjusted, definitions of words in the text are immediate, bookmarking and annotations are available. The text and the screen are pleasing, easy to read, even in the sun, and the button to turn the pages has been placed optimally for animals with eight fingers and two opposable thumbs. The Kindle remembers where you left off reading in all your books, up to 350. As indicated above, that experience is available on a range of devices from smart phones to laptops.

I am not blind to some advantages of printed books. Especially for technical books, the random thumbing through pages after having given up on the index is still a favorite practice of novices and professionals. The cause for the practice is the combined failure of the table of contents and the index. It is one of the great areas of serendipity achieved routinely when all hope of finding crucial information should have long been given up. Such lucky shots are lost with electronic books, and that has been lamented in technical circles ever since more and more documentation went online twenty years ago.

It turns out that the printed documentation for the AEGIS Destroyer would have exceeded the capacity of the ship to carry it, for example. Perhaps the technical people were happy to rediscover the power of the "grep." "grep" is a UNIX command widely used by programmers at a time when most programs that were to run on a central computer would be stored in a common read-only directory. If you needed to check the syntax of some programming statement, a "grep" would bring up all the lines of "other people's code" with that statement. Those were still the artisanal days when we are all living on the commune.

The thumbing, for all its virtues is difficult to defend: "Well, I open the book at random and start flipping pages till my eye catches something that might be useful, and Bingo!" Granted, much of human intellectual activity goes along these lines, but the arguments have a mystical quality touching on the nature of the subconscious. That is gone now since clicking pages, while functionally equivalent, is not as satisfying to the subconscious. It has been replaced by searching, supplemented by complete indexing of the book.

Searching and finding in online documentation can be learned and productivity can be increased. Ever since O'Reilly published its CD of Perl documentation, all my thumbed Perl manuals but one that was once yellow have been relegated to shelves out of easy reach.

In non-technical areas, thumbing is clearly not best practice. If there are 282 references to "Intention" in a book, you will be able to inspect each reference with a search. Neither thumbing nor sequential reading are a great help due to the limits of hu man memory. Only a general impression of "intention" can be achieved unless one takes the trouble to pinpoint and inspect every single last occurrence. Of course if you are thoughtless and hope to gain by intermixing "Intention" with "Intentionen" (German) in the name of lemmatization of plurals, you can see that list of references as well. The same applies for "truth" and "truths." All in all, in the question of thumbing vs. searching, the rational arguments are on the side of searching.

Really Old Books

Similar considerations apply for the "really old books," which are by definition, books published before 1923 and securely in the public domain. There are several caveats. The economic advantages are all on the side of the "buyer." In electronic form, thanks to Google, old books are generally free, although there has been an attempt by print on demand companies to hoard electronic texts and offer them for sale as alternatives to actual antiquarian editions. Some are repackaged electronic files available for free elsewhere. This phenomenon can be observed in full flower on abe.com, on amazon/kindle and in general Web queries. For public domain books, Google is really our last best hope for getting these volumes for free electronically so we can print them out ourselves should we be daft enough. There are other players in the free archive game, many players, but the very nature of free, legally free files, is that they migrate where they will, even behind toll gates.

The second caveat is not price but quality. The maxim of: "If it's free it's not worth anything" applies not only to European higher education, but also to scans of antiquarian books. It is actually a mixed message, a complex message. Google scans are generally delivered as PDF files. For most scans, the PDF files are generally good with notable exceptions. The problems range from missing pages, missing tables, illustrations and maps, blurred pages, round or square holes in the text, halves of pages missing, parts of fingers obscuring the text, tight binding causing margins to curve or disappear entirely; the list could go on. The fact is that not all old books are easy scans. Great care and some virtuosity have to be applied to a variety of printed books that will not fit easily on a platen. In some cases one even has to sacrifice the book to save the scan.

An additional problem with old books is that the printing in many cases is not crisp. In addition, specific glyphs used in the nineteenth century and before wreak havoc with OCR programs. In many German and English editions of that time, it is difficult to distinguish the difference between the letters f and s. (e.g. Ricaut, 1686) After some considerable work with the problem over many hundred pages of my own scans, and working at high magnification, I have come to the conclusion that typesetters did not really care whether an s might have a soupçon of a crossing mark or not. Nor did they care if an f had no hint at all of a cross bar. Only context can decide between an f and an s or a transcribed z. This is actually not so great a problem since programs can be written to disambiguate normal use. It is however a very tricky job with Middle Eastern proper names and place names, especially given the uncertain methods of Romanization and the notorious ambiguities of naming places in the Middle East, places that had been renamed many times, even before the Greeks showed up, the ancient ones. One can also not know if a crisply printed f or s has not been subject to erroneous transcription previously. All these problems can be solved, but only through dedicated, highly trained and motivated effort, which is not cheap. One cannot expect the file handling jocks at Google, who are working with image files that were created at a rate of seven seconds for two pages, to achieve even remotely adequate OCR of difficult printed texts.

It is charming to see some scans of nineteenth-century German texts from the BSB in Munich that were done with great care, with beautiful PDFs and beautifully prepared epub, with a touching note about "preserving our textual heritage" embedded in the electronic text, only to notice that European diacritics were not turned on during the OCR phase or were lost on the way to the e-pub reader. That is bad. Even worse is that I would even consider the notion that we should do away with diacritics for all European languages; it would simplify the collating sequences. For data mining there must always be some work done on collecting alternate spellings (but not necessarily plurals) under headwords. European telephone books, increasingly relics, have made a veritable pig's lunch of the issue by sorting the diacritics after the vowel. Germany has reorganized its spellings most recently to such a degree that no one, not even teachers in the Germanophone countries are certain how things are to be spelled. This is tolerated as inevitable by a continent with low expectations for sensible solutions. The geeks and geekettes in the lab are clamoring for English headwords for everything, but I realize that this is an extreme position—inevitable, but extreme.

Of paramount importance is the electronic text "underneath" each image of a scanned page. With modern books that are in print that is generally no problem. In some cases they are "published" on paper and simultaneously published as an electronic file. In addition, OCR of crisply printed text with wide margins is now close to 100 percent accuracy. Errors occur chiefly through specks on the paper, motes on the platen or rare badly inked individual letters. There are no easy solutions to all the technical problems with turning books printed before 1923 into acceptable electronic text. Without the clean electronic text, many options for researchers are limited. The "search" of a text becomes a crap shoot less reliable than thumbing. Word lists become unusable for automatic processing since so many letters are missing that only context can provide clarity.

In short, the delivery of PDFs is a halting initial step. This fact is often missed in discussions of Google scanning. One has to be careful here. There are no arguments here against scanning. A badly scanned book is no argument for not rescanning that book. Even a bad PDF with the first five pages missing of a rare volume in front of my eyeballs right now is better than that same volume in printed form in San Diego possibly with the same missing pages ripped out, especially if I am sitting in Baltimore.

The arguments are only for more scanning, better scanning. In order to make these arguments we need dispassionate analysis that scanning is worth doing and that the resulting method-ological opportunities will advance humanistic studies. These arguments are hard to make while the fight is going on. During the fight, bad OCR is a weapon that can be hurled at the opponent; nostalgia for the antiquarian book can be used to kick the opponent in the shins; the list goes on.

INTRODUCING THE PALADINS

Before we can go on to the analysis, we have to get some understanding of the fight. The fight is really a good old free-for-all. Much of the fight goes on in badly spelled sentence fragments in blogs. There are however two especially worthy combatants who have brought many retainers and much pageantry to the lists. This discussion will start with the contributions of Professor Darnton, Harvard, and Professor Grafton, Princeton, to the melee. From there, we shall continue on to a general introduction to book digitization, its usefulness by means of specific examples and some attempt to mediate the seemingly irreconcilable differences between book digitization and the mission of research libraries. The projections are in preponderance for a long and winding road with a happy end.

The Texts of Darnton and Grafton

This first part of this presentation will focus on a set of texts by Prof. Robert Darnton, Director of the Harvard University Libraries and Professor of History at Harvard and a set of texts by Prof. Anthony Grafton, Professor of History at Princeton and editor of the "Journal of the History of Ideas." The two series of texts are unusual in that the treatments of the subject of book digitization by Google and digital humanities in general have come in rapid fire, with only a few months in some cases between essays. While one would expect journalists to publish at that rate, it is rare for the extremely learned to give us updates of their thoughts at such intervals.

Nevertheless, the words on digitization by two eminent scholars, clearly in the league of the extremely learned, must be examined closely. We have an opportunity, though no guarantee, to get some answers that one will not find on the average blog: 1) Is digitization a help to humanities studies? 2) Does digitization help the extremely learned, or is it for beginners gathering initial acquaintance with a field? 3) Given the disorganized lethargy that characterizes many academic ventures, does Google (or digital humanities) have a positive impact on the range of activities from the acquisition of information to the formation of knowledge to the attainment of learning? 4) Is there an assumption at work in the more exclusive circles of the academy which asserts that academics working in their traditions are the sole stewards of knowledge and learning, and any technology and any other upstarts that hope to open wide, democratic avenues to knowledge and learning are sadly deluded and will not get the time of day, their degree and much less their tenure? The last question is loaded; it serves merely to show my own bias. It seems that "De la Gramatologie" has had no real impact other than to mobilize the aesthetes, and thank the deities for that, very much indeed.

In the essays discussed below I shall examine some ambiguous views of the facts on the ground. Clearly everyone understands that life, as we know it, artistic, intellectual, academic, commercial, mechanical, agricultural or even the life of parents raising children can no longer be done without all sorts of electronic devices and online resources. Given this fact, let us examine how the extremely learned evaluate their work and that of their students with these devices and with online materials. At first blush, after a brief glance at all the print works to be included in Prof. Darnton's "Electronic Enlightenment," there seems to be at least one field in which digitization will benefit the most initiated experts.

Of course we shall have to separate Prof. Darnton's role as a scholar of the Enlightenment from his role as director of the Harvard University Libraries. We shall have to be alert for a divided soul: the defender of the institution which depends, or better, once depended exclusively on printed matter versus the modern scholar who depends increasingly on electronic repositories, perhaps even on electronic methodologies. My own experience has been that digitization adds significant value to humanistic artifacts, for example to texts and images, but I will save the detailed arguments for later.

Similar issues will confront us with Prof. Grafton, who makes a case for the non-digital resource as such, the vellum, the aroma of the codex, the quiet of the eye scanning the printed page, and other non-electronic sensory details increasingly rare in a world lousy with networked laptops, including his own.

We are fortunate in having several polished essays written over a period of time that will provide us with a long and lingering look at the opinions and judgments presented.

At the end of the book you will find links to the texts that are available online. There will be no page references to the online texts; please download the texts and use "search" to pinpoint quotes. You may use this presentation to explore techniques of reading in the electronic age. Suggestion: download the texts (including the header information) into a single file, read the file, make notes in the file and keep it at the ready while reading my commentary.

The first section starts with Prof. Darnton's 1999 essay in the *New York Review of Books*, "The New Age of the Book." That essay is really only a prelude from a time ten years ago when large scale digitization was unthinkable; it is a bit of history from a time when Prof. Darnton suspected no dark technological clouds gathering over the academy. It serves as a contrast to the later pieces. Of greater current interest are two other essays by Prof. Darnton in the NYRB in 2008 and 2009. The section on Prof. Darnton will conclude with his speech at the Frankfurt Book Fair in October 2009 where he vehemently and repeatedly attacks Google's scanning of books as monopolistic. The Frankfurt lecture is not available in electronic form but is published in a collection of Darnton Essays, "The Case for the Book," Public Affairs, New York, 2009 (e-book by Amazon). The collection of essays goes back to gather up all his shorter pieces on books, their history and more recently their great peril. It includes the well known 1982 essay from *Daedalus*, "What is the History of Books?" One more NYRB essay by Prof. Darnton managed to slip under the wire, December 2009, "Google and the New Digital Future," an update on the path of the settlement through the court in November. Lets hope Prof. Darnton takes a couple of weeks off this winter.

The second section will treat essays by Prof. Grafton from 2007 to 2009, beginning with the 2007 *New Yorker* piece "Future Reading" and the 2009 greatly expanded version of that piece, "Codex in Crisis," published separately in a limited print run in 2008 and included in *Worlds Made by Words*, 2009, Harvard University Press. A brief glance at Prof. Grafton's 2009 essay in *Daedalus*, "Apocalypse in the Stacks?" will round out this flurry of text on Google and the larger issues the book digitization project by Google has precipitated. The picture will be supplemented by some early voices, Prof. Jeanneney, former Director of the French National Library and others, from as early as 2005. One should not forget to mention an editorial by Sergei Brin in the *New York Times*, 2008, which appeared shortly after the announcement of the "proposed" settlement, better called the "embattled" settlement today. Brin's short uncomplicated defense of Google's work is a welcome antidote to the fears and despair one can read from the texts of the opponents.

A final note to the reader: I have resisted embroidering this essay with footnotes of explanation. Most of the things mentioned, obscure or technical or obvious, including "Google Books" can be googled with satisfactory results.

Rather than print the illustrations, I will embed only the links. All potential illustrations and other supplemental materials can be seen on the humancomp.org Web site.

http://www.humancomp.org/batke/sagbs

The short bibliography at the end of the book presents all the links to the essays reviewed in the book. For those who tire of the discussion of who said what when, and what that may mean, it may do no harm to skip to PART TWO, a brisk narrative of my own take on Google Books and the larger issues.

So, the discussion can begin without further elucidations.

PART ONE: A CLOSE READING OF DARNTON, GRAFTON ET AL. ON BOOK DIGITIZATION.

Background: Printed Words and Electronic Text

Book digitization was once a strange craft practiced by a small group of technologists with a background in the humanities. In the early eighties one had to have fairly advanced skills to turn printed text into electronic text. Images were out of the question except on expensive workstations. Most people who had those skills had little interest in text other than that found in computer manuals; they were programmers, system managers, or analysts who were busy taking care of an important and demanding business—they were a generally surly bunch who did not suffer fools, which for them, was a broad category of humanity.

There were, however, humanities PhDs and ABDs who found their way into computing due to the collapse in the academic job market in certain fields during the seventies. They found a place in computer centers and soft-money computing projects to pay the rent and put bread into the mouths of their starving children. We were a *lost generation* left hanging after the widespread vandalism on the humanities curriculum in the sixties and seventies. I started work in 1983, as research associate (PhD, UNC 1979) in Humanities Computing at Duke University.

The specific issue of the day was picking a desktop computing platform. We narrowed the choices to the Victor 9000 versus the IBM PC. The chief criterion was the screen resolution, 800x600 for the Victor versus 640x480 for the IBM. We needed the higher screen resolution for all sorts of non-Roman alphabets: Greek with breathing marks, Hebrew with vowel points, Amharic with over 150 glyphs, and Cyrillic with the requirement of three vertical lines and a connecting bar. Clearly, the Victor was years ahead of its time with its character set editor, multiple key-stroke binding, integrated audio, and variable-speed disc drives. We bet on the Victor. We lost the bet when Victor disappeared three weeks after we took delivery on twenty units, foully murdered by 640x480 screen resolution. The vice chancellor was not pleased.

We won a bet on book digitization with the Xerox Kurzweil Reading Machine, although the vice chancellor would have been happier had we not spent $100,000 on a device that went down in price to $10,000 a few months later. Raymond Kurzweil had sold the Reading Machine to Xerox, the black hole of technology, to concentrate on music. We were now in the good hands of Xerox marketing. The terminal came with a refrigerator-sized cabinet with massive, loud cooling fans. The scanner was the size of a large bathtub. The cabinet contained just one smallish rack for half a dozen cards, and the bathtub contained just one motor, a pulley, and a light source. The Xerox technician explained that they could put the cards and the scanner into a box that could sit on the desks, but Xerox found that institutions resisted paying $100,000 for something that didn't have at least one cabinet with big cooling fans. Those were heady days, the 80's; we were on the bleeding edge of technology.

We were also on a campaign to increase the productivity of academics, not just those in the humanities, that paid off on a scale hard to measure for its enormity. Few will remember checking for erasures in dissertations by holding each page up to a lamp in the offices of graduate schools. Few will remember the agony of professors, secretaries, and students alike when finding new errors in a page already retyped twice. Few still know what carbon paper is. Few will remember the extreme athletes of typing who could do 160 words per minute without errors and the horror that crept over a student as a professor demanded that "develop" should be used for "grow" in a typed seminar paper; one can imagine the time spent hunting down the words. That was the time to put up a fight, cost what it may.

Early WP

My first introduction to word processing was in the early seventies when I had my MA thesis typed on an IBM Magcard typewriter. I had an epiphany when I saw the Selectric type by itself at superhuman speed; it was like being a caveman seeing a Zippo light a fire. I sensed then that humanity would eventually get the upper hand over texts.

I discovered "Text 360" in 1978. It was a jealously guarded secret of Computer Science professors who used terminals in their offices to write successive lines of text into data sets that were still mimicking punch cards. The lines could be edited, formatted, and printed at high speeds into presentable typed pages. For me this was a no brainer; I went to my Chair who sent me to the Dean who authorized $10,000 of computer time for my dissertation. I still see the shaking hand of my Chair as he signed the paper after listening to me for an hour explaining the notion of "funny money." He made several phone calls and was still muttering: "Ten thousand is ten thousand," as he signed. That was, after all, half the budget for Teaching Assistants in German.

Things developed quickly, and along came a formatter from Waterloo, Ontario, that could handle all the formal requirements of the ladies checking pages; Daisy Wheel printers completed the illusion of a published text.

Of course, there were opponents who detected falling standards, decried writing on the screen, and advocated character building through the preparation of typescripts without erasures. It was pretty clear at the time that everyone from students to university presidents would embrace word processing, sooner rather than later.

Perhaps it would be interesting to speculate, just for fun and with all due respect, how exactly Prof. Darnton's 1982 essay "What is the History of the Book?" was prepared. Did he write on legal pads, type the pages, edit, and retype? Did he have help? Did he cut paragraphs with scissors and paste them together to add or reorder? Had he also discovered the IBM 360 in the computer center? Or did he use the Electric Pencil on a TRS-80? Or did the essay spring whole from his brow, just to be written longhand into an examination booklet without a word or comma out of place ready to be set in print? Is the 1982 paper demonstrably better for having been retyped several times than his subsequent papers that were done electronically and just printed several times? I ask these questions only to remind or inform some readers that producing a sensible, neatly typed paper of thirty pages was once a formidable challenge that not everyone could meet.

For the technological humanists, there was no question: the tyranny of the text was over—on the production end, at least. Misspellings could be found automatically. Individual sentences could be rewritten without concern for page cusps. Words could be exchanged with a few keystrokes. Pagination was automatic and flexible, as were footnotes. Confusing multiple edits on a handwritten page were at an end because a clean printed page was ten seconds away. One could be confident that one would not introduce new errors while removing existing errors.

Beyond WP: The Undiscovered Country

Yet we, the humanities techies, were not satisfied with rev-olutionizing text preparation with essentially souped-up typewriters; there was the undiscovered country, the potential of big breakthroughs of substance, the digitization and indexing of printed primary and secondary texts. In the eighties and nineties there was still great resistance to the notion of electronic versions of the raw material of research. Curiously, this resistance was somewhat dependent on the field. Departments of Religion had little problem with electronic texts of the Bible. They were eager to look up the Word and all the words of the Word. Interpreters of literature were less eager at finding their words, lest they contradict favorite ideologies. In any case, for the technological humanists, it was just a matter of time.

I spent many hours with the Kurzweil, scanning books and doggedly pursuing a fuzzy vision that I could atone for my own suspect, species-based reading habits with computer indexing. That bet was a winner, paying mostly in personal satisfaction; it seems that no one was really interested in a nail-it-to-the-wall interpretation of Broch's *Death of Virgil*; everyone had failed with it just as I had in the sixties and seventies and was happy to blame stream of consciousness. Nobody was interested in the mapping of the first sentence of Gadamer's *Truth and Method* on the rest of the text. No one cared for the word frequency anomalies in the seven books of Husserl's *Logical Investigation*. I had to agree: there was plenty to be absorbed in technology with a new generation of gadgets and widgets every fifteen months. I did scan many texts, learned how to clean the files and work with word lists, and learned the difference between the interests of literary computing and the interests of computational linguistics.

I do remember going to the cabin of Mark Rooks, a veritable pioneer. (Actually, the cabin was part of an old mill in the county around Chapel Hill.) He was scanning British Empiricists at the time; there were books everywhere and a desktop scanner hooked up to a Northgate. His vision was to sell "Past Masters," a collection of philosophy texts bundled with a search engine— pretty weird for the time. The project morphed into *Intelex* of Charlottesville, which leases a large collection of texts to universities.

Similar projects such as the TLG, the Patrologia Latina, the Dartmouth Dante Project, Goethe, Kant, the Greek philosophers in various languages, Buddhist scriptures, and most journals, even the collected works of Karl May are available bundled with sophisticated list-based searching. Everything is just sitting there, holding its breath, waiting for a Caesar Augustus, a Charlemagne, a Bismarck, to do real, large-scale integration. The fuzzy vision has become clearer, yet the problem of text has not been solved; it has only become more complex—but so has particle physics. The bottom line is: whatever has been done on paper will probably have to be redone once we get everything online.

Careers are still being made with the methodologies of the early nineteenth century; once that loses its fascination, systematic digital work can get its just due. We will always need professionals who develop a deep understanding and love for the material artifacts of our past, but that should not stand in the way of digitizing these objects and letting the methodologies of electronic storage and analysis get at them. There is no real battle to be fought here; over the last decades, funding agencies have increasingly supported projects of digitization and declined projects without a credible technical component—examples abound.

Once, the task was to bring all the manuscripts, and whatever old stuff had been found at that time, onto paper so that it could be printed and studied. Elaborate rules were set in place for how that transfer of information was to be accomplished. Now the task is to put the paper, as well as the images and whatever else was too obscure for our predecessors to bother with, into electronic form—all the paper, all the images, everything.

The Digitization of C. S. Peirce

Of course, every essay about digitization includes some list of examples of digital projects. Prof. Darnton has certainly distinguished himself in that arena by being one of the founders of the *Electronic Enlightenment*, a database of eighteenth-century correspondence of gargantuan proportions. That is all I have been able to glean from trying to peer over the wall; "free to all" does not apply here.

I would wish that Prof. Darnton had taken us on a little tour of the place to show just one small example so that the reader could get full confidence in his virtuosity with digital resources. Digitization is not just about money; it is also about establishing the methodological integrity of textbases and databases. As with any area of the humanities, only real hands-on experts have standing to go into details—the avoidance of egg on the face is paramount. Generally, instead of trenchant examples of digital work, we get rephrased snatches of books, which were reviewed long ago and serve as a holding pen for safe prose, quoted back to us. I would like to stay in the present and not divert past 1970. Anything that happened before then is interesting only for those who cannot go out in public without silk breeches and a powdered wig, or perhaps heavy wooden shoes and a large felt hat, or a toga, or one of those cute leather miniskirts of Babylonian librarians.

I would like to bring forth a real example to enrich the discussion; it is current, it is American, it is long past due, and it involves one of the Harvard libraries. I also don't want to get too specific. I realize that struggling projects need room to breathe, and destructive criticism is not helpful, especially to the moribund. But some projects need a boost, not really a reincarnation, just a little of the old phoenix. So let me give the example: Charles S. Peirce was a great philosopher with amazing things to say about thought, philosophy, and science. He was a laboratory hands-on scientist and experimental thinker with great currency internationally. His papers are sitting somewhere in Houghton, the photocopies in Indiana, microfilm and fiche widely available. I have no real standing to make definitive statements about his work, but I can relate my own involvement with his texts.

As I started working my way around the edges of his work a long time ago, I was very unhappy with the *Collected Papers* (1931–1958). Coming from German Studies, I always assumed that excellent editions are available for important figures. The eight volumes of Peirce papers are organized by topic and represent the best efforts of the editors to present his work in a coherent manner, something Peirce himself was never able to do. It is unquestionably a work of love, and it was conceived as a fitting monument to honor one of Harvard's (in the extended sense) most original thinkers. But the generations a-following don't want monuments, not even splendid monuments; we want to be able to wade into the papers ourselves.

For me, the non-chronological sequencing, to the point of splitting up essays, was the most disturbing. My trust level was breached. In short order I fired up the Kurzweil and started scanning the non-mathematical volumes. I spent many hours piecing the essays together and trying to understand the chronology of his writing, although I clearly was working with limited material. Remember, back then, working with indexed text files of philosophy was intoxicating and exhilarating; it was a feeling of being at the very forefront of what had ever been done with text.

I was developing familiarity with the major essays and could throw around the volume and page numbers; my most fervent wish was that Peirce could have had a computer and learned how to write algorithms. I was struck by the utter limitations of a human mind trapped in time–from my perspective decades later, equally trapped. The human condition was specially painful to observe in someone so earnestly struggling to escape those limitations. At some point I gave what electronic files I had to John Deeley who was working with Mark Rooks preparing a full version of the *Collected Papers* for *Intelex*.

I also made contact with some of the principals of the Peirce *Chronological Edition* being done at Indiana. I was all aglow with the importance of digitization; images of the individual sheets of paper with the electronic text underneath were a clear priority for me. For months dragging into years, I had to listen at various meetings to arguments as to why this would not work with Peirce. When finally the principle of scanning was agreed to, scanning could be done only with a certain expensive scanner that would reproduce different color pencil marks and ground in crumbs of pound cake. And only the diagrams would be scanned; who would want to scan text? Attempts to raise money for the device failed. I suspect the Web site that holds the few prototype scans has withered and can be seen on Internet Archive.

When it became clear to me after many months of quiet confidence in my position that my arguments for digitization were not getting through and were becoming annoying, I took my hat and left, metaphorically. I still bought the volumes as they came out, shaking my head at the notion that a total of thirty such volumes would appear over the next twenty years. I also shook my head in non-comprehension at the expensive printing and the various supplementary materials divided over several volumes. I never had arguments with the actual work; I had no arguments with what was being printed, but I can imagine that a close examination of the source texts by others might yield yet more divergences. It was a classical edition: *here it is; we have done the work; it is thick and it is heavy; if you want to argue, come to Indianapolis or go through the microfilm.* I should add in all fairness, that the first six volumes of the *Chronological Edition* are available from *Intelex*, a fact that raises more questions than it answers.

I was horrified at the glacial pace of the work that turned geological after volume 6, especially given the intense international interest in Peirce's work. My insight was that this was about the people doing the work and not about the work. Procedures were in place at Indiana that had such a pedigree that no change of direction could be expected, not then, and not now after a decade hiatus. The editors would use advanced word processing to mark up their variants and other textual features, they obviously had to have electronic texts, but the notion of morphing into an electronic text project—no way.

My interests turned towards continental thinkers, primarily the early Husserl. Peirce slowly aged out of my system. At some point, the volumes stopped being published, and the edition project ground to a halt around 2000. It is instructive to go to the Web site of the project; there are signs of minor decay, weeds growing in the cracks, and no real explanation where the project has been for the last ten years. Volume 8 has been sent to the printers and is expected early 2010. Volume 22, the Lowell Lectures, had been nearly finished by a team of Germans but was abandoned for lack of funding; the raw materials and the copy that was finished were returned to Indiana. Work on volume 11, *The Century Dictionary* is going on in Montreal.

It is also instructive to read the report given by the new head of the Peirce Edition to the Peirce Society in December 2008.

The gist is: external funding has run out, the NEH is putting us on hold for our suspect technology among other reasons, the university has agreed to take over some of the budget lines, provide a bridge grant, and secure the position of the new director of the project in the Philosophy Department. Yet the financial crisis is hitting everybody hard.

The video tour of this project takes us to a room where long strips of paper are stapled together and fastened with clothespins to strings of twine strung from wall to wall. Notes are attached with paper clips up and down the strips of paper. Against this background the associate editor explains the problems of matching up the styles of handwriting and dating undated pieces of paper. Good people doing heroic work, truly.

Personally, off the top of my head, I would snip out words from images of each handwritten page and layer them in Photoshop. There are more sophisticated strategies, but this would rid the office of most of the string.

It will be interesting to read the 2009 report, if (and when) there is one, to see the progress. I maintain my position: I want the digitization of Peirce. I want to see digital images of every image on the thirty-two reels of microfilm. If that means opening the boxes in Houghton again for a couple of days each, so be it. I also want to see a digitization of the *Published Works* microfiche with the supplemental materials in clean electronic text. I would consider this just a common courtesy to researchers around the world and a fitting tribute to the work of Peirce. A large ugly stain on the otherwise brilliant vest of American philosophy and on the universities that declined Peirce's services could be removed.

I see Peirce as a prime candidate for state-of-the-art text mining. It would be absurd to do this with the collected papers. It might be possible to go to the excellent Wiki bibliography on Peirce and gather enough electronic files from Intelex and others to create an acceptable data set. For all I know, someone in Norway or Poland or Korea is doing that; Peirce is big, and I have not really kept up. But we need those bundles of papers turned into electronic text. We have to face the fact that all the legendary Peirce scholars who have had that legendary feel for the hundred thousand loose pages have retired. There is still considerable expertise in the anointed successors, but it is hard to believe in the chances for the next twenty volumes. Given that the Peirce edition was started in the seventies and it took thirty years of adequate funding and work by the best people in the field to bring out six volumes—you do the arithmetic. Were I still working on Peirce, my first reaction to volume 8, when (and if) I ever get it into my hands, would be to spend three hours putting it into electronic form or reformatting the electronic version for my own analysis tools. I am not holding my breath.

There are other projects like the Peirce edition in various stages of activity that must make a pact with technology, real technology that gives them a presence in electronic space. If Google can scan 10 million library books, then Harvard can scan 100,000 loose-leaf pages and let people around the world examine and pore over them, not 1.5 FTEs in Indiana. It can be done; it must be done; it will be done; the alternatives are too absurd to contemplate. We should use the current interest in Google's digitization project to expand the discussion.

* * *

The purpose of this digression on Peirce is to show that there are still non-electronic backwaters. The purpose is to undercut the assumption that electronic work is kidnapping scholarly work and degrading our heritage. One may even counter that the electronic veneer is rather thin when it comes to many areas of study. The issues surrounding Google's digitization of books is so much in the news that one forgets how young these efforts are. I have some problem with arguments that all sorts of traditions, even institutions, will be left hanging in the balance if Google continues to scan library books. In my view, it is a marvelous demonstration of the feasibility of something that will need to be done with even greater energy, greater precision, and greater virtuosity with text files than Google has been doing for the last five years. Of course there are others who cannot see the purpose; printed texts are just fine. Yet whatever arguments we shall see over the next pages, fortunately we will not see the one that would have been unspoken in everyone's mind: "It can't be done so don't worry about it."

Of course there are many who will see failure in Google's effort even if fifteen million books are delivered around the world with the blessings of the courts this year. This book will have been missed, that collection will not have been done, and, oh, these documents were not scanned. The universal library is a sham, QED. It is not really about Google at all, it is a collapse of the imagination; the Google people are just of good sense and energy, doing what should be done. If it can be done, it should be done. People of good sense and good will should look at the work of literary estates, editorial projects, rare languages dictionaries, national encyclopedias, and whatever else out there is crawling at a snail's pace, and inject some urgency. If necessary, let us buy up Freud and Heidegger and Steinbeck and Einstein, and whoever else for a generous price. It is important that these texts, all texts, circulate freely in the electronic universe. We have plenty of evidence and analysis from Prof. Darnton that the founding fathers intended such a liberal use of texts, explicitly.

Those who say "forget about it" can just come and check it out in fifty years. We are in the early stages of this process, but considering how far we have come from the modest beginnings of the Duke Language Toolkit, from putting the first Hebrew characters or the first Amharic character set on a personal computer, I amend that to: "Come back in the Twenties."

Perspective on the Current Discussion

It is clear from the current discussion on Google and its work, especially from the high-profile essays and the creampuff reviews, that some Olympian luminaries and those in the second and third tier would just as soon Google went away. The Google digitization project of library books has forced the issue; it has accelerated the process of digitization and created realities on the ground that are hard to ignore. One can ignore a database of all the paintings in the Louvre or the Metropolitan; one can ignore the digitized Patrologia Latina, or the collection of all Dante Commentaries, or the TLG, or the Digital Scriptorium. One cannot ignore ten million library books. Most annoying are any number of enthusiastic advocates that are trying to mobilize general enthusiasm among amateurs; after all, budgets have to be fought for and standards have to be maintained—talk of a revolutionary future should be kept at a safe distance. Sit down, sit down, sit down, sit down, sit down; Sit down you're rockin' the boat.

Instead of insisting on a nostalgic view, our Olympians should sit down with technologists and develop a roadmap for digitization in each particular field and raise some money, time's a-wasting. The one-on-one engagement of the scholar with sources will not be abridged through digitization. Most routine, even brilliant, work on sources can be done via images; let us not distract ourselves with remembrance of times past. A close look at the work done in the past will show that scholars have always worked with copies; go to the Victoria and Albert Museum in London, and you will see the 3-D new media of the past, full-size plaster casts of all manner of monument. There is a full-size plaster cast of Trajan's Column there, no kidding, in two pieces to get it under the roof, other examples abound. For the updated version, visit the McMaster Trajan Project Web site. All the "cartoons" [read: the line drawings of the relief] have been digitized and ordered in an exemplary interface. There you can see the figures as only the artists were able to see them. In addition you can read explanations of what you are looking at.

There are many problems of display and analysis, wonderful problems, in all fields of the humanities, and technology is eager to help. The national divisions in Europe have led to separate realities in their view of history, literature, and art. Only comprehensive interlinked chronologies tied to the text of sources can begin to allow synthetic perspectives. Many non-European cultures are trying to understand our strange ways. Essays polished to a high sheen may not be the best strategy. Our best tools are the database and the algorithms that can process the data into new media output embroidered with text, a very neutral formulation. The field is progressing quickly.

Today, the discussion on digitization in the popular press and in the organs of literate opinion (e.g., *The New Yorker*, *Daedalus, The New York Review of Books*) is going on at a very elementary level. The discussion is being carried on by people who can elaborate digitization, spin digitization, paint some future created by digitization, describe the victims of digitization, but some discuss the issue without betraying any overt essential experience or personal stake in actual digitization. This holds for arguments pro and con. That is truly good and just since digitization has gone from the artisanal to the forefront of the technology section, opinion on the subject must be shaped, and everyone has a say.

But let us be clear: I would never set a student on a series of hardcover books for some extensive complicated research if there were the possibility that this student could get the text of those books in electronic form. OK, the books should be looked at, thumbed through, even read, smelled if you please, but the actual work should be done with electronic text on the computer with various programs in multiple windows on multiple laptops. Would you send someone to work on Dante Commentaries without using the Dartmouth database? Would you send someone to work on Gibbon without downloading the electronic text from *Gutenberg*? I would even go so far as to suggest the student scan important texts. Not to invest in scanning with today's technology for a big project would be simply irresponsible, lacking due diligence.

Rows of quiet students sitting in oak-paneled reading rooms becoming extremely learned with stacks of books before them is a piece of nostalgia that should be put in a huge golden frame and nailed to the wall.

I do think some actual hands-on experience with electronic methodologies is desirable before using authority gained elsewhere in this area. But it has to be a certain kind of experience; everyone can scan fifty pages out of a modern book in ten minutes and achieve an error-free electronic text. The desired experience is not a mechanical one of producing text or of watching as text is produced in the bowels of a library. The desired experience is that of gaining insight into a text that one has lived with for a long time in its printed form by turning that text into an electronic text file. The experience is inspecting a wordlist of that text, querying the text interactively from that list, and being able to find diverse entry points for reading based on questions raised by an overview of the complete semantic content; the experience is of achieving a new level of interpretation on that text.

We are, after all, talking about methodologies of text interpretation, about discovering thematic patterns, persistent vocabulary, and technical terms, and we are talking about escaping personal biases. We are fighting against the bogus certainties that entrap us. Electronic research can give more consistent access to text and it can help expose our ideological habits.

Hands-on experience is also required of venerable scribal work (to work the other side of the street). Anyone who has not transcribed an early book or manuscript cannot appreciate the detailed engagement, the veritable fury, and the complete immersion in strange language and thought habits that such a labor involves. Transcribing goes levels above any form of reading. And I should add that, in my current work, the transcription is being done from digital color images with one horizontal window each for the image and the transcription into an electronic text file. I find it reduces eye-skip, a perceptual problem that did not stop with the fifteenth century. The resulting electronic text is, of course, invaluable; no monetary value can be placed on it; it is the ticket to another world.

I see people with white gloves working in manuscript collections, all of them working carfully in slow motion, and I cannot but think how much better they could work with high-resolution images, having several pages open at the same time, jumping to different sections, enlarging pages, eating a sandwich, looking at the vocabulary, daring to flip back twenty pages to check on a word. There is no clear us-and-them division when it comes to work in the humanities, and the digital image will not cheapen the work.

But there is a larger picture; experience with databases is required. The required experience is the taking of data, studying that data for an extended time, discovering the important data points, and the developing of structures to hold those points. One proven technique is to conduct a seminar for the technologists on the subject to be put into d-base form (Persian miniatures, the Trajan cartoons, or Judeo-Arabic texts) over several months to develop a common language. I will not describe the process further, but it is not unlike planting something, something that can grow beyond the current intentionality of the creator so that future generations may harvest it. Essays of descriptive analysis will not be able to compete with d-base designs.

The polished monograph, by comparison, is a form of aggrandizement that may yield some crumbs of insight to a lucky few. Google Books is full of such dilapidated monuments from the nineteenth century; the essays of our time will experience a similar fate. There are enough examples of humanities databases in electronic space that we can assume a passing familiarity. That passive familiarity must be made active in order to seize the opportunity technology presents us.

Until very recently, anyone writing about digitization would write about it from inside the field and would know what a scanned file looked like, how to clean it, how to archive it, how to index it, and how to work with an interactive retrieval system—or the writer would be a database designer reporting on progress on some digitization effort.

Now, digitization has hit the big time in the world of media; at universities everywhere, humanists are trying to come up to speed on one of the topics of the day, but they do so without any real experience, and thus, the results are predictably superficial.

Since humanists not only speak, but also write, we have a curious turnaround: previously, technologists have written to humanists, or "technological humanists" have written to humanists; now we have "non-technological humanists," some with very high reputations in their non-technological fields, writing about technology to their colleagues and to the world. And all will be raptured by what they read—except *this* technologist right here. What do these people have to tell us, and why should we listen?

One can give a preliminary answer before we go to the texts. The popular press knows that pointing an accusing finger at corporations, even at a corporation not yet in its teens, makes good copy. Those who practice the higher forms of journalism are not above using rhetorical figures to patronize contemporary efforts. So we might be told that due to "hype and rhetoric" it is "hard to grasp" what "Google and Microsoft, and their partner libraries are actually doing" with digitization [Grafton, "Future Reading," 2007]. In the next paragraph the magic lantern is turned on to take us to the third millennium BC for two sentences. In such a magic lantern show we might be told that Mesopotamian scribes invented key words or abstracts and practiced alphabetization. Good point.

In my magic Web show, there is an international team working on a database of clay tablets where you can see high-res images of clay tablets along with the transcriptions or line tracings. Of the 500,000 extant tablets around the world, some 250,000 transcriptions have been digitized, and roughly a third have been photographed. The database spans more than a dozen collections from Berkeley to St. Petersburg with the NYPL in the middle; just google the Digital Cuneiform Library. Were I extremely learned, trying my hand at belletristic journalism, I would visit Eglund or Damerow and have them tell me about database design and the new experimental search and the directions of digitization for the future. At first blush, judging by the incredible images and tracings, I see no compelling reason to handle the tablets themselves; I could be wrong. I also see no reason to be amazed by a historian remembering something, admittedly not entirely random, about clay tablets.

A preliminary answer to the question above is: the strategy to cast aspersions at digitization by using Google's status as a corporation with billions of dollars is not effective except with those reflexively against corporations. To be fair, Prof. Grafton strays into these waters only occasionally, but he does so forcefully. Prof. Darnton seems to find the greatest comfort there of late.

Unfortunately, the extremely learned have sensed the weakness in their arguments against the feasibility of studying digital representations and for the immaculate virtue of the book printed on paper. There is still a bit of preaching to the Luddite choirs, but the only viable option has become shouting "monopoly" loudly and often. We are not talking about an existing monopoly that has been restraining trade and making goods expensive for everyone while making a few fabulously rich. Clearly, monopolies and cartels are established and are functioning in higher education; a rigorously enforced merit-ocracy would wreak havoc in our society. No, we are talking about a suspected potential monopoly that has to date not taken a nickel out of anyone's pocket for providing a ubiquitous searching service, but that must be stopped at all costs in the minds of some, nipped in the bud before it can prove itself to be a monopoly—or a boon for all.

This paper is primarily for technologists, perhaps literate technologists, who actually may care what is being thought out loud in highbrow journals. Its purpose is to present a strategy for evaluating these texts and their subtexts that throw a somewhat jaundiced eye on the enterprise of technology. Once upon a time, the humanists, I mean those not working on international d-base teams, were willing to stay in their offices, so the caricature goes, grumble over their ancient texts, grow apoplectic over mistakes made four hundred years ago, viciously attack someone in print, and slouch back to their lair plotting their next foray. They let the computer people do their work and conquer the world, so the caricature goes, which they promptly did, and then cashed in their stock options and moved to Belize.

However, the Google thing has gotten a little bit too big for most; the balance in the world has been upset; they think it's time to put on the brakes. It started small with Google the search engine. Suddenly, any obscure reference in any field of the humanities from British painters to Italian mathematicians could be googled with satisfactory results. One of the great arenas of the learned, the display of extreme trivia and the ability to delight the gathered throng therewith, lost all appeal once students started googling details from their lecture notes. That was bad enough; however, when Google started scanning library books in the millions and getting away with it, it became time to put on a concerned face.

We shall look at the texts of Darnton and Grafton closely to see if any conclusions can be drawn from what important non-technological humanists are writing.

What is a Close Reading?

A close reading is not unlike dealing with certain kinds of computer programs. I had an acquaintance at Duke in the early eighties, who was a brilliant designer and teacher of *machine code* and *assembler code.* (Feel free to google any of the concepts mentioned.) Although he had no academic degree himself, he attained high rank before retiring early to life-long luxury from the user fees for his code. He did not let the details of the code that bogged down the rest of us distract him from what the program was intended to achieve. He could read and mark up assembler code as though he were proofreading "Mary Had a Little Lamb" copied by a mildly dyslexic first-grader, (who is of course mainstreamed and getting the best medication against anxiety and much positive feedback). "Change this, use that, move this here, move that there, cut this, add a section here…" and on it went for fifteen pages of green bar; it was amazing, humbling. Generally, the program would work now, and if it already worked, it would work better; that was important back then with limited regions of core. He could look at chunks of machine code and see assembler statements; he could look at chunks of assembler code and see functions in a higher level programming language. What he did at the machine and assembler level, we could do in PL/I or Fortran to create a sequence of statements to execute some logic on a data stream.

We shall try something similar with texts. Words are the machine statements, they carry a charged meaning; they load certain registers, sometimes occult registers, that are loaded with psychological effects discovered after years of trial and error by rhetorically savvy humanists. This machine code of words can be grouped into assembler statements of sentences, which can be grouped in turn into paragraphs, the programming statements, where we can finally follow the logic. We, the readers, are the data processed by the text and spewed out in neat little tables according to the whim of some extremely learned person who wants to put his mark on the Google discussion and make sure we leave with correct thought. If we can see where the logic is going, recognize the charged registers, we, the data, can still say no; we will not be enraptured. Contrary to the rhetorical program, we will go elsewhere, into the shining infotopia for example. Our main task will be to discover the bad machine language that will make wobbly assembler code and produce badly formatted output. If writers, even extremely learned writers, write about technology, then we should expect the discussion to be informed on a certain level. We would not want to be informed about Erasmus from someone with only a passing acquaintance from Wiki. We can ask that much.

For those who find the computer metaphor above silly or too elaborate, let me suggest the metaphor of the sheepdog trial. A herd of sheep is to be gotten up the hill, down the dale, around the tree, and into the pen by one dog and one person. We are those sheep. If we arrive at the pen as intended, we will have accomplished our close reading; many will have wandered off, perversely, listening to the yip of a different sheepdog and causing points to be deducted from the score of the person.

SECTION ONE: DARNTON

The Professor of the History of Books

The first essay by Prof. Darnton under consideration, "The New Age of the Book" (NYRB, 1999) is really a bit of pre-history from an earlier time when the information age had not hit with full impact. It reminds me of a false dawn that goes through various hues of gray and blue and pink till the sun actually breaks through, finally, after we have tired of the anticipation. In 1999, Prof. Darnton was still in History at Princeton, and he presents a dispassionate analysis of the trends in computers and academic publishing. Oh yes, there are problems here and there, fiddlesticks; the world was still basking in the glow of Bill Clinton and Monika.

Perhaps that long false dawn gave academics a sense of security that technology would be content with its minor role as secretary and mail-person—that the sun would never rise and boil away life as we know it, if that is indeed what it is actually doing.

Prof. Darnton happily and cheerfully dismisses the vision of McLuhan who prophesied a "post-printing" universe. He quotes Bill Gates relating that, "Reading off the screen is still vastly inferior to reading off of paper. Even I, who have these expensive screens and fancy myself as a pioneer of this Web Lifestyle, when it comes to something over about four or five pages, I print it out and I like to have it to carry around with me and annotate." [Darnton, 1999] So even He, the Gates, prints pages—probably because he had not mastered strike-through and double-strike-through editing in Word. Who did? Of course, he did misjudge the importance of the Web initially and had to play serious monopolist to exterminate Netscape and conquer the browser, but I digress.

Darnton credits the Lewinsky affair and the Starr report for bringing electronic text and the Internet to the full attention of the

American public. The main characteristic of electronic text is that it is considerably faster than print. Television is not mentioned because people wanted to read extended texts about the scandal, and the TV loops, salacious as they were, did not satisfy the hunger for detailed information.

Before turning to his topic of scholarly publishing at the near dawn of the electronic age, he illustrates the wide dissemination of information through the Internet. Not only did the Starr Report get six million hits in twenty-four hours, but the NYPL processed ten million hits on its Web site per month (1999) while dispensing fifty thousand actual books per month, according to Darnton.

Darnton's analysis of academic publishing is quite detailed and holds out some hope that some of the problems can be treated with technology. Most striking is a section concerned with turning dissertations into books, which are required for career advancement, I have been told.

> "Certainly, we can dump unlimited numbers of dissertations onto the Web. Several programs exist for providing this service – and it is a genuine service: it makes research available to readers. But as a rule, this kind of publication provides mainly information, not fully developed scholarship, at least not in most of the humanities and social sciences." [Darnton, 1999]

At first, I was a little shocked at the cavalier manner in which the realities of academic publishing were presented. I have no great illusion about my own dissertation of thirty years ago, which is slumbering peacefully on the Web, but at the time I did gather all the dissertations on my topic together to glean information, and I would expect anyone working on Doderer to do the same with mine. I was a bit nonplussed by the notion of "fully developed scholarship."

I sense a trend of conformity to fashion, correct thinking, and a support for specific paradigms and the dominant theories of heavy hitters. The notion of "fully developed scholarship" will have to be googled extensively.

Prof. Grafton makes a similar point about preparing submissions to the JHI:

> "The referees' reports are almost always very substantive and often quite long and detailed. In many cases, they help us help authors, by suggesting exactly where and why they need to modify claims, examine further primary sources, or engage with further secondary works. Once revision has taken place, our one full-time employee who manages the flow of files, copyedits the text, as does one of the four editors" [WMW, 2009, p. 314].

Prof. Darnton continues to explain what makes a book:

> "Anyone who has read raw dissertations knows what I mean: with few exceptions, they are not books. A world of difference separates them. To become a book, a dissertation must usually be reorganized, trimmed here and expanded there, adapted to the needs of a lay reader, and rewritten from top to bottom, preferably with the help of an experienced editor." [Darnton, 1999]

As I think back to a time before Google, or netbooks, or Wi-Fi, I wonder if some of our problems in the humanities do not stem from just this sort of grooming that scholarship has received. There is a distinction that I want to resist between *information* and *fully developed scholarship*, and a distinction between *books of scholarship* and *books of information*. Granted many dissertations are mentored by people without specific expertise in the topic; this was the case with my own. Certainly, peer review by actual experts could contribute significantly. However, as in my dissertation, I did have the monographs and articles of those experts, and I would have been hard-pressed to find more. And I did want to tweak some noses deliberately at the very least. I do wonder if the earnest plodding through information that raw dissertations provide is not a more genuine source of scholarship than the sanitized monographs churned up professionally and rhetorically by editors. Or is it that the star scholars of the day are not writing for their few true peers, but seeking stardom on bestseller lists?

Perhaps, precisely the emphasis on smooth formalism, if I understand Prof. Darnton correctly, the university press style that sweeps all before it with its apodictic rhetoric, creates an illusion of completeness that can only falsify the very nature of research and the very nature of the problems humanities are to study. If some semi-interesting half-baked idea is polished up with proper references and unassailable style, how can the colleague or the layperson understand the ambiguities of the research task? Are we beguiled by makeup that hides some hideous skin condition?

Perhaps there is some additional learning going on there, the post-doctoral learning of how to turn a sow's ear into a publishable silk purse. The Germans call the post-doctorate publication that leads to the rank of Professor, "Habilitation," from the Latin "habilito, habilitare," which I have been told means "to enable or to make suitable." Now I know they refer to the work editors.

But if the subsequent submissions by actual professors to JHI are also sows' ears, as we learn from Prof. Grafton in "Codex in Crisis," then scholarship really becomes a matter of style over substance. This attitude could explain a great deal. We are seduced by an illusion of knowledge, a mockery of deciphering sources, and a sham of testing hypotheses. I don't want to believe that; I don't think that has always been true; it is just that Prof. Darnton's explanation is so convincing, and Prof. Grafton's substantiation is so disarming, so matter of fact.

I remember when I was a graduate student coming across any number of mimeographed and stapled monographs that seemed to have had no benefit of professional production techniques. In the field of German studies, minimally bound monographs in mono-spaced courier type were still widespread, especially for detailed questions. Have we succumbed to a cult of academic celebrity scholarship where the "anointed select" just e-mail their rough pages to the University Press, and then show up at the book presentation and accept prizes? I am amazed at the long list of acknowledgments in many books and collections of essays.

For all the analysis of the process of publishing that Prof. Darnton gives us, there seems to be some fundamental reflection missing. Of course, it was the era of unclouded Clinton prosperity. We miss it sorely.

Prof. Darnton obviously has experience in the guild:

> "Editors often refer to this reworking as "value added," and they add only some of the value that goes into a book. Peer review, page design, composition, printing, marketing, publicity - a variety of expertise is necessary to transform a dissertation into a monograph." [Darnton, 1999]

This reflection puts academic presses into the same mold as the commercial publishers. They seem to buy dross cheap and sell heirlooms dear, exceptions notwithstanding.

I will not paraphrase his analysis of the position of academic presses in detail, the points are concise and easily called up, only to quote two sentences about the state in 1999:

> "Scholarly publishers, harder pressed than ever, continued to produce a large number of titles, but fewer of them were scholarly. They tended to be books about popular local themes or birds or cookery or sports or "midlist" books - that is, the quasi-trade works that commercial publishers

were neglecting in order to concentrate on books with mass appeal: exercise books, how-to books, and the assorted schlock that clutters up most bookstores today." [Darnton, 1999]

I personally happen to love books about birds and about cooking, but I wonder what the point is of university presses competing in the "mid-list." Is it some communal spirit? The university community has a police force, several stores, many restaurants, a hotel, several ball parks, theaters, a dairy, and a bakery if it is an agricultural school, and of course a press, since books are its stock in trade.

I have not followed the development of university presses into the present, but given the tenacity with which university presses can be trusted to cling to their fiefs, I would doubt that any set of statistics or analysis of the subjects treated would move them off the dime. I suspect that publishing something with a first line academic press is still the glittering jewel in a career, and having a press is only slightly less important for universities than having a football team; academic considerations simply have to give way to the greater good. Blogs, no matter how well managed, still will not get you tenure, and I am happy about that, but I am willing to examine the medium further. It would be an interesting case study to examine the original submissions and the various recommendations to publish something and compare that to the shining jewel coming out the other end of the publishing process.

The sciences have managed to free their scientific communication from style and rhetoric, environmental screeds excepted. Perhaps they have developed a more subtle form of rhetoric that ensnares the readers by cleverly embedding keywords, for example, search terms that would make all the chlorophyll biochemists come running. Generally, I have heard, the requirements for being able to read scientific communication are so stringent and demanding that only certifiably plausible propositions can be assimilated by experts in closely related fields. The coin of the realm seems to be verifiable processes; things that are worthy of citation, in other words, things that one can *stand* on. If it does not meet these expectations, the paper will age out of the citation index.

The notion of publishing scholarship for the lay reader does not automatically resonate. Pardon me, but stochastic disorders in spin glass is no more a hobby than Ottoman Historiography. The experts in the respective fields should not write for the hobbyists, but bring the hobbyists to a professional level. This is clearly understood in the study of magnetism, which is content with low ratings. Are the standards of humanistic scholarship more flexibly inclusive? When I was being taught, the Germans differentiated between scholarship and belletristic writing that was more of a prop for monolithic bourgeois culture, something called *Bildung*, which one was expected just to have. Serious research made no compromises. To edit scholarship so that it appeals to laymen in order to support a business competing with non-academic publishers seems almost worse, academically speaking, that graduating the slow readers who can run a 4.2 40. My own copy editor, on the other hand thinks it is worse than placing slow runners on the first string of a football team, from the perspective of sport. Prof. Darnton's rhapsodies on the virtues of professional editors have not been able to ensnare me; they have made me look with suspicion at every sentence, searching for an honest word.

It would be a feat of daring to take a field of study, let's say Shakespeare, starting with the folios and identify verifiable, plausible claims about Shakespeare and his plays. It would be a database estimated at no more than several hundred thousand records. Or pick Marlow if that is too many.

Prof. Grafton has recently heaped some scorn on attempts to separate small chunks of information out of a larger rhetorical landscape [WMW, p. 316]. Ten years ago Prof. Darnton was willing to at least try the idea on for size.

"Instead of simplifying this process [publishing], electronic publishing will add further complications, but the result could be a great increase in value. An e-dissertation could contain virtually unlimited appendices and databases. It could be linked to other publications in a manner that would permit readers to find new paths through old material. And once the technical problems are worked out, it could be produced and distributed economically, saving production costs for the publisher and shelf space for the library." [Darnton, 1999]

I quote this argument at length only to create a baseline for further discussion of digitization. Prof. Darnton has clear sympathies with the book:

"Consider the book. It has extraordinary staying power. Ever since the invention of the codex in the third or fourth century AD, it has proven to be a marvelous machine - great for packaging information, convenient to thumb through, comfortable to curl up with, superb for storage, and remarkably resistant to damage. It does not need to be upgraded or downloaded, accessed or booted, plugged into circuits or extracted from Webs. Its design makes it a delight to the eye. Its shape makes it a pleasure to hold in the hand." [Darnton, 1999]

This paragraph is marvelously dated as a decade old. As fast as network backbones were back then, performance varied in the offices. Downloading was still a chore, waiting and waiting and then wondering where the file went; upgrading was like painting the bathroom; and, no matter where you were, there were always weird things that had to be done with network cards or IP numbers. It was the false dawn of the information age. Nobody worried about the books; they were very much with us and still are. Of course, Brin and Page had already started digitizing books at Stanford at the time.

What is not to like about a book? I have personally dragged books all over the world. I have shipped books from Europe to America, and I have shipped those same books back so they would be near me. My dream of dreams is to own a bookmobile, or a Leer Jet with faux-oak aluminum shelves: a bookjet.

But I have also digitized books, and by doing electronic searches of books, I have come to the conclusion that books hide more than they reveal. Yes, it is possible to thumb through a book, but it is impossible to find a sentence you read a week ago unless you are very good or very lucky. It is even harder to construct an argument out of a series of books without creating a major construction site on your desk.

The similarity of *reading* to *lived* experience, vicarious in reading, of course, brings the same problems of remembering and evaluating lived experience, to remembering and evaluating reading. It becomes a matter of oscillating between poles. The clearer the ideological framework of the reader, the more certain the selection of experiences from reading. The more empathic our experience of the other becomes, the more open we become to the voice of the other, the more difficult becomes the selection of experience. One pole produces sharp analysis from a clear perspective; the other pole is lost in the ineffable. Generally we wander around somewhere in the middle, or we are carried by editors.

Especially second or third readings have to be brought into new channels. This is where indexing, but above all, interactive querying can be helpful. There are no arguments to be made against the book as the basic tool. But we have been trained by the book to think in a certain way not always helpful or productive. The first thing one must learn when reading on a Kindle is to stay with the divisions the author provides and not to mark time with page numbers. A book without page numbers is a difficult challenge at first. The problem subsides over time, but I still find myself wasting time skipping ahead to see if bandits are lurking before the end of the chapter. One could imagine the same effect reading from a scroll. The Kindle is an experience of an endless page.

The new generation may not have the unquestioned allegiance to the printed book as those from a time when there was little media competition for certain forms of vicarious lived experience. In a world short of new media, the mind instinctively goes to books to listen to the voice of another. In a world full of new media, where vicarious experiences are not to be avoided, books will have a subordinate role. Some will find peak experiences that they miss in routine media exposure; some will concentrate on retrieving information from books that they cannot get from new media.

Much work must be done to get clarity on the practice of reading. If an above average undergraduate with a high verbal test score spends five minutes scanning information in a JSTOR article of fourteen pages, is it possible that five minutes were all that was required to grasp the argument and see through the editorial costume? I trust the cybernetic academic organism to do these reading studies in great detail, eventually, and I have confidence that the young people of today, who are much smarter than I was at their age, are able to perform great feats of reading.

Prof. Darnton demonstrates his second sight with a resounding final paragraph. After citing efforts to get dissertations online and to improve the quality of e-books, in which Prof. Darnton has been instrumental, we read:

> "The world of learning is changing so rapidly that no one can predict what it will look like ten years from now. But I believe it will remain within the Gutenberg galaxy - though the galaxy will expand, thanks to a new source of energy, the electronic book, which will act as a supplement to, not a

substitute for, Gutenberg's great machine."
[Darnton, 1999]

I am sure it would not have occurred to him that a mere nine years later Google will have scanned ten million books, some from Harvard University Libraries, the institution of which he will have become the director.

The Historical Librarian

The second essay under consideration here, "The Library in the New Age" (2008), Prof. Darnton wrote as the newly appointed head of Harvard University Libraries. The world looks different from the oak-paneled (I should hope) offices in Widener than the twentieth-century gothic of Princeton that looks like a cinderblock junior high school on the inside (some rooms are exceptions). Gone is the quiet confidence of ten years ago in the inviolable immutability of the book. "The Library in the New Age" starts with a barrage of questions: How will we cope? What will happen to my own dukedom? How do we understand it all? Alas, the questions are followed by a rhetorical strategy: the profession that there is no answer forthcoming from the orator, when in actuality, we are merely being made to wait in suspense.

The sun has risen; the information age is upon us. An actual librarian, who has come up through Library Science, who has taught Library Science for twenty years, and has been active in the day-to-day arrangement of library resources, would of course react differently than a historian with a concentration in the history of the book.

An actual librarian has managed a major computer center for the last twenty years. When computer centers on campus were throwing away their heavy computing iron in favor of networked PCs, the library was left as the last centralized computing platform. Librarians have been in the middle of the struggle to come up with cost-effective computing strategies for everything from the OPAC, the circulation data, rows upon rows of networked computers, the CD-ROM collection and on-line resources. Contrary to popular opinion, it was librarians, not corporate fat cats, who were on the front line of Google's early digitization effort.

In contrast, books represent a relatively minor problem: let's install some compact shelving; let's move some of this stuff to warehouses and write some modules for our circulation software to facilitate delivery of off-site materials, and oh, buy a small truck. Perhaps my vision is spurious, but I have seen libraries lead in strange projects such as building a *Second Life* campus and providing virtual space to the business school for meetings. Librarians have never had the option to say no to anything; nor have they had the option to arch an eyebrow or to indulge in nostalgia for the codex.

The historian turned librarian can maintain the big picture. First we need a theory; before we can have a theory, we need a chronology. Let us start at 4000 BCE, just like in Sid Meyer's *Civilization III*. Just like in *Civilization III*, writing is "the most important technological breakthrough in the history of humanity," according to Darnton. [Darnton, 2008]

In *Civilization III*, writing is important because it leads to philosophy, which will give you free "knowledge" such as currency, code of laws, construction, or monarchy. The reason for the free knowledge, in Sid Meyer's mind, is that humanity was emboldened to understand the world, which really makes philosophy the original science. Alas, it stayed that way till an unfortunate phase in our relatively recent history when scientists were burned, quite literally, by the dogmatic-texts people—this caused a schism in the otherwise happy world of philosophy. Eventually two teams were formed: the text people and the science people. Not everybody can play for the science team.

I quote some random examples of the first sentence of Aristotle's *Metaphysics*:

1. All men by nature desire to know. W. D. Ross
2. All men by nature are actuated with the desire to know. M'Mahon
3. All men naturally desire knowledge. Trendennick
4. Alle Menschen streben von Natur nach Wissen. Bassenge
5. Alle Menschen haben einen angeborenen Wissenstrieb. Schwelger

My apologies for the English-speaking colleagues of the past, who, for reasons hard to fathom, used "men" as a collective to mean "humanity." No doubt there is an explanation that reflects positively on the English. The indication seems to be that the Germans are better classical philologists that the English, although they probably did not mean to include women in their quest either. Clearly "anthropoi" cannot be translated as "men." For that there is another word I have been told. There is no "anthropos" in that sense. Lest anyone think the inventors of philosophy were enlightened proponents of equal rights, a little poking around Google books in "Full View" leads to all sorts of references that they considered "gune" or "gyne" a particularly nasty scourge sent by the gods. A little more poking around in "Full View" will give the impression that the root of our words (Greek, Persian, Latin, Arabic) for man and woman were initially crude diagrams scratched on the bathroom wall by first graders. But I digress.

Darnton's chronology leads us from first writing in 4000 BCE to the blog. The blog leads us to the notion of "unstable texts," much like the game of telephone we used to play as kids on rainy days. After a little personal sharing from his time as reporter, we are dipped again into a history on the unreliability of news at a time when a transatlantic voyage took two months. We still have a long way to go before all the sheep are herded into the correct pen. There is a section on the acquisition practices of the Folger library and a convincing series of paragraphs showing the wisdom of having bought forty copies of the First Folio (The total now stands at 71).

We are to appreciate the instability of texts. Voltaire continually rewrote. He even cut deals with pirate printers:

> "In order to spice up his text and to increase its diffusion, he collaborated with pirates behind the back of his own publisher, adding passages to the pirated editions." [Darnton, 2008]

A subtle subtext emerges: anyone toying with the idea of the solidity of the printed word on the printed page bound into books had better look closely just what kind of catch-as-catch-can industry publishing has always been. Authors, publishers, type-setters, and binders conspire to produce WYSIAG—not "What you see is what you get," but rather, "What you see is anybody's guess."

It is wonderful to be herded by a master; here we have excellent code at all levels. We have *not* been told that blogs lead to stupid rumors of epic proportions all around the world (which would have caused some of us to bolt); we have been told that the formation of America once hung on a stupid rumor. We are *not* told that most everything newspapers publish is trash not to be trusted; we are told that newspapers have always published trash and have never been trusted even on the occasions when they don't publish trash. We are told that the first editions of Shakespeare were merely a rough approximation and that even Voltaire hacked around at his texts.

We have thus come to the end of the first section of Darnton's 2008 essay securely boxed in by the notion that the Internet, with all its seeming excesses, is merely one point in a long development and is neither extreme nor unusual.

Exit the Historian, Enter the Librarian

The purpose of Darnton's snapping at our heels was to prepare us for the defense of the research library. In the second half of "The Library in the New Age" the code, in the sense of assembler code, becomes tricky. We are about to be strong-armed. Some virtuosity in reading will be required to understand the following passages:

1. "To students in the 1950s, libraries looked like citadels of learning. Knowledge came packaged between hard covers, and a great library seemed to contain all of it. To climb the steps of the New York Public Library, past the stone lions guarding its entrance and into the monumental reading room on the third floor, was to enter a world that included everything known." [Darnton, 2008]
2. "Students today still respect their libraries, but reading rooms are nearly empty on some campuses." [Darnton, 2008]

There is a problem with this code. In the first quotation Darnton writes: "looked like" and "seemed" and "was to enter." These are very weak choices, deliberately chosen to give the very questionable notion of privileging the perceptions of students, while not even talking about the students of the fifties, any real force. And what is meant by "included" everything known. Why included? What else was there to which "everything known" was "included." Let us try this: "The library included everything known and water fountains, as well as many things only vaguely suspected and others that turned out not really to have been 'known,' only 'asserted' and later proven false." Does this sentence render the situation?

Else one might have written with some conviction: "In the 1950s libraries were citadels of learning. The great libraries contained all of knowledge. One entered into a world of everything known."

In the second quotation Darnton writes: "some" and "nearly empty." Again we see extreme soft-pedaling. And precisely what is his assessment of the library's status for today's students? What is it to be "still respected?"

We shall have to help this juxtaposition along a bit:

1. In the view of the students and professors of the 1950s: the research library is the absolute temple of knowledge and learning. Learning was there, nowhere else. If learning was at some other institutions, it was because they also had a library. If any learning were produced at said institution, it must be carried to the research library before it can become proper learning. Anybody who thought learning could be done privately without institutional imprimatur starved to death unnoticed. Only rare exceptions were noticed. The papers of the emaciated dead maverick were then carried to the research library after the unfortunate's death. That is the way it was, correct me if I am wrong, until the post-WWII demographic, computers, and digitization shook things up.
2. Due to the Internet, today's student views knowledge as something to be accessed via computer, a world-wide electronic continuum of information in which libraries still play a respectable role. If some bit of information is not online, one has the right to complain but also the obligation to get it online.

I think this opposition is largely rhetorical, anecdotal, and commonplace, in short, a cliché. The way it was back when the Cleavers were the only house on Wisteria Lane cannot inform the head of a great library—hence, the soft formulations. The fact is, we have moved on. The fifties are interesting only to kids with purple hair who wear *Converse* rubber and canvas sneakers. It seems that the extremely learned think they have earned the right not to be moved along.

What is it precisely that makes this picture of libraries in the fifties so endearing? I suspect it is an extreme personal nostalgia. We shall see this nostalgia even more when we get to Prof. Grafton's texts.

This sheep is beginning to get restless. Something is up. Are we going to end up mutton after this herding? Better start quibbling fast.

Although I don't remember the tomblike quiet of the libraries in the fifties, I do vividly remember reading rooms in the sixties and seventies where any number of extremely annoying things were going on. I can only guess that the difference between the extremely learned and the rest of us was that we were distracted, and they were not. They don't remember the staccato of leather heels clacking the length of the reading room.

The first paragraph of the juxtaposition above loads the registers "knowledge" and "learning." The second paragraph loads "knowledge" and "information." "Learning" is not mentioned in the second paragraphs. "Information" is not mentioned in the first. Something is up. I suspect that the moderns (the post moderns have long been reabsorbed) are to be sent out with a lot of information and only a little knowledge. Are we to pine for learning?

We are also given "ordered … standard categories" opposed to "endless extending information." We shall see this over and over. Neither Darnton nor Grafton have any problem with the several million books at the New York Public Library. They walk leisurely up between the lions feeling no pressure from the vast accumulation of "content" there.

Let's say they have a productive scholarly life of 60 years, 10 years as a kid, plus 13 years as a student with a quick dissertation, would retire them at 83, still a good 10 years left. Let us say each reads 10 books a week, which would give us 520 books a year. Let's be generous and double the pensum to 20 a week with a week off for Christmas and a week off in the summer; that gives us a thousand books a year. Assume they keep this up till age 90, throw away the first ten years and the dotage after 90, and we are looking at 80,000 books, probably a fantastic number. Given that there are several million books at NYPL, why does no one speak of endless impenetrable stacks? There are masses of books that are never looked at. The extremely learned are working through sampling techniques; the part stands for the whole—*pars pro toto* it is called, I have been told. Let us at least give these unsampled texts a chance to be mined.

Let us not assume that just because there is an entry in the catalog and some grey librarian has attached some subject categories cribbed from the publisher's data that the text has been absorbed into "learning." Darnton argues that in today's debased form, "Information is endless, extending everywhere on the Internet, and to find it one needs a search engine, not a card catalog." [Darnton, 2008] Is that really bad?

I fear that being learned is much like being an athlete. Every athlete knows who can be beaten and who is going to be difficult or impossible to beat. The key is to cultivate a reputation of being hard to beat. The athlete does not represent perfection. Perfection is temporary in the rare superlative cases, it is fleeting in the great ones, and it is elusive for most. But one can concentrate on beating a weak opponent, and there is satisfaction in that. Great scholars are like that, at least until the eyesight goes, the memory becomes unreliable, and their ideas become inflexible. Perhaps we should return to public disputations with the clear understanding that one will win and one will lose and that knowledge and learning are to be used like weapons.

Certainly, the student of the fifties, and those of decades later, had to come to terms with the library. Everything from the facts that keep you alive in exams to the theoretical perspectives that earn top marks were found there. The task was not an easy one, and no real effort was made to be helpful to novices. Lesson one: if you don't copy out the number from the catalog correctly, chances are you will not find the book. Go back to square one. Lesson two: do not think you can spare the cutter numbers if you are looking for a specific book. Take the time at the drawer, not in the stacks. Go back to square one. Fortunately, there was beer.

When I first started working in circulation at Wilson Library, UNC, the stacks were closed to undergraduates but stack permits could be attained with a display of sufficient gravity. Starting as a book pager was probably the most brilliant move in my early life as a student. I kept in shape by running up and down stairs, and paging took me to parts of the stacks where I would never have gone in my own interest. Shelving books was a similar amazing learning experience.

Of course, sitting in the back, behind the curtain, was an IBM 29 Keypunch Machine. The rails were being laid for the future. Independent of cataloging, circulation was putting a punch card in every book. Eventually that punch card would be run through a machine that would designate that book as checked out to the owner of the hard plastic user card that was inserted in the machine. The circulation records were printed on green bar, one line per book. That is how it started. Eventually, data was integrated by linking up the circulation data with the OPAC data so the book record in the online catalog could tell you the book was checked out.

For those of us going to classes in the sixties, there was never the remotest notion that knowledge was exclusive to the library. We were being pointed to things all over the world; in the library we could only get vague hints of what had been out there and what was still out there in the world that we had to know about. Case in point, we needed to know about art and architecture. For those few of us who grew up in Europe, the library had little to tell us about those subjects. Since I was old enough to clamber up the steps of a streetcar by myself, I had been going to the museums in Vienna, which were free for kids on Sunday. After the museum I would go to church, generally a different one each Sunday, developing an intuitive sense for Gothic and Baroque and having doubts about historicism at an early age. And what did the music library have to tell a kid who had been going to the opera and the Musikverein since he was old enough to clip on a short tie?

So this sheep will not be herded easily into the re search library veneration society. I did at some point under stand the difference between the European "seminar library," the "university library," the "national library" and the American "university research library." The seminar library started in German universities long ago and referred to the subject specific book collections that individual departments collected for their professors and students, or the books that professors collected and made available to their students. That meant that the latest research would be available for the people who knew the field well enough to know when a certain book would be ready for publication and to expect the author to mail a copy fresh off the press. The university and national libraries were generally large, old collections going back to early modern times, reading room based, with stack access only to the very select few. Yet they would keep the books they could be bothered to find for you to read in the reading room, where you read them, vainly wishing for silence.

The American research library not only had people from all departments in the university ordering all the latest books, the stacks were open, and they would let you take the books home. Reference librarians were genuinely interested in helping. That was the brilliant thing: what was reserved for the top 5 to 10 percent of the learned in Europe was open to anyone who could walk through a door. Guards to restrict access appeared later, especially in urban environments, but not everywhere. I am as big a fan of the research library as Prof. Darnton is of Google, but let us not overdo it with the happy memories.

Still, knowledge and information were not exclusive to the library. Poor copies of the world, of civilization were in the texts in the library, copies that would have quickly aged out of a citation index, would we dare to have one. The Web generally has better copies, more useful copies of the world than my library ever had. Oh, what I would have given back in 1967 to have clicked through a complete catalog of the Louvre or of everything by Vermeer or Rubens. I knew where the black-and-white pictures of art were (700s). A lecture from the slide library was a rare peak experience back then; many slides were in gray scale.

One night after several beers, three of us graduate students drove from Chapel Hill to Washington so we would be there at ten when the National Gallery opened. We had talked each other into an irresistible urge to see Vermeer. I still have pictures of us lolling somewhat dazed on the Mall waiting for the doors to open.

Certainly when I was young I compensated for my lack of experience with an amazing lack of maturity, as students do today, but I do envy the effortless access that today's students have to the artifacts of world culture. The professors of today will have to build on this foundation as my professors built on what we could find in the stacks.

There is a time in the life of a student when information has been internalized, exams have been passed, some competence has been demonstrated, and the next step has to be taken. Here the register of "learning" must be loaded. It is no longer enough to know a work by Balthasar Neumann; one also must know what has been said about Balthasar Neumann through the epochs. This really is where books come in. Most students in the fifties never got there; most of my fellow students in the seventies dropped out to go to Silicon Valley, or get an MBA, or work for the UN, happy they had read deeply in German.

Listening to the extremely learned, one gets the notion that the educational institutions in the universe are destined to produce only the extremely learned. I think the Google people understand instinctively that the extremely learned are an exception but would probably not articulate that because it is too confrontational. Instinctively, they see a need to bring the books out of the stacks to join with everything else that has escaped to cyberspace years ago.

Let us forget for the moment any quibbling about the fifties and sixties and what those libraries were really like. Forget for the moment about the idea that the Web actually does produce new media representations of everything in the world that we ever might want to see from art to artifact to nature. Let us return to the shepherd and see where he wants to take us; it will not be mutton land, I am sure.

The master herder wants to get the trust of the suspicious sheep. He shows us a range of electronic projects—one particularly that would remodel his field of expertise and allow high-school students five years from now to write an essay on Voltaire that would have won a major prize in 1982. He presents similar examples for other fields. I am not in a position to say much more since guest accounts are available only to institutional librarians. For my vision of things, it is enough if these resources are made available to institutions. I don't need to click deeply outside my areas of familiarity.

However, at some point we should talk about just how much money is flowing out in user fees, not to stop the flow, but to renegotiate once the production costs have been recovered. Even the Mass Turnpike closed its tollbooths in due time, as did the Richmond-Petersburg Turnpike. We don't want Chadwyck-Healey and others eventually to choke on money with their user fees for electronic books.

I find it somewhat unconscionable that production costs for print are inflating the prices of electronic journals. These things should be all electronic and the practitioners of extreme nostalgia can print them out on their own paper and with their own toner. When printed, they actually don't look bad, and that goes for the online *Jenaische Allgemeine Literatur-Zeitung* of 1813 or *Daedalus* from MIT of 2009. I am not in a position to speculate what could be done for the printers and the truck drivers; I suspect they have seen the handwriting long ago and are installing routers.

The purpose of all this herding, we discover, is to show that Google, good old information-at-your-fingertips Google will not make research libraries obsolete. Personally, I am relieved; I thought it would be much worse. I certainly will follow him down that path without any need of nipping at my heels.

Darnton's Final Arguments: Eight Points

Argument one (1) is that Google in its present incarnation will not scan all books; it will miss some and researchers that rely on Google will be sadly misled. Other minor arguments trickle in: items in the library may not be scanned because at present, they appear to have no value. The fact that librarians through the ages have thrown away things that we wish we still had is being used as a caution. Point taken. Style points are high, substance points are medium.

The cataloging of books has benefited dramatically from the advent of computers. I see no reason why the Director of HUL should not break a lance or two to make sure that if there is some book lurking somewhere in the continental US and Canada that has not made it into its institution's OPAC, that book shall be found and the straggler be summarily cataloged. Furthermore, I should make sure that these OPACs, all of them in their entirety, find their way into WorldCat or some other online catalog with sufficient computing power. We must be sure that if a book is available somewhere, there is a central location where that fact can be established, preferably faster than at present with WorldCat, preferable in my study on my computer. I think something like that would make a good plenary address at some important conference.

I would remind everyone that the excuse "But the book was not in the stacks" was never an adequate excuse for anything, nor will "But the book was not on Google." Once WorldCat or its clone is complete, it will be a matter of comparing Google with WorldCat and taking Amtrak to Harrisburg to look for the uncataloged hiding among the Amish. More to the point would be to link up Google scans to the institutional OPACs as has been done to a degree at Harvard with HOLLIS, at Michigan, at the BSB in Munich and elsewhere. Programs can be written to do that automatically. Let us take the last few steps on a journey that was started years ago in Ohio. Catalogs of the world unite.

There will be serious re-engineering to be done in libraries. As more new books come out in electronic form, cataloging as we know it will become a lost art. Should the orphans find a secure home in some distribution system, I fail to see where original cataloging will find a niche. It is one thing to find fault with what Google may or may not do in the future; more to the point will be to decide what catalogers will catalog. Keeping the presses going perhaps with user fees from electronic resources will not last very long. People making budgets will wise up rapidly.

I remember a long six month exercise in re-engineering at Homewood Computing at JHU in the eighties. The inescapable fact was that the hundreds of thousands of dollars that the IBM VM hardware and software required were to be stricken from the budget. The unthinkable would happen: the machine room would be cleaned out; those who had been feeding heavy computing iron would have to learn to feed something else. The IBMs were replaced by a couple of racks of servers largely self-feeding. Ten years earlier, the TUCC centralized computer system that served Duke, UNC and NC State, the facility where I had cut my computer teeth, had closed with no loss of services. Technology is disruptive to comfortable lives—amen to that.

Point two (2) covers the raw numbers of books to be digitized. Given that we still have several billion years before the sun boils us away, I would say that five hundred million volumes of old books, double it for the Europeans, triple it for the Asians, does not scare me in the least. Google started digitizing books five years ago, and people are just beginning to sense the money that could be made. Give it at least another ten years—or as much time as the letters of Voltaire and his buddies take to get online.

Point three (3) covers copyright and continuing production. I do not think that at present we are governed by people who can take a larger view of the public good when it comes to competing private interests. Copyright legislation in the last ten years has proven the point. Our only solution may be to make some people rich so we can get at the texts we must have for our work. At present, the orphan scans are more useless than the books currently for sale electronically on the market.

Darnton paints a picture of continuing production that will overwhelm Google; the question is posed: "How can Google keep up with current production while at the same time digitizing all the books accumulated over the centuries?" [Darnton, 2008] One may ask in return: "Who if not Google?" As head of HUL,

Prof. Darnton should be in a position to shape the future. I see no great future for half a million new titles in print runs from a thousand to a hundred thousand being trucked around the country.

Let me veer off a bit. From Amazon/Kindle I can get texts for more than I could ever possibly work on, at least for starters, from data mining to programming to multivariate analysis to standard works on Ottoman history, in literally ten seconds. The Kindle store currently lists 300,000 items. Some of them are clearly amateur efforts, but many are real mainstream publications that cost fifty dollars printed and can be bought for download at a third of the price. And let us not start with the old reading-on-the-screen saw. Kindle texts are functionally equal, actually functionally superior because of search capabilities, to books. The texts have been optimized for the Kindle; they are searchable and can be annotated and bookmarked. The learning curve for using them is not steep, and the new habits that have to be developed are not especially difficult. The new habits enforce a certain discipline that can have only a positive effect on intellectual work.

The interface of the Kindle is highly developed, honed to an amazing degree to provide a seamless experience. To repeat myself, within minutes of taking the Kindle out of the box, I had downloaded a book on data mining that I own in hard copy and was skipping through the chapters, lying in a hammock by the pond in my backyard, much to the amazement of the geese in the distance. The interface provides a smooth experience; the built-in dictionary that defines every word under the cursor automatically is a brilliant idea for advancing verbal skills. That is also widely available on the Google Web pages as a translation service. There are other devices that have recently hit the market that promise to be the Kindle-killers. In their attempt to hype their functionality these wannabes forget that what really matters is access to e-books. The users of the Nook will be greatly disappointed to find that after a subject search their choices consist of three e-books from BN and the rest "Books Scanned by Google." They may even begin to appreciate the crude effectiveness of the "5-way-stick."

Clearly this is a direction with promise. I see no reason why all the latest research should not be available instantly on this device, or on the new and improved versions. Any intellectual robber barons imposing taxes on the commerce of ideas will have to be routed out of their strongholds in the name of the public good. We should also beware of the formation of cartels to inflate prices; just because Apple users are used to paying double for their computing does not mean the rest of us are eager to join their general profligacy.

I should add that users of all stripes are filling in odd times during the day with reading e-books on smart phones. It may be a quite natural development in the user community at large, especially since the phone is always in hand. Peeks into the personal e-book library may become an attractive alternative to the high drama of Twitter.

However, there are problems that must be solved. The typing of searches, numbers, and symbols must be made easier, especially for someone in a hammock. Kindle is on the move. The international Kindle has a distinctly improved keyboard with finger-sized round keys instead of Chiclets. In addition, the navigation buttons have been improved for left-handers.

At present, PDFs will load and run but only very slowly; they will, however, run faster than flying to Berkeley and going to the library. The Kindle must become more like a real external drive with subdirectories and file handling. But let us remember that the Kindle is not intended to be a computer; it may be that miniaturization will progress to the point where the distinction becomes mute. I must admit that there is a difference between reading on a 700 gram (1.5 lb) laptop and the Kindle; it is not a question of weight but rather the fit in the hands. The Sony reader clearly needs more work, especially the software. The Nook has some problems that begin with trying to get it out of the box without the two page instruction sheet on how to get it out of the box. Make sure you get that sheet if and when you buy one, or a hammer. We can expect this field to become very competitive and bring forth innovation before the inevitable shakeout.

Concerning the other points. D-lib had an article some time ago that we are outstripping our capacity to store our electronic production [Mest et al., "Time Challenges," D-Lib, May/June 2009]. A large percentage of our storage is taken up by unneeded even unintended duplicates of files. As the Web continues to grow, Google is really the only candidate that has a chance to keep up with that growth. It would of course be clever to position research libraries to carry some of that burden—if they are up to the task and not looking for third parties to carry the load.

We should ask Prof. Darnton: if every book at Harvard that has an entry in HOLLIS also had a link that would make the text downloadable to a netbook or a book reader would that not solve some problems. If new books were routinely issued in electronic form, as many are—with the exception, most notably, of the collected essays of the extremely learned (nudge, nudge)—then we are well on our way to infotopia. A new generation of book management software could be developed that tracked large collections as well as private collections and managed over-lapping servers. Complete bibliographies could be bundled and downloaded; no, no, Virginia, not the references, the texts. Whatever could happen, it will never be as bad as the Municipal Archive of Cologne collapsing during subway construction in 2008, damaging documents going back to the Carolingians no doubt, or the 100,000 seventeenth- and eighteenth-century books burning in Weimar a couple of years ago.

Arguments for the status quo in the face of the Google challenge should be abandoned in favor of expanding the challenge and shouldering additional burdens to achieve infotopia.

Point four (4) juxtaposes the ephemeral nature of technology companies to the *Rock-of-Ages* research library. Why are we defending the Rock of Ages against the onslaught of the ephemeral? Clearly libraries have received a shock. For the first time ever, the notion of repositories of hard copies has been challenged. Even the most ardent defenders of nostalgia for the past and the most vociferous critics of Google could be seduced in a New York minute by a PDF of some book from the nineteenth century that they have wanted to see for years and have not been able to find or afford. Or more enticing even, just go take a look at what stuff was published back then that you did not even know existed. Get online people, all these texts are already there.

Ladies and Gentlemen, this is going to be hard to stop; the only chance is to get on the bandwagon and start playing the tune. I should add, if Google disappears tomorrow, the scanned book files will remain objects of value, objects of desire, and objects of scheming, and they will be delivered to users.

Point five (5) addresses the mistakes of Google. Yes, mistakes will be made. Mistakes have been made. Mistakes have always been made, in writing, in printing, and in binding. As word processing has shown, in the electronic world, it is finally possible to correct mistakes. Mistakes are not a sign of an unalterable defect, they are not original sin, and they are to be corrected. There is still the notion left over from stern mentors of yore that certain mistakes are signs of such grievous unprofessionalism that dismissal of the unworthies is the only alternative. A closer look at the work of the stern masters is that they were themselves masters of the muddle, hence the errata pages and the not infrequent eviscerations in the journals. The electronic gods forgive gladly. Granted, there have never been as many misspelled words as there are in blogs and Web pages, but there may be someone who will design some "bon-ware" that will sneak around and correct spelling errors.

Point six (6) covers the potential of a digital data loss disaster. I find the argument somewhat strange. Let us say that working with electronic book files will win the day as word processing has won the day. Let us say that a great majority of people would rather work on their laptops and Kindles rather than filling their bags up with books. Stranger things have happened.

Let the library manage redundant data-storage for its holdings, rationalized so that electronic files are not treated with the same possessiveness as printed books. A couple of disk arrays per institution should do it; software could rout the electronic files by the most efficient path to the user in seconds. Google does not own any books. Then let us build a bunker and put the books in there to make sure that nothing happens to them till the sun burns out. We might take our electronic files to Alpha Centauri or the Delta Quadrant if we still think they are worth the bother.

Point seven (7) offers a suggestion.

> to: Google, Human Services
> from: Darnton, HUL
> re: bibliographer
>
> Urgent!!!! Get one!!!
> cheers, Robert

If I had a highly motivated workforce working with texts, I would not want a bibliographer gumming up the works. I could use a couple of OPAC jocks who can see beyond the MARC record and ordering by date or alphabet—although I would get a couple of dozen of those as well.

Seriously, we are getting to a gravely serious problem here that has been prepared by Prof. Darnton throughout the essay. Texts are inherently unstable.

> "No single copy of an eighteenth-century bestseller will do justice to the endless variety of editions. Serious scholars will have to study and compare many editions, in the original versions, not in the digitized reproductions that Google will sort out according to criteria that probably will have nothing to do with bibliographical scholarship." [Darnton, 2008]

Without asking in detail whether such work is worth doing, let us accept the challenge.

Prof. Darnton is carving himself a nature reservation for endangered species; "endless variety will have to be studied." Let us leave aside for the moment the clear inadequacy of the current Google scans of older books and the utter uselessness of the underlying text representation for many old scans. Let us instead pretend we have started a project to digitize eighteenth-century best-sellers. We have identified eight editions of some work published between the years 1738 and 1753. We have managed to photograph every page, the front, the back, the inside covers, even the inside of the spine. We have also prepared an electronic text. Arguments such as "that seems to be a lot of work" do not count with "bibliographical scholarship," where no amount of effort can be too much—we do love it so. Once that work is done, the variants can be presented automatically in table format. If some typesetter cut a line here or there to make the pages come out right, the software can be tweaked to discover that and identify the sections in a special column. Routine mistakes in typesetting can be culled out, as can more substantial reorganizations. Trees of derivation can be constructed based on methodologies developed for medieval manuscript traditions.

I would not think that a lone scholar working with printed copies of the eight editions could come up with a definitive list of variants. I don't know what the measures of success may be for bibliographical scholarship. Perhaps it is only to establish the date and place of printing. Comparing text files for variants may go beyond bibliographical scholarship (let us say "BS" for short), but that is what computers love best above all the world. They should have a run at this kind of work.

So we shall have to grant that in its present form the Google scans are not suitable for BS. On the other hand, the future of BS clearly lies in comparing electronic files. So we have to ask, is the Director of HUL finding arguments against the current practice of scanning, or is he carving out a conservation area of the eighteenth-century best-sellers for human labor in perpetuity?

There is a telling quote from Professor Darnton:

> "nothing suggests that [Google algorithms] ... will take account of the standards prescribed by bibliographers, such as the first edition to appear in print or the edition that corresponds most closely to the expressed intention of the author."
> [Darnton, 2008]

Given the problem of "the text submitted to the publisher by the author" and "what gets printed by the publisher" and "what rewriting was done after the novel flopped" and "what extra drafts are found" after the death of the author - given these well known problems—it is a little rhetorical, not to say disingenuous, to imply there is some solid theory or methodology of BS in this area. In the area of German Studies (Germanistik, Literaturwissenschaft) much hair has turned gray as every German writer from Herder to Günter Grass has been examined from these perspectives; there are still many scores to be settled. The computer is our last best hope for clarity.

This section (7) seems to display a serious misunderstanding about the nature of "page ranking." I find it somewhat strange that such a misunderstanding [read: lack of understanding] should come from the director of a library from which we expect leadership, especially in dealing with Google. Does Prof. Darnton really expect the generalized page-ranking algorithm to prepare a list for *serious* scholars to download, and say thank you very much indeed, let me send this off to the PMLA? Could Prof. Darnton imagine doing a few hours work with the advanced search function to get all the editions he wants within a mouse click and pasting the links on an HTML page? Or could Prof. Darnton imagine creating a Web site where the actual PDFs for the editions were arranged chronologically completely outside Googleland? A great example is the list of Google Books links to the Patrologia from Notre Dame. Bundling lists is already a major activity. The fact is that many of the not extremely learned out there, and this includes me, are simply smitten with the access to the past that Google Books gives us. We have finally gotten that stack permit to NYPL. You may not get "fully developed scholarship" from us, but you can count on dedicated efforts to organize sources.

It is a problem writing outside one's field to which Prof. Darnton is not immune. The voice wants to resonate and be convincing, alas, everywhere. Yet it does tend to get thin and tinny in some ears. I remember when a new edition of Musil's *Mann Ohne Eigenschaften* completely reorganized the first edition based on manuscripts in the literary estate. There were many unhappy campers. There may be several dozen examples of this kind of work with modern writers. Someone may want to rewrite Joyce, or Hemingway, or Sartre. Many philosophers have been rewritten; for some we have no real idea what was meant for publication and what were random notes made by the philosopher on a bad day. If someone wants to do this kind of work on eighteenth-century bestsellers, *brava, bravo*—but there are no anti-scanning arguments here.

Indulge me for a paragraph or two. An extended quote may help to hear Prof. Darnton distinctly. In this section, Prof. Darnton tries to peer into the black box.

> "Google plans to digitize many versions of each book, taking whatever it gets as the copies appear, assembly-line fashion, from the shelves; but will it make all of them available? If so, which one will it put at the top of its search list? Ordinary readers could get lost while searching among thousands of different editions of Shakespeare's plays, so they will depend on the editions that Google makes most easily accessible. Will Google determine its relevance ranking of books in the same way that it ranks references to everything else, from toothpaste to movie stars? It now has a secret algorithm to rank Web pages according to the

> frequency of use among the pages linked to them,
> and presumably it will come up with some such
> algorithm in order to rank the demand for books.
> But nothing suggests that it will take account of
> the standards prescribed by bibliographers, such as
> the first edition to appear in print or the edition
> that corresponds most closely to the expressed
> intention of the author." [Darnton, 2008]

The wrestling is full earnest; it is in the style of an OPAC user. First, Google lacks a bibliographer, an assumption. Second, the scanning is assembly line fashion, haphazard. Third, ordinary readers will be overwhelmed. One might ask, how do ordinary readers deal with the thousands of editions of Shakespeare plays in the Harvard University Libraries? In Google, user statistics accumulated over time rank pages of Hamlet, and the results of a general query may not differentiate between editions and scholarship about Hamlet, convenient for the ordinary reader. At Harvard, better get a PhD in English and write a dissertation on Shakespeare. Yet that is not the right question. The extremely learned cannot ask the right questions in this area. On one hand we are concerned about the ordinary reader finding some Shakespeare, no problem with Google in its present state. I would rather go to Google than sit through an introductory lecture at Harvard. On the other hand we are concerned with the bibliographical fine points of text traditions which are generally not touched by OPACs but explicated at length in specialized monographs that take years to prepare.

It is quite legitimate to be skeptical of Google's efforts. However, to write with authority about what goes on inside the black box requires some concerted effort. By that token, I would not make glib arguments about the "page ranking algorithm" and make dire predictions on how it will develop or not, unless I had spent some considerable time with it, or poked around in some textbooks on the subject, or gotten off at Kendall Square occasionally. There may well be "some such algorithm," but I would trust Brin and Page and the engineers to make sure the algorithm in question will have a chance to grow into effectiveness; the one on movie stars is not bad at all. I have not tried out toothpaste on Google; I'm good! You can be pretty sure you will not get the first edition served up first by Google, but HOLLIS also has no clue which is the first edition of something.

But a passage from one of our eight hypothetical editions may be on the first page of any number of queries. It really depends on the semantic content of the novel, the bags of words on individual pages and on whatever features the text miners at Google may find important and helpful. It may not be helpful for working in BS. One thing to remember: page ranking revolves around the search term that will bring you pages. Don't use it if you already know you want a specific book, the whole book, and not a page on "chamber maids."

I cannot repeat often enough that the lessons finally learned on the OPAC, how to find a book in an electronic catalog, should not be applied to page ranking by Google. Has no one wondered what it means that Google presents books opened to a specific page? Page ranking is not there to find specific books; it is there to point to relevant passages in the text. Text is a continuum, and a vast index points to pages in the continuum. Pages are a convenient but arbitrary unit. It may be considered hubris by the extremely learned, but there it is: the kids from Mountain View want to divide up books into pages and mine pages based on a vast, ever-growing index. It is an ambitious project, but the head of HUL cannot afford to sneer at the idea, or, let us say more gently, he would not sneer once he developed familiarity with the concept.

The library is a service organization, as is the computer center. The Chief Librarian cannot dismiss processes in exciting new fields of the science of text because of his expertise in antiquarianism or his seat on the Oxford UP board. That voice may persuade some, but to a text miner, it is just a pair of silk breeches with a powdered wig that does not know where the coal is to be found.

In section eight (8) we weary of the battle. The wad is gone, lost in the last salvo, but the battle still hangs in the balance. The acrid smell of burnt powder swirls in dank fog around the combatants …

Speaking of smell, how are we going to get the sheep around the tree and into the pen? Let us be disarming. First, the red herring in crème fraîche with capers: the importance of the smell of books. This is a theme we will encounter with Prof. Grafton as well. I am doing just fine without the smell of old books as a guiding principle; having grown up in Europe, my nostalgia goes towards steam locomotives and freshly filled honey wagons or a really ripe brick of Limburger. Then we get a bit about eye of newt and snout of toad and whatever else was mixed into early paper.

> "Books also give off special smells. According to a recent survey of French students, 43 percent consider smell to be one of the most important qualities of printed books—so important that they resist buying odorless electronic books. *CaféScribe*, a French on-line publisher, is trying to counteract that reaction by giving its customers a sticker that will give off a fusty, bookish smell when it is attached to their computers.

> When I read an old book, I hold its pages up to the light and often find among the fibers of the paper little circles made by drops from the hand of the vatman as he made the sheet—or bits of shirts and petticoats that failed to be ground up adequately during the preparation of the pulp. I once found a fingerprint of a pressman enclosed in the binding of an eighteenth-century Encyclopédie— testimony to tricks in the trade of printers, who sometimes spread too much ink on the type in

order to make it easier to get an impression by
pulling the bar of the press." [Darnton 2008]

After several more paragraphs of rhapsody on the physicality
of books we get a pat on the back and a resounding: "...but its all
about the text isn't it?" Well thank you very much inded, so it is,
isn't it.

But then, like an addict, despite disavowals, Prof. Darnton
takes one last lingering draught of the elixir of the aesthetics of
the ancient artifact, and he projects into the future, when
handheld technology will have bloomed fully:

> "Perhaps someday a text on a handheld screen will
> please the eye as thoroughly as a page of a codex
> produced two thousand years ago." [Darnton,
> 2008]

Of course Prof. Darnton projects that date of mature handheld
technology a few centuries further. The first codex will not be
two thousand years old till 2300. I have never held a codex
produced one thousand seven hundred years ago, nor really hope
to do so. The high-res images of the "Codex Sinaiticus" on the
Web site of the same name are as close to the physicality of the
fourth century as I will ever be allowed to get; I am fine with
that.

Let us pretend we did not pick up on that. Let us stay with our
designs to please the eye with a papyrus scroll from some site in
the Middle East on the 2029 version of an iPhone and throw all
our concentration on text.

It is most emphatically about the text, it is about herme-
neutics, figuring out the text, giving life to the thoughts that were
put down on paper so that they be preserved, whatever the
motivation, whatever the genre, whatever the medium.

When I look at the not really ancient sixteenth-century
Ottoman chronicle that I am working on currently, I see
Leunclavius considering on the pressing problem of the day. The

images of the pages are crisp on my laptop, the book itself is hidden well in its padded box; I see only words and sentences. Time 1590, place Vienna. There was war with the Ottomans, perpetual war, interrupted only so the Thirty Years War could get on the agenda. Fortunately the Sultan's agenda was also full. There was clear and present danger with the outcome uncertain for another 120 years. In many ways it was understood that the foe was clearly superior, on many levels. Tribute will have to be paid, many thousands will have to endure slavery (for many, a good career move), savage encounters will have to be won or the alternative suffered dreadfully. Yet there was an attempt to understand the foe, a clear, respectful understanding, a caution against complacency, a caution against underestimating capacities and will, aspects that could be communicated to others so the foe might be understood and eventually beaten. There is some indication that Leunclavius died at the Siege of Gran in 1596 and his papers were lost, but his book on the Ottomans was in the library of Prince Eugene, who came up with a clear two pages of instructions to his staff a hundred years later that allowed fifty thousand of his soldiers to rout two hundred thousand soldiers of the Sultan routinely. It had nothing to do with bravery, esprit or fierceness; it had everything to do with calm discipline and technology.

When I go through all the facts that Leunclavius had accumulated and the earnestness of his narrative, I can see how knowledge can become power. I can understand that my understanding of Leunclavius is perhaps not as deep as that of his contemporaries for whom the question was central. After all, I know who won those rounds.

I would assert that many of our predecessors had a better grasp of the past than our most learned contemporaries. Would I attempt to read Aristotle as had Brentano (Franz)? Would I read Nietzsche as had Heidegger? Those boats have sailed and all that is left is text about text. In the humanities we are put in a position of epigones. Yet technology has given us perspectives never before experienced. As I work on the texts of Leunclavius, it occurred to me that it may be enough to have done a semantic inventory of Leunclavius. Perhaps putting his chronology in step with the chronologies of Hammer and Zinkeisen and the few Ottoman chronicles that have been translated could prepare the seedbed for a generalized trans-cultural Hapsburg-Ottoman chronology. I don't mean the latest agreed-on version of that chronology that can be memorized, but a chronology of the actual statements of *reported fact* as experienced and related by Leunclavius and his Ottoman contemporaries.

In this project, Google has been very helpful to me. I have complete editions of the two most important sources in the nineteenth century, priceless and invaluable in electronic form (to the chagrin of the expensive volumes banned off my desk). I have just begun to enumerate all the histories the Hapsburg Empire created in all its territories that Google has scanned up to the end of that empire. I would never have dreamed that I could take a library of these texts into my hammock to amaze myself and the geese. It is possible to say that the wealth of sources has made the project practically unmanageable; certainly it has made it much more complicated for a single researcher. Yet, sources are now in my electronic workspace that appear in none of the recent bibliographies. It will be a matter of deciding if these fallow fields should be recultivated, or if they have been abandoned because of the toxic soil.

Prof. Darnton is the master of the last paragraph. Some harsh words have been said; some hidden agendas have been insinuated, but now, *mes enfants*, it is July 14, and it is time to celebrate. Vive everything! Vive the library, printed matter, books, electronic impulses, data sets, digital repositories, e-journals, and information systems.

We have arrived; above the shed for us sheep is printed in big letters, "Shore up the library." Cautionary essays are so hard to write because the message cannot be clear. On one hand, the future is running away from all of us and with it the constituents of Prof. Darnton's responsibilities; on the other hand, he would like to reverse the process and have them leave their lattes at the door and file back into the reading room. I don't see research libraries threatened. I see them meeting the challenge if they continue their proactive course towards delivery of electronic resources.

I can only smile at the notion of picking up a book for a good read. I would much rather go to *Gutenberg* and pick out a Trollope or a Stifter and load them in my Kindle for free. I can pick from all of literature. Or I may just buy something for two dollars from the Kindle Store, maybe a Virginia Woolf, or maybe Darnton's book about the dead cats. I get nervous when I don't see a cursor. I am trying to establish a competing paradigm. Look here! I have access to the most unbelievable bookstore with my Kindle. It is not "an undifferentiated mass" that I have to dig through. After all, I have an idea roughly where I want to read. And if not, like any good store, Amazon pushes books to the front, though generally not for my demographic. But they do remember what I bought and are trying to please me by finding ever more data-mining books and works on phenomenology.

But here we have the chief metaphor of the extremely learned: the good read versus the mass of millions of Web sites and electronic texts. A stack of several million books side by side in cramped dusty quarters, the agoraphobe's favorite place is just fine; it is the *locus amoenus* of the medieval romance, the place of "the magic of words as ink on paper." By contrast, Web resources are portrayed as masses of undifferentiated material and processes that one must search, navigate, harvest, mine, deep link, and crawl. One should appreciate that many features in text do not just come up and bite you, neither in the stacks nor on the computer. Words can hide in text, even from experts. The automatic processes of harvesting repeated phrases, for example can yield surprising information. A harvest of repeating phrases in Virginia Woolf's *Jacob's Room* will yield two identical paragraphs many pages apart. It takes a while to come up with an explanation.

Listless is the air in an empty room, just swelling the curtain; the flowers in the jar shift. One fibre in the wicker arm-chair creaks, though no one sits there [Jacob's Room, eBooks@Adelaide, chapter 3].

Listless is the air in an empty room, just swelling the curtain; the flowers in the jar shift. One fibre in the wicker arm-chair creaks, though no one sits there [Jacob's Room, eBooks@Adelaide, chapter 14].

I suspect a large percentage of readers never even noticed. I noticed it only by accident since I thought I had scanned a page twice, back in the early days. For me it was not a question of defective reading, but rather a question of having a good friend in the computer. I have actually never met anyone who has read *Jacob's Room*; literally, the book is "passing strange."

The electronic activities mentioned above: search, navigate, harvest, mine, deep link, and crawl, although a random and disparate selection of technical vocabulary from the field, are nevertheless representative of processes that will undertake focused forays into the historical dimensions of text; for example: a search for specific answers or a trawling for hidden features. Some modern techniques are based on the insight that the hidden patterns in text cannot be discovered through sequential reading. Hence learning algorithms that can pick up patterns that elude human perception.

Alas, Prof. Darnton's logic leads him surely to its consequences. It is a vision I do not share. I have so many reservations that I have a problem considering this logic an example of proper vision; it is backsliding of monumental proportions; I will paraphrase:

1. No computer screen gives satisfaction like the printed page.
2. The Internet delivers data that can be transformed into a classical codex.
3. The electronic file of page images can be saved from its manifest awfulness by turning it back into bound pages through print on demand.

Boink, we are back in early modern times sitting in the mud, eating roughage. The circle is complete, so speaks the head of Harvard Libraries; please, all exhale.

Logic is bitter, but it will have its due. We will chuck searching, and we will print many millions of defective books because many citizens will not buy new glasses so they can finally read the computer screen on a two pound laptop or a one pound Kindle. Will the professor be pleased by the print-on-demand page when the rays of the sun play over the contours of the hardened toner?

Then comes the great non sequitur to which we have alluded above:

> "Perhaps someday a text on a handheld screen will please the eye as thoroughly as a page of a codex produced two thousand years ago." [Darnton, 2008]

Does anyone really want that? Is that really necessary? What were codexes back then that made them so beautiful? Or is the mere voice, decoupled, running away with us here? Does the director of HUL feel he must play the role of antiquarian to the bitter end? Is he caught holding up one end of a dialectic that is long past synthesis?

The last paragraph brings it all together, and Google gets the roast: "I also say: long live Google, but don't count on it living long enough to replace that venerable building with the Corinthian columns." [Darnton, 2008] That is the parting curse of the antiquarian, I am glad it did not say "Doric columns," that would have been devastating.

Let us move on.

Enter the Paladin: 2009

We have one more sheepdog trial ahead of us: the finals of the Google Settlement Trial; there will be several heats. I have professed utter indifference to the original lawsuit; I have professed utter disinterest in the settlement. If I thought any reasonable logic operated in those proceedings for the benefit of the common good, I would change my tune. Yet I accept that the clash of interests must take place, and paladins must do battle.

The fact cannot be escaped that Prof. Darnton has become a major player in the Google digitization game. He became head of HUL in 2007; the second paper discussed above came out in June 2008. Toward the end of October 2008, the settlement between Google and the authors/publishers was announced.

What little information leaked through my earplugs at the time filled me with some horror. Some medium-sized bureau-cracy is to be set up to take money from people wanting to read fifty-year-old books on behalf of authors who may or may not be alive. The money is to be collected in order to encourage them or their heirs to step forward and accept their rewards. To manage all this and deliver the goods, Google gets a third. At that point I lowered the "cone of silence."

A day after the announcement of the settlement, Prof. Darnton wrote a letter to the HUL staff informing them that the terms of use for the orphan books were simply too uncertain and potentially restrictive that Harvard would not participate but would leave options open. I have not had my ear to the ground on this topic because my disinterest was genuine, but I can imagine some fur flying. I think this move by Harvard made everyone sit up and pay attention.

A few months later, in February 2009, Prof. Darnton published the essay "Google and the Future of Books" in the

NYRB. (In October of that year a collection of many of Professor Darnton essays on the topic of books was published by Public Affairs, NY, under the title of "The Case for Books.") In March, the first reactions to the Darnton essay were published in the NYRB; there was a stout defense of the settlement by Darnton's counterpart at Michigan and a letter of thanks from representatives of literary estates, thanking everyone concerned for finally designing a cash flow into their moribund enterprises. (NB: Interpretation all mine.)

So let us go through the 2009 essay to see where we are going to be led. Prof. Darnton starts with a summary of the announcement of the settlement. He has a clear view of his responsibility: to open the collections at Harvard to all. [A quick aside: what about the recent requirement for Harvard logins to open electronic books? What part of the word open do I not understand?]

In all the uncertainty, Prof. Darnton does his favorite thing: he looks in the rearview mirror. We are taken to the eighteenth century and the Republic of Letters.

I think we can safely say that from the very beginning Prof. Darnton was glued to the rearview mirror. We are on a forced march with all sorts of literary and historical figures waving from the side of the road. There is no real reason to follow that presentation in detail; read it yourself. For us it becomes interesting when the discussion turns to the letter of copyright law.

To make a long story short, the British tradition was set into definitive law in 1774 after the last challenge expired.

> "At that time, Parliament set the length of copyright at fourteen years, renewable only once." [Darnton, 2009]

> "When the Americans gathered to draft a constitution thirteen years later, they generally favored the view that had predominated in Britain. Twenty-eight years seemed long enough to protect

the interests of authors and publishers. Beyond that limit, the interest of the public should prevail." [Darnton, 2009]

[Since my personal interest in copyright is negligible, I have not performed what some would consider due diligence by tracing the evolution of European copyright law. I only know that if an author is killed in the service of France, the heirs get an extra 25 years on top of the normal 70. At this point my own logic circuits begin to wobble.]

The focus shifts to the current US. In 1998, Congress set copyright for the life of the author plus seventy years, affecting all books after 1923. Really, this is when I tuned out and decided to realign my interests out of the twentieth century. As a specialist and advocate of digitization, when digitization was not cool, and living in New Jersey at the time, I could only say: "Forget youse!"

Prof. Darnton shifts gears to examine journal publishing. He sketches a timeline from the "professionalization" of the sciences in the nineteenth century to the division of disciplines into departments and separate campus real estate. Somehow we have to get to journals, university presses, and library budgets. The story is brutal; journals are becoming ever more expensive and are taking ever more of the available budget and forcing cuts in acquisition of monographs; this in turn squeezes the presses, which depend on the library market, and this squeezes the young scholars who have to be published.

Of course the real concern is to secure the place of the library as the heart, lungs, and brain of the university.

When Darnton returns to Google, the mood is sour:

"When businesses like Google look at libraries, they do not merely see temples of learning. They see potential assets or what they call "content," ready to be mined. Built up over centuries at an enormous expenditure of money and labor, library

> collections can be digitized en masse at relatively
> little cost - millions of dollars, certainly, but little
> compared to the investment that went into them."
> [Darnton, 2009]

What is the intention here? OK, library collections have been built over time at substantial cost. OK, they can be digitized for relatively little money by comparison. OK, Google looks at a library and sees "content." What should they see? Circulation statistics show that over half of the books in Widener have not been checked out since the Carter administration, and a quarter since before WWI. Correct me if I am wrong. "Content" ready to be mined is not a dirty word. Text mining is an important new academic discipline; departments of information science all over the world are ramping up to deal with the intense interest. The fact is that information generally has the form of text, be it Web pages or book pages. Data mining became interesting when Google showed it could harness unbelievable amounts of information and give millions of simultaneous users a satisfying query experience. Does Prof. Darnton want to tie HUL to the tracks of that train?

The notion that he is against content mining because he is against commercialization, which is inimical to the public good, is hard to follow. Better to restrict the books to the physical proximity of Cambridge, Massachusetts, require Harvard logins to the odd e-book in order to guarantee access free to all?! It may be that he is actually just holding out for a better deal. By playing the monopoly card and mixing in Jefferson and Franklin, maybe the settlement can be scuttled and the orphaned books can be adopted by parents who will let them play for free. Or perhaps, the actual foster parents who gave the orphans a loving home all these years, the library, will get a cut.

We have to vivisect the argument:

1. Due to the 1998 Act of Congress, books from 1923 on into the foreseeable future are covered by copyright. If an author died in 1940, the book will come out of copyright this year, but this is by no means the whole story. Prof. Darnton heaps much scorn on the work of Congress in this matter:

   "I acknowledge the importance of copyright, although I think that Congress got it better in 1790 than in 1998." [Darnton, 2009]

Clearly Darnton thinks Congress has made a dog's breakfast of the issue.

The damage is so great that the public has lost the only defender of its rights.

   "No invisible hand would intervene to correct the imbalance between the private and the public welfare. Only the public can do that, but who speaks for the public? Not the legislators of the Mickey Mouse Protection Act." [Darnton, 2009]

It is possible that due to the self-disqualification of Congress, Prof. Darnton feels that the mantle of protecting the public has fallen on his shoulders.

2. Prof. Darnton is clearly miffed at publishers of journals. He quotes the figures for the most expensive journals but fails to mention that the market will bear these costs. The invisible finger has wagged and declared that Neurology can be expensive. Since he is on the purchasing side in the equation of journal prices, why does Prof. Darnton not lead a revolt of the research libraries against rapacious pricing?

Yet he seems to accept the *fait accompli* of journal prices, a sort of "fool me once, shame on me." But he will not be fooled twice. Unfortunately, Google was next in line.

> "To digitize collections and sell the product in ways that fail to guarantee wide access would be to repeat the mistake that was made when publishers exploited the market for scholarly journals, but on a much greater scale, for it would turn the Internet into an instrument for privatizing knowledge that belongs in the public sphere." [Darnton, 2009]

Here the vivisection becomes problematical. Mistakes were made with journals, they have become too expensive, and the libraries, including HUL, have paid up because they like to see their professors on the list of authors. I think no one expects wide access to journals about neurology. In the quote directly above, Darnton does link journal prices to the prospect of Google exploiting the market. So it all hinges on this: does the settlement guarantee wide access at reasonable prices so a digital copy of the first edition of *Catcher in the Rye* does not end up costing $49.50?

Darnton writes that "…no invisible hand would intervene…" [Darnton, 2009] to balance public and private interest. So we have to look also at the invisible hand—as best we can. For some, the invisible hand is the capitalist who ruthlessly destroys the lives of the little person from afar as some unseen force that wreaks havoc. Laissez-faire has gotten a bad name for that. For others, the invisible hand is a market force that depends on everyone employing rational self-interest, which is the best hope of the public good. There must be another, more subtle reading of the image. In our case, we have an implication that there is an invisible hand that "could" correct imbalances, but in this case, it "would" not. Or perhaps Prof. Darnton implies that there is no invisible hand at all and we are in the good hands of the Jubilation T. Cornpones the public sends to Congress.

Prof. Darnton has come to the same conclusion as many of us; it is about dividing the money. But given the 1998 Copyright Term Extension Act, how could it be about anything but money. The authors and publishers—and Donald, Mickey, and the Green Lantern—lobbied back in the nineties, and they won. Back then, all of us who bothered to think through the consequences realized they would not be good for electronic versions of texts.

Darnton has this to say:

> "No one should dispute the claim of authors and publishers to income from rights that properly belong to them; nor should anyone presume to pass quick judgment on the contending parties of the lawsuit. The district court judge will pronounce on the validity of the settlement, but that is primarily a matter of dividing profits, not of promoting the public interest." [Darnton, 2009]

3. Darnton has morphed into the defender of the libraries and the defender of the public interest:

> "You cannot legislate Enlightenment, but you can set rules of the game to protect the public interest. Libraries represent the public good. They are not businesses, but they must cover their costs." [Darnton, 2009]

The picture is becoming clearer. If the digitization money is split between Google to cover its delivery cost and the authors and publishers to garner their entitlement, the libraries are left sitting on stacks of dusty, smelly books.

It is one thing to argue that no learning can take place without the actual physical books. That is not a keeper. The only alternative is to argue that as the stewards of the public good (as related to information, knowledge, scholarship, and learning), the libraries, henceforward called the parties of the first part, will be abridged in the performance of their public service by a big, vile, odorous, greedy monopoly, henceforward called the party of the second part. That argument may actually work. Of course, the authors and publishers cannot audition for the role of monopolist; they are already dressed up as the impecunious heirs of deserving authors and as public-spirited publishers operating at a loss for serving the public weal. They are gratefully huddled over at stage right for having finally been given their just due by Uncle Congress. So let's put a black suit, white spats, and a gold watch-chain on Brin and Page and their lawyers.

To cement the casting, Darnton has to set the scene, something out of a dinosaur movie.

> "[At the formation of the Internet] … commercial interests did not sit idly on the sidelines. They want to control the game, to take it over, to own it. They compete among themselves, of course, but so ferociously that they kill each other off. Their struggle for survival is leading toward an oligopoly; and whoever may win, the victory could mean a defeat for the public good." [Darnton, 2009]

Darnton says this:

> "We need … to win back the public's rightful domain. When I say "we," I mean we the people, we who created the Constitution and who should make the Enlightenment principles behind it inform the everyday realities of the information society." [Darnton, 2009]

It looks like nothing so much as a repeal of the Mickey Mouse Act and a rewriting of Copyright Law with a Democratic

Congress and a Democratic President. I would not hold my breath.

The argument goes on for another nineteen paragraphs, which we can summarize briefly. There is the insinuation in the form of a trumpet blast from the ramparts, that Google and the authors and publishers have intertwined themselves with a golden chain. If the settlement is accepted as is, they will shovel money at each other, and no one shall be able to rend the golden chain asunder, even if it turns out a disaster. And who will complain? The publishers, a powerful often misunderstood group, are extremely happy with the Mickey Mouse Act, as are authors, musicians, comic book writers and whoever else got an entitlement. Where is the constituency for a fight?

Several paragraphs express intense regret that the Library of Congress, the National Endowment, and a consortium of research libraries did not do this job in the nineties to create the National Digital Library. I can tell you why this did not happen; despite many people (like me) trying to persuade anyone and everyone who would listen that digitization was important—with few exceptions—the scholars, professors, administrators, and librarians thought it ridiculous, absurd, and potentially grounds for dismissal. OK, we were allowed to do small tests, to set up a Glimpse site for American novels here and dabble a little there; but a national mobilization? It was not happening; I was there.

So along comes Google. Google not only demonstrates the feasibility of digitization, but it scans up to the original goal of fifteen million in five years. Of course, it is not exactly my type of scanning, but it is a great start, and the messes can be cleaned up in good time. The world watches in stunned silence. So we are faced with "unintended consequences" according to Prof. Darnton. I would say they are not unintended at all. The publishers and authors intended to get paid some day, and that day has come. Google intended to deliver the books of the world because no one else could be bothered, and they were willing to invest a small percentage of one year's net to get it done. That is how monopolies operate, is it not?

Here we have the lament of the would-be contender:

"We could have created a National Digital Library - the twenty-first-century equivalent of the Library of Alexandria." [Darnton, 2009]

The point is, *we did not*, although I did build the library of Peter with my own energy and resources. For my part, were I a star humanist instead of a veteran of technical professional grades, I would be ashamed to say what should have been done at a time before Google showed it could be done. I think legions of professional technical grades would have flocked to the banner if there had been just even a murmur that such a project was plausible.

In this essay, we are not given a rousing last paragraph. The vivats are spent. Prof. Darnton's says his first two years at Widener had no real duties but to argue with lawyers; it seems he has exhausted his sunny disposition. In his view, the vision of the founding fathers has foundered due to the lack of imagination of librarians and politicians everywhere. The settlement will create revenue streams into perpetuity for private interests to the detriment of the public good and nothing can stop it.

We are left with the thought: "The Enlightenment dream may be as elusive as ever." [Darnton, 2009] Fade to black.

Let us assume we are dealing with rhetoric here. Prof. Darnton has chosen the pessimistic view—though he has tried to establish that he is upbeat about technology. He is very unhappy with the Congress. He accepts the free market, but he longs for a time when there was no free market; he longs for a time when there were just some thinkers postulating a better world. Over two hundred years have passed with the ideas of the founding fathers in play. It is not helpful to immerse oneself in the ideas of two hundred years ago if one forgets that the only test of those ideas is their in echo the present. In this present, two recent Stanford PhDs have scanned fifteen million books without breaking a sweat. They have linked millions of information sites together so anyone, in any language, can ask a question and be presented with a plausible source of information. I have used

Google constantly for years without ever paying a dime. That is the public good writ large. Jefferson would be pleased.

The fact that money will change hands and people will get rich is part of the process. Money was made during the revolution and during Washington's presidency. Had I lived back then I might have wanted specific things for free, but they were not free.

If I have to pay ten dollars for a PDF of a book I want, then I will pay it and not begrudge the authors their $7.30 or Google its $3.70. I might think that a dime might be a better price, and I will say so. I have received such benefit from the work of Google that I will not let a rather inflexible interpretation of the nature of enlightenment or a two-hundred-year-old interpretation of the public good distract me from the task before me and my computers.

If money is distributed in return for services, then I say *tally ho*, I am for it. If the price is too high, it is time to haggle. I think it is good that money should be diverted from cigarettes, cheeseburgers, and pay-per-view, to authors, publishers, and Google.

But it may not come to that. Prof. Darnton states several times that he has not grasped the full implications of the settlement. He is clear about one thing: there is nothing in it for the libraries. Actually, if the settlement works as the rumor mill has it, there will be a substantial downside for libraries.

That downside, for all of Prof. Darnton's protestations, can only be postponed; digitization, as illustrated by his own work with the letters of the eighteenth century, will not be halted. Projects such as the Peirce *Chronological Edition* that have a 2050 completion date of another twenty-four heavy volumes cannot be the hope of libraries. This kind of book production will grind to a halt.

Whether the settlement stands or falls, libraries will have to continue to re-engineer. In the meanwhile, I see no problem with the paladin of the libraries to pull out all rhetorical stops to scuttle or change the settlement. Perhaps the best thing would be for someone to walk away from the settlement; let's have a couple rounds of real litigation and give those lawyers some sleepless nights. However, if the settlement can be modified to give the library from which a book was scanned just a dime for every dollar of revenue, the future of libraries may be bright, and libraries would have an incentive to scan. If they would give me personally just a penny on the dollar, I would write a very nice thank you note.

I fervently hope that Prof. Darnton will prevail and not let the seeming defeat of the forces of good as projected by his reading of the enlightenment sour his appreciation of the present. There are good reasons why historians should stay historians, and why it is best to be a historian in the later years of life. At that point, the immersion in the past can be full and will have no consequences for the present. If the attitudes of the historian are projected on the present, the effect will be unpredictable. Perhaps others will be inspired to forget all the problems of a past when Jefferson dreamed of the unfettered white men exceeding their potential, and they will be seduced by the sound of words that have since changed their meaning. Let us leave the notion of "Free for All" sitting above the entrance of the Boston Public Library and let us return to a world where a rational business plan requires recovery of costs. Infrastructure and the cost of maintaining infrastructure has changed from the time you could ride the speckled gray up to Monticello to look something up in Mr. Jefferson's volumes of Voltaire. I see no appetite for expensive public electronic projects. I see no competence in the public sector to achieve such projects. I do see some considerable idealism and some considerable competence in Google in the area of information. That is the beacon of today.

The present has its own dynamic only vaguely and incrementally derived from the past. We have the rhetoric of the Enlightenment, but we also have the rhetoric of Nationalism, the rhetoric of Industrialism and the rhetoric of Global Information. There is no bridge back to the Enlightenment except through specialists on those texts. Before a reading of those texts can be brought to bear on the present, they must be supplemented by any number of other texts that hold that emancipation did not end at the Siege of Yorktown. Let us not forget that the enlightened thought of that time was bought by the labors of a large underclass in Europe and also in the Colonies, and that their acts of revenge were brutal.

It does no good to orient ourselves by the sentences of the past. Jefferson said as quoted by Darnton:

> "I look to the diffusion of light and education as the resource most to be relied on for ameliorating the condition promoting the virtue and advancing the happiness of man."

It is hard work to trace the changes of the meaning of those words through the previous two centuries. The ramifications of those words are all around us, at Harvard, at UVA, in Palo Alto, and in Mountain View. We cannot find the present deficient with reference to the past. History should teach us—if I may become insolent for a moment—that the present belongs to the young. Even Jefferson's quote was a radical formulation that contradicted educational practice in his time. So we need radical formulations for the educational practices of this day; these formulations abound in electronic methodologies; the extremely learned should stay on the bus.

Spinning Google For the Europeans

We have looked at three essays of Prof. Darnton, and we should have no illusion what he sees when he holds a codex. He holds it up to the light to let his aesthetic sense be inspired by the craft of the papermaker. But I don't actually believe that. Prof. Darnton has assimilated plenty of information in his time. He has drawn inferences from texts and developed theories and models of how the past worked.

Science has played catch-up and produced algorithms and learning systems that would also like a shot at developing models of the past.

Darnton looks at Widener and sees a temple of learning with all that metaphor implies: initiations, a clergy, sacred fires, accumulated wisdom, funny hats, and secret handshakes. Brin and Page look at Widener and they see a medium-sized collection of Unicode characters grouped into words displayed in individually numbered pages. In short, they see something they can work with. The fact is that the books in the combined HUL libraries are crucial text resources. It is acceptable to hold that collection hostage for a time in order to influence a legal and political process—it is a great bargaining chip.

Yet, let us not be confused, there are no viable arguments here that hold up innovative research. A way must be found to make sure that before too long the content of HUL becomes available for text mining. Google is setting up a research unit at Stanford to start charting a way to mine the current corpus of fifteen million. This will not be that hard. At present there are several dozen professionals in the field who have written full-blown textbooks on data mining, going from old style corporate database mining to the text indexing and text mining pioneered by Google. There are thousands of very smart people flocking to that field, and departments are ramping up around the world.

Whatever the outcome of the settlement—whatever the coming dislocations in the library scene—the science of text analysis by computers will not be halted or even delayed.

So we come to the address at the Frankfurt Book Fair of October 2009. Many Europeans travel to the States; it would be better they did not. It would be better if there were only twenty-year permits. Want to come to America? Sign here, just like a Roman Legionnaire, welcome for the next two decades. This would solve the problem of Europeans coming to New York or LA for six weeks, the typical period of paid vacation in Europe, and then returning with all sorts of defective information.

It really takes twenty years or more of living in America for a European to be able to evaluate what all the Europeans who left Europe in the last three hundred years have really been up to.

Since this is not going to happen, we have to put up with European notions of what America is and what it should be, what it should and should not do. I responded with trepidation when I heard that Prof. Darnton would speak at the 2009 Frankfurt Book Fair. I need not have worried; America does not interest Europeans anymore since the financial crisis. China was the headliner at the Book Fair, and all the buzz was about whether anyone had stepped on Chinese toes and what horrible things should be done with that person.

Prof. Darnton's talk did not receive the widespread reception I expected; as I said, the details of American life are currently less interesting in Europe.

The text of the lecture is in *The Case for Books* [pp. 43–58]. To consider all parts of the little book would lead us too far afield, we shall focus on the introduction and on the Frankfurt lecture.

In the introduction we get a few pages of professional biography. That is helpful since it makes clear that Prof. Darnton was not a closeted scholar, despite regular highly regarded publications, but was active in all sorts of professional areas from television, publishing, to electronic projects.

Most interesting for me is his story about being hired by Harvard in 2007. Lest we had labored under any misconceptions, he relates that his new job was light on administration, which would continue to be done by the Head Librarians of the approximately one hundred libraries in the Harvard System.

Of interest to us are the passages about Google:

> "… in July 2007, as soon as I moved into my office, I learned that Harvard was involved in secret talks with Google about a project that took my breath away. Google planned to digitize

millions of books, starting with those at Harvard."
[CB, p. ix.]

We can assume that both Prof. Darnton and his editor would
not let random sentences slip past their watchful eye. So what
about the tenses here? Of course he learned about the secret talks
in July 2007—they were secret. Of course, given that everyone
was expecting a settlement in the publishers' suit, one could have
intimated that the partner libraries would be part of the
discussion—another secret, of course.

If we remove parts of the sentence, as is done in diagramming
the sentence, we come up with:

> "I learned … [of talks] … about a project that took
> my breath away." [CB, p. ix.]

Had I known about Google Books before July 2007, I might
have written:

> In July 2007, as soon as I moved into my office, I
> learned that Harvard was involved in secret talks
> with Google about a project that I first
> encountered at the Frankfurt Book Fair in 2004
> and had been using to find obscure gratis
> nineteenth-century sources on the Enlightenment.

Sergey Brin, one of the Google founders, declared in his
defense of the settlement in the NYT in 2008 that Google had
scanned ten million and counting. So how can Prof. Darnton's
editor let "Google planned to scan millions of books" be
associated with July 2007. That sentence should read: "Google
had been scanning millions of books, including some at Harvard
since 2004."

What precisely was it that took his breath away, and when
was that breath first taken away? If Prof. Darnton learned about
GBS in 2007 when he moved into his office as is implied, then

why did Harvard hire him? On the lighter side, I can just hear the search committee:

> "Hey, let's go over to Widener where Darnton is moving into his office and let's tell him about Google Books, but bring the oxygen, it may take his breath away."

I started first downloading files from Google Books in 2007, I had of course heard about the project and the legal issues, but I was not prepared for what they had achieved by 2007. Nor was I prepared to grasp that all these PDFs were free. There is no shame anymore of missing a piece of what is going on so long as you recognize it eventually. So, we can see Darnton working hard on his essay of 2008—the relatively mild tone implies that things will work out—but the 2009 essay signals a shift as the implications of the settlement seem to have sunk in; time to gird the loins and defend the opposition to the settlement.

In the introduction he alludes to his changing perception of Google.

> "The more I learned about Google, the more it appeared to me to be a monopoly intent on conquering markets rather than a natural ally of libraries, whose sole purpose is to preserve and diffuse knowledge." [CB, p. x]

Darnton uses a weak formulation: "it appeared to me," which gives me hope, since I would very much like to believe that Google is indeed a natural ally of libraries.

The public domain books available on Google make it the natural ally to the independent scholar living in Europe. This spring I was in Munich looking for a monograph by Konstantin Schlottmann on von Hammer published two years after Hammer's death. For reasons hard to understand, no library in Austria seemed to have the book; when I found it in the catalog at the BSB, in Munich, a note in red said the book was being scanned by Google and would be available again anon. Sometime later, I downloaded the book, saving a bunch of euros on xeroxing. I cannot imagine the librarians at the Bavarian State Library see in Google the enemy at the gates.

"Monopoly" is not mentioned in Darnton's 2008 essay; in the NYRB essay in 2009, it is mentioned several times as a phenomenon of the eighteenth century but only very obliquely in reference to Google. Thus we can only surmise there has been a serious escalation of Darnton's skepticism by October 2009.

At Frankfurt Prof. Darnton enumerates the three reasons Google is a monopoly. The points are somewhat legalistic and don't represent a *smoking gun.* I am not sure anyone who is not a lawyer will appreciate the reasons except for the first one: Microsoft has dropped out, leaving Google alone in digitization. No doubt the audience understood that Prof. Darnton enumerated three reasons why Google is a monopoly. To quote: "in plain English, Google Book Search is a monopoly." [CB, p.45]

The lecture meanders on: Google will know more about us than the CIA and the FBI combined, Google's first responsibility is to make profit for shareholders, Google will be a perpetual toll collector on books, we are all victims. Fortunately, the Europeans are more interested in China than in Google, so Prof. Darnton's reception was muted in the press, just a few quotes about Darnton repeatedly saying "monopoly."

Darnton sketches out five points to improve the settlement: monitor prices, put librarians on the registry board, free up the orphans that are not claimed, have the justice department certify Google is not a monopoly, and guarantee privacy.

It would be even better if Congress would rewrite copyright law, pay off the authors and publishers, and pay Google for its trouble, quoth Darnton.

So there is really only one thing left to do with the audience at the Frankfurt Book Fair: to sound the theme of monopoly vs. openness. That is going to be difficult for the director from Harvard. They may be more interested in China, but that does not make them dim. They understand monopoly; they encourage monopolies as integral parts of their economies. They also understand privileges. Someone might get the crazy idea that Harvard, Yale, and Princeton might be a monopoly in a general sense, perhaps even a cartel, quite specifically. They also understand cartels. Perhaps Google who has never turned away a query, is being maligned by elitists, a particularly nasty invective in European education. So the Europeans are in a bind. Are they more afraid of Google and the hegemony of American technology, or are they more horrified by American elite education producing cohorts smarter than theirs?

So a little smoke, a little mirrors and the bait and switch. The smoke is the reminiscence about the good old days at Oxford. The logic is difficult and requires some local knowledge of the Oxbridge scene. For an American, the layout of the colleges is hard to understand—with its walls, closed gates, and exclusive domains. At first, it seems like it might be just to keep out the tourists—but I have been told that the spikes on top of the high walls was for keeping rival theological factions from murdering each other in their sleep in the good old days.

Prof. Darnton constructs an anecdote that makes the obvious physical manifestations of exclusivity seem charming. The young spry Darnton, after curfew, clambering up the pole, over the roof, down the drainpipe, and on to his straw sack to sleep it off. After this anecdote, which he acknowledges as the most grotesque example of exclusiveness, the nice Georgian buildings at Harvard seem like something from a public university. But don't let that fool you; the natives will know you as surely as the Shogun's retainers knew Richard Chamberlain as an outsider. Nevertheless, the scene is set. As Darnton says:

> "Openness is the guiding principle that we will pursue in order to adapt the library to the conditions of the twentieth century" [CB, p. 50].

And I agree, I have received great help from HOLLIS, the Harvard library catalog. I can call it up any time to check a reference and, until recently I downloaded PDFs from the catalog entry, very convenient. (Now a Harvard ID is required).

There is no way that this story can have a happy end without a switch. Thankfully, Prof. Darnton has prepared a *seguito*, really an *attacca*, that will get him out of railing against Google and into the positive territory of praising the openness of Harvard. The theme is *openness*, and he segues into Harvard's new pre-publishing program for all research.

We can safely abandon our stalking of Prof. Darnton here. Through the three essays and the lecture, an optimistic untroubled pioneer in all sorts of digital experiments has become a burr in the fur of Google. His indictments are becoming increasingly shrill; it is hard to imagine any room for escalation. His position at HUL has put Prof. Darnton into severe intellectual conflict. Defense of the research library is his first priority; thus, large-scale digitization is the enemy. I can hear him say: "Openness is everything with us here at Harvard, never mind all you have heard to the contrary. We will pre-publish our research to prove our openness even if it means hitting the research library where it hurts." [My words]

We will stay tuned.

Hold the Presses: "Google and the New Digital Future"

Along comes a news flash: Prof. Darnton has published another essay while my manuscript is at the editor. What to do? Wade in.

The new essay concentrates exclusively on the legal aspects of the Settlement. This is no longer Prof. Darnton speaking, it is merely Darnton, court reporter for the NYRB. Gone is the genteel, learned historical introduction. Now we have a paragraph of "What happened this day in history?" The day is November 9, a filing in District Court by Google and the authors and publishers of the Amended Settlement, a veritable non-event, legally speaking. Curiously, on November 9, the pilgrims sighted land, the Kaiser abdicated, and Bonaparte ended the French Revolution and other things happened on that day and the next.

So we are in for another round of direness about the "profound effects." I for one would like to see just what this "orphans" depository would look like, especially with the unclaimed orphans for free and some other of Prof. Darnton's suggestions implemented. Having spent some money buying new e-books, I would like to see what fifty bucks would get me of digitized orphans. I have enough faith in the system in general and in Google in particular that the system can be made workable. After all, I do hate to see all the incredible waste of people young and old spending time and money xeroxing library books. I know, I have done it myself, plenty; there are boxes in my study to prove it.

After admitting that November 9 was a dud in District Court, if not for the French and Germans in history, he begins speculating; what is a journalist to do at a non-event? Darnton starts by casting doubts right and left: price, effect on other media, privacy, legal finality, the profit motive, the exclusion of libraries. Of course there are precedents: Chadwyck-Healey and others seem to have taken ownership of e-texts. These texts are being leased to institutions for sums of money that are not widely discussed.

Darnton mentions some few of the briefs against the Settlement. First on the list are France and Germany, who argue against concentrating power in a commercial enterprise, an American commercial enterprise. They seem to prefer local concentrations studded with the respective national flags. Those not smitten with the idea of establishing French and German fiefs in orphaned books worry that Europeans will increasingly become spectators on the sidelines in a game in which they are not playing. The game, let us remember is to create a vast index of pages. Let us hope that cool heads prevail and the current culture minister Mitterrand will not let the patriots set policy.

It is hard for Americans to understand the depth of national feeling and all the potentially irrational things that such feelings bring forth. It is fine for President Sarcozy to give money to the BNF to digitize books; if the text of those books are not in the Google indexes, they might just as well have stayed unscanned in the stacks. The notion of taxing Google advertisement within French national boundaries and giving the money to young people for music discounts will not be easy to grasp for someone not French.

There is talk that the French have raised money to create a French indexing enterprise, in the range of ten million Euros. Talk is that it would take three years to develop. They must be joking: the notion of a French engine starting from scratch with presumably French search terms is not credible given the global nature of information. I would farm the project out to Palo Alto.

Darnton goes on to summarize the revised agreement. Lacking good in-depth journalism on this topic, the NYRB is providing a real service, and Darnton is doing yeoperson's work, alas. I will not summarize his points which try to divine what the judge will bless, what the judge will damn and what the Justice Department will see peeking through its blindfold. We will know soon enough, and I am prepared to spin my own spin.

Darnton closes with the recommendation for an Act of Congress to digitize the Library of Congress over the next ten years. It shall be called the "Porcine Aviation Act" and will cost a mere 750 million for starters.

There is a follow up blog for the unsated (NYRB, January 1010) that contains a thorough and fairly devastating rebuttal from Michigan followed by some harsh words from Prof. Darnton that Michigan and its partners are essentially outlaws. Oh, I do love a fight; people forget themselves so completely. I will not try to reach into the future; I feel it is premature for exhaustive speculation until the court has spoken.

See: http://www.nybooks.com/articles/23518

Let us move on.

SECTION TWO: GRAFTON

Another Humanist Weighs In

The New Yorker article "Future Reading" [2007] by Prof. Grafton gives a rather ambiguous view of the Google efforts with books. The short companion piece "Adventures in Wonderland" in the online *New Yorker* adds to the ambiguity. It gives a brief tour of some dozen resources in digital humanities, no doubt to embolden the readers of the online *New Yorker* to read the November 5, 2007 print issue online. Things have become complicated at *The New Yorker*.

An expanded version of "Future Reading" is included in a recent collection of Prof. Grafton's essays. The essay has been renamed "Codex in Crisis" and attempts to put Google's book digitization into a larger context of prophesies related to the universal library, the specter of corporate empire building, and the trend toward electronic publishing. We shall begin with the story narrated in the *New Yorker* piece and conclude with the various new themes woven into the revised and enlarged essay.

There is a *coda* in two parts to round out Prof. Grafton's treatment of Google. First, an hour lecture at Google headquarters making the "Codex in Crisis" essay palpable to them by presenting the astonished techies with a separately bound copy, February 2009. Second is a short blog piece in *The New Yorker* which brings us to his latest stratagems and spins in defense of the book.

The *coda* is followed by an *encore* in *Daedalus*, 2009, that surpasses the previous performance, "Apocalypse in the stacks?" It is a detailed reading on how intellectual work is done today, and the resulting challenges facing libraries. Google is mentioned only as one among many contributors to the deteriorating situation. Whatever I may nit-pick in the earlier pieces, it has been smoothed out, disinfected, declawed, and sent to finishing

99

school in Switzerland. It is a testament to the art of editing, but also to the art of rhetoric, to style, and to the art of listening to feedback—but primarily it is a wonderful example of pulling the chestnuts out of the fire.

To take away some of the suspense, let me characterize my reading. The series of texts from 2007 illustrate a scholar wrestling with the questions of the day. Perhaps the first essay was a bit flippant, a bit careless; perhaps the expanded version was a bit too aggressive, trying to rescue the original crashed and burning in a free-fire zone by bringing in the big guns and blasting everything to bits. The Google lecture is an attempt to establish rapport with the villagers, pacifying their hearts and minds. *The New Yorker* blog is just a couple of mortar rounds to make sure the area is secure. The *Daedalus* piece is a marvelous analysis of current intellectual habit, a phoenix rising from the ashes, but it is still rendered with an undertone of disapproval. Alas, for us, the chestnuts had turned black with the original essay; in any case, even the extremely learned can't hit a home run after six strikes—only one topic per at bat.

Preamble

There is enough subtlety in the 2007 *New Yorker* essay that one could consider it a guarded endorsement as well as a general debunking. One fact cannot be escaped: when Professor Grafton speaks, the humanist profession listens; thus, it is invaluable that someone who can speak with authority addresses the subject of digitization—someone who clearly has no interest in hyping the field. It is to be welcomed as an important record, even should we have no sympathy with his analysis. The analysis, in short, is a defense of the book, more specifically, a defense of the non-digital resource in all forms—clay tablet, papyrus, birch bark, vellum, parchment, twenty-weight, onion-skin—to stay with texts. We are emboldened by Prof. Grafton to look beyond the digital representation, back to the original artifact.

I cannot help but wonder if this is not an undertaking that would occur only to one who does not work with digital resources as a rule and pays attention to them only to the degree of being dissatisfied with the emphasis they receive. This characterizes a substantial majority. I mean to say that digital resources, though potentially a source of delight, perhaps even an amusing and profitable side light, perhaps even something to be used in teaching, or for fact-finding tours, or for expeditions outside one's field, do not play an integral part in the serious professional life of such a person. For them, the center of gravity lies in sources that have not had exposure, much less been digitized. The idea that value could be added to serious sources through digitization is obviously out of the question; I mean serious sources that reside in archives so ancient and exclusive they do not have electricity, and you actually have to wear sandals to enter; a choir of chanters chained to the wall sets the mood in the flickering light of extremely large candles set on extremely large candle holders. The great volumes are arrayed on treadles, an early random access device. Forget digitization, database design, and brilliantly conceived interfaces.

Allow me a hypothetical to set the stage: Widener is a material library that contains many million items cataloged for many generations so that there are at least two or three persons alive at any time who can find everything that has not been actually irretrievably misshelved or stolen. Would this overwhelm the average scholar? Let us say this material library were to install a modern mechanical archive retrieval system, as it is seen at the Albertina in Vienna for example, where a robotic system retrieves items by Dürer or Rubens and brings the items to the custodians on velvet rollers. This is done for security and convenience but has become somewhat of a joke because it would take six months to remove everything in case of flood or fire. Would such a hypothetical system, made to work faster and installed at Widener, overwhelm a Widener user? Were a large corporation to give substantial funds to Widener to photograph books and make hot links in HOLLIS to the electronic files so that the resulting page images could be downloaded to G3 laptops around the world, would this create an unacceptably shallow work area where an entire generation of students with Harvard logins would be ruined?

Since the knowledge explosion some two hundred years ago, the sources of our professional learnedness have been piled in a somewhat organized manner, here there and everywhere all over the world. There have been enough printed catalogs of most of the piles to allow a small class of Mandarins to pretend they have a handle on what is where and what it means. Along comes the computer, and the servants of the Mandarins furtively combine all the catalogs into one networked electronic resource where all the cataloging information for all the books at all the important libraries save one in New Jersey of all places, could be accessed from any terminal in the world; this started in public universities and became widespread circa 1980. That many institutions did not maintain the room-sized catalogs with the pencil glosses made by generations of librarians ranks low on my personal list of crimes against humanity. Some did photograph the cards, especially in Europe, and still deliver the images, electronically, I am afraid.

But the servants of the Mandarins were not done; they had a vision of transforming the entire system of piling things here and there and everywhere until more and more images of the actual items, not just their catalog record, could be seen from any computer in the world. More and more Mandarins shed their silk robes, put on jeans, rolled up their sleeves, and started digitizing. There is still a long road before them; they will have to learn database design, query languages, interface design, and con- siderable statistics before they can be satisfied with what they will have wrought, and they don't really want to hear that. I personally think the profession is up to the task, having labored since the mid-seventies to prepare that vineyard.

Along comes a brand new major corporation—but not the nineteenth century robber barons who endowed universities (very bad people, indeed). It is a corporation run by nerdy kids who decided to scan vast numbers of texts and gave away the files for free. How bad is that? I had heard about Google's project when it was unveiled, but I was surprised by the rapid progress and the immediate dramatic effect that would have on my own work with the German sources of Ottoman history.

In 2007, I started downloading PDF files of rare items in my personal library for which I laid many euros on the table, literally; they don't take credit cards at my book dealers in Salzburg. I was overwhelmed with a sense of gratitude and vicarious accomplishment.

"Adventures in Wonderland"

Along comes "Future Reading" in 2007—my brow wrinkles as I try to comprehend. A reading of "Future Reading" is made complicated by "Adventures in Wonderland," which is not much more than a listing of projects, doubtless to make sure everyone knows that Prof. Grafton is well informed—something we might be tempted to doubt were we to read "Future Reading" by itself.

In "Adventures in Wonderland" we read:

> "Google's simple, fast interface will do much to make its books rapidly accessible, even in poor countries with old computers and uncertain connections." [Grafton, 2007-2]

I assume we are talking about reading the books online, which I have personally not tested in the third world. We cannot be talking about the Adobe PDF Reader. Given that the average Google PDF file is 20 to 30 MB, it downloads in 9 seconds in a typical U.S. faculty office, in 3 to 10 minutes with the average connection in Europe, and I don't even want to know how long it would take in Morocco. What you can do with a 20 MB PDF on an old computer depends on just how old the computer is and on screen resolution. If anyone in Morocco or Argentina wants any piece of literature in English or German, let them go to *Project*

Gutenberg and download a zip file of the ASCII of *A Tale of Two Cities* in 2 minutes and read it on their phone. Incidentally, about *Project Gutenberg* we can read only this:

> "*Project Gutenberg* … offers a vast range of information about collateral projects, e-book readers, and more." [Grafton, 2007-2]

Quality control called; they are in Aruba partying with the fact-checkers.

"Adventures in Wonderland" does give the interested reader starting points for exploring the field. It has a *bloggy* feel and an uncharacteristically awkward style reminiscent of a junior intern. Of course it could have been called "Adventures in the Past or History or the Human Record or the Human Treasury." But "Wonderland" gives a Disney slant something insubstantial, plastic, with hot dogs and Slurpies, something unserious. The connection to "Alice in Wonderland" eludes me, at least on reading the title; I suspect allusion to "fantasia" instead of fantasy. Hot links are embedded in the short text to facilitate navigation to the projects mentioned.

Towards the end of "Adventures in Wonderland," Grafton recommends a blog sponsored by the American Historical Association. That material is presented without much comment except to recommend the Townsend blog as the view of experts. [http://blog.historians.org/articles/204/google-books-whats-not-to-like]

Actually it is a Johnny-come-lately blog covering the same ground covered many times before. To recommend such a blog, which is more a shambolic argument outside a pub in Wood Green by librarians from North Islington, is unhelpful to the knowledgeable and confusing to novices who will be tempted to take sides, only to get a black eye, as will any extremely learned one who may want to join the fray. If the AHA wants to get someone to write a report, let's spend some time writing it, but don't give imprimatur to a blog of people gesticulating in print in the name of the AHA. This is just the sort of loose cannon approach one would expect the extremely learned to eviscerate.

Reviewing the Townsend blog would lead us into the blogosphere, where we do not want to go except to say that academics should stop complaining about the quality of Google Books if they are gleefully willing to drag any number of rare sources off Google Books as some *second-story person* who has just cracked the British Library Cube and made off with rarities.

It is also no good sending someone to catalog mistakes, a silly task if done with relish; no one wants to take a lash for every error in *Early Medieval Europe*, or even in JHI. That could smart. Would Prof. Townsend be happier if Google worked at academic speeds, and he could wait to garner his lootings for a decade or so? We should be grateful; I certainly am, and I am willing to come to the defense of the maligned, even if they are billionaires.

Finally Prof. Grafton mentions the digital materials available from the Vatican Library, modestly not mentioning his own involvement, but we are expected to know all that. See: [http://www.loc.gov/exhibits/vatican/intro.html].

It has not been easy to piece together a coherent picture of Prof. Grafton's opinions and judgments. There seem to be several masks he wears for specific occasions. There was a time when the extremely learned said what they thought and let the world lump or like. I would not have separated the two pieces in the November 2007 issue of *The New Yorker*, although I find some of the projects cited and what is said of them not *on message*. Integrating "Adventures in Wonderland" into "Future Reading" would have been harder to write, but it might have encouraged Prof. Grafton to deal overtly with positive aspects of digital humanities, as he is clearly willing to do on occasion. It would have given a more adequate picture. There are at the very least two personas, two masks, perhaps even two persons.

I would not have let Townsend make my arguments but would have attempted to make them myself if I thought them germane based on experience and myself competent to make them, or stay out of the discussion. Let us not skim the blogs! But we are getting ahead of ourselves; we have some text to dissect.

The Dissent

One should, however, consider the notion that one of the extremely learned, one who can be seen on Facebook reading Latin out loud in public, briefly and strangely, to an audience who can no doubt parse spoken Latin, although he is demonstrably extremely learned, in this case for all to see, may not be the best person to discuss modern phenomena. Perhaps the extremely learned, in the act of becoming extremely learned, have absented themselves from modernity in their imagination and in the formation of their neural pathways to such a degree that their judgment on contemporary culture may be askew. For direction on modern policy we should perhaps look in the range of barely to suffciently learned.

Prof. Grafton can write enviably well about anything. But we should not confuse easy acquisition of facts, practiced interaction with students, belletristic acumen, and a doggedness to keep whacking at the ball, with trustworthy vision of what road is best traveled—especially if that vision is essentially pessimistic and nostalgic. Even the judgment of the extremely learned on libraries and their future direction may be weighted with concerns that have nothing much to do with modern efforts. It may be that the extreme scholars have forgotten how to differentiate the past from the present; that is why we value them so, for their ability to bring the past to the present.

Yet, how can these academics not be front and center on important questions of the day? Clearly they must be courted; is dissent possible?

So, we start the dissent gingerly. Let us consider that we would rather have Prof. Grafton delight us with stories from areas of the past to which only he has access, than to weigh in on popular culture, on policy, and on technical issues. We would be happier, and he would be happier. We should keep that thought in mind as we try to understand what he tells us about Google, and we should weigh that against what he tells us about the history of scholarship.

The authority, speaking *ex cathedra* from Conde Nast in Midtown Manhattan, uses that forum to debunk digitization by many means—sometimes overtly but often by damning it with faint praise. As one of the early ones to leave Goshen on the digital humanities wagon train [1983, Kurzweil at Duke Humanities Computing, op. cit.], I must admit that I am disappointed at his reading of digitization in general, but heartened by his awareness of the volume of work in all fields. It is not a matter of selectively choosing quotes to make me feel better about my work; it would be possible to do that. It is not a matter of knowing that Prof. Grafton himself uses digitized resources; rather, there is a general pessimism that implies that those who headed west to build a new shining city on the hill are contributing significantly to a deteriorating intellectual situation. Best they should have headed back east; best the great navigator had stayed in Genoa. Even in his talk at Google, he expresses only worry that the work of Google, which he praises genuinely, though briefly, will lead to an irretrievable loss for the students awash in a world of information.

There is a development to be charted from the 2007 *New Yorker* pieces to the work he publishes in 2009. We would like to follow that path and not dismiss the early texts by means of references to the later ones. Obviously Prof. Grafton is more accommodating in his lectures than in his writing—student evaluations are filled out at Princeton as well. He allows himself to demonstrate in passing the deep integration of technology in his own work—and how could he not? We shall not be able to skip glibly past the fact that such demonstrations are not part of his published text, and thus we can draw conclusions only from what we are given to read. But it is heartening to learn that he considers himself a consumer of PDFs and an advocate of some forms of search technology; he owns a Mac laptop.

"Future Reading"

In the *New Yorker* piece "Future Reading," the narrative strategy is to juxtapose the meticulous abnegating work of archivist scholars through the ages culled from the mist of time, with the blue-sky scenarios of enthusiastic champions of digital humanities, whose rhetoric is not supported by actual scholarly achievement and hence to be met with embarrassed eschewal.

Grafton starts with a rhapsody on Alfred Kazin and his work at the NYPL in the thirties. This *in medias res* makes sense in a New York (and *New Yorker*) context. It is a city of short memory that must be reminded periodically of forgotten favorite sons and daughters. Yet I don't know if Alfred Kazin would really relish his role in this essay as a counterpoint to computer users. It is like celebrating the last person to win the slide-rule trigonometry championship, who would go down in smoke today next to a ten-year-old with a TI-60.

In addition to the labors of Kazin, we get a sampler of morsels of other scholarship. Certainly it is entertaining to be given one or two paragraphs each about a series of library problems spanning the last three thousand years; the relevance is in the intellectual entertainment and the improvement of the mind through osmotic absorption. The agenda here is to dip the readers of *The New Yorker* in real Graftonian scholarship to make it easier for them to spot the insubstantial hype by comparison. However, analyzing the current trends in digital humanities through the selected statements of proselytizers only is not unlike judging religion by the statements of extremist missionaries. Trenchant insight into the current opportunities is kept to a polite minimum in the published text. Perhaps the present is much too unruly to warrant the attention given to the lovingly exegeted past. One could get the impression that if the universal archive—the total history of all things animal, vegetable, and mineral—is not achieved within the next decade, an economy-size can of *debunk* will have to be opened. The can-opener is always at the ready.

Let us look at a quote from the second paragraph:

> "It's an old and reassuring story: bookish boy or girl enters the cool, dark library and discovers loneliness and freedom. For the past ten years or so, however, the cities of the book have been anything but quiet." [Grafton 2007-1]

An example of this veiled debunking strategy is the juxtaposition in the second paragraph, of the cool dark library of the thirties and sixties where one can discover freedom (and loneliness), against the contemporary metaphoric "cities of the book" that have lost their quiet because of scanners and networked computers. "Quiet" must be used metaphorically here as well; digitization is generally hidden away and the noise of networked computers is confined to the clicking of some keyboards, alas, a ubiquitous feature of modern life. [NB: "Future Reading" is made of twenty-six paragraphs divided in four sections. Quotes can be pinpointed by searching the online text.]

I sometimes get extremely irritated at what goes on in public reading rooms, and that includes NYPL: the talking, the whispering, the obvious boredom on the faces, the clandestine nose picking, the nervousness, the gestures of impatience, the questionable hygiene practices, the clicking and clacking of heels, and most recently, the ringing of cellular phones. The British Museum is no longer a fit place to work because of the tourists and the shrieking voices of small children trying on the dome; the British Library, trying to emulate the American elite by its openness, is overrun by all sorts of scholars with secondary interest in books. These developments, lamentable as they are, have nothing to do with digitization. I always preferred my carrel.

Perhaps we should all adjourn to our personal studies and let the halls become unmetaphorically quiet again, so we can get some real work done on our computers. Let's face it, we spend much time going to these places because they have the only copy of something that we want to look at; thus, they can afford to take their sweet time about showing it to us. I personally don't see why the Pope makes such a big deal of giving Tom Hanks the pamphlet by Galileo and making him promise to will it back to the Church after his death and all that; have someone photograph the pages of the thing in a few minutes with a cell phone, including the margins, and e-mail it to him. [Google this if you have not been to the movies lately...]

There is something unfortunate in conjuring up romantic images of the library since it ignores the fact that bookish boys and girls today can also discover loneliness (and unprecedented freedom) in front of the laptop screen as they follow links into vast source materials in the humanities that just didn't exist twenty years ago.

A similar proportion of young people today discover books and learn to read well. Some will find free editions in PDF format—something Alfred Kazin would have loved. The thirties were not immune to unmotivated students; for every Alfred Kazin there were two hundred budding *Joe Palookas* playing sports and drinking beer, and any number of *Sallys* who did not go to university at all. Much of what went on in those "cool, dark halls" was not unlike what goes on in front of laptop screens, time is wasted in hormonal reveries; it may not even be wasting time, just time spent growing. And let us remember, we are talking about books and a vast amount of humanities raw material from around the world—presented on laptop screens in living color and streaming video—that today's students can work on even when the libraries are closed. Prof. Grafton acknowledges that, but he does not allow us to feel good about it.

Clearly, one should not be too nostalgic for the thirties considering the worldwide academic industry of publishing nationalistic trash at that time. To hold up nostalgia for the research opportunities and tools of the 1930s is a harmless but extremely quixotic undertaking permitted only to the extremely learned. To pick out one brilliant student from the 1930s and find an entire generation of netbook owners wanting by comparison is strange. In any case, it is rhetorically ineffective, even if it is based on actual experience with the Princeton students of today who pass as the best and the cleverest.

The 1960s

One should also not be too nostalgic for the sixties. True, library budgets had not collapsed yet, and what was on the market was bought by elite institutions. But the influx of the baby-boomers did stress resources at state universities; we did notice that.

The sixties and seventies were also a time of great vandalism, not just petty vandalism against books and institutions, but vandalism against the very core of the humanities. For example, Theudoric of Berkelensis and Rufus of Michiganus and many others clad in bearskins and power ties appeased unruly mobs of drunken warriors and did away with language requirements, chucked Western Civilization, dumped Chaucer and Milton, and kept only a few Shakespeare movies. The older philologies were cut to the point that at Hopkins there were no more courses past the eighteenth century.

The selective nostalgia of the Golden Age of Humanities is in great need of correction to honor the uncounted language pedagogues who eked out precarious livings on the nightshift at Seven Eleven and rented single-wides in trailer parks.

Of course the drunken warriors loved shedding onerous burdens; I did, at least until I got my PhD in Germanic Languages, and there was one job listed by the MLA in the year of my defense, a one year replacement at Northern Iowa, reportedly being fought over by a crowd from Harvard and Yale. We were the "lost generation," driven out by the rampaging hordes; incidentally, we did find comfortable careers on Wall Street, in Silicon Valley, and in digital humanities projects.

From this perspective, digital humanities, the TLG, and Google Books seem like a reformation, or a counter-reformation—a return to Taoist values after a cultural revolution. It forces us to conclude that Prof. Grafton is indulging in his personal nostalgia for a time when a select few were protected by their institutions or by their surpassing brilliance from the fierce onslaught on the curriculum. This personal nostalgia, embroidered with cameos from the history of libraries and the development of scholarship, is to be wheeled into battle to cast aspersions at Google Books and those excited by its prospects? I think not.

Professor Grafton is suspicious of the profit motive of Google and others who have long since dropped this profitless potato. In the following example, Grafton is careful to identify massive digitization with Google and not with the partner libraries doing the work, lest he be forced to mention what kind of work is being done:

> "A second enterprise, the Google Library Project, is digitizing as many books as possible, in collaboration with great libraries in the U.S. and abroad." [Grafton, 2007-1]

Both Harvard and Michigan have clearly made the Google partnership their own. Michigan has designed its own catalog, and Harvard has scanned only out-of-copyright texts and integrated the links into their OPAC. I assume similar approaches around the world.

> "In fact, the Internet will not bring us a universal library, much less an encyclopedic record of human experience. None of the firms now engaged in digitization projects claim that it will create anything of the kind. The hype and rhetoric make it hard to grasp what Google and Microsoft and their partner libraries are actually doing." [Grafton, 2007-1]

The implication is that "firms," specifically Google and Microsoft, are the Internet. It is common practice to substitute Google the search engine for all the stuff that Google brings to your screen. It appears that Google and Microsoft are the Internet. Of course, everyone knows that is not so, but in the course of writing, certain Luddite slips can happen even to professed non-Luddites. Scholars around the world are creating the universal library; Google organizes the taxi service to the relevant sites, and Microsoft provides the vehicle.

We hear commonplaces about business practices that ignore the fact that large-scale digitization is a boon for all:

> "Google and Microsoft pursue their own interests, in ways that they think will generate income, and this has prompted a number of major libraries to work with the Open Content Alliance, a nonprofit book-digitizing venture." [Grafton, 2007-1]

The fact that hundreds of thousands of Google scans have migrated to the Internet Archive could not have been known in 2007—it happened in 2008—but it could have been predicted; after all, the files are free. This fact has escaped the notice of most users to this day.

> "Google, controversially, is scanning these books (out-of-print, orphans) although it is not yet making them fully available; Microsoft, more cautiously, is scanning only what it knows it can legitimately disseminate." [Grafton, 2007-1]

I am willing to believe that Google would have given "Full View" access to the orphans—unless authors, heirs, literary estates, publishers opted out. Predictably, it became a donnybrook, and a grotesque settlement was worked out. I see it as Google caving in to *extortion by negotiation*; and they should cave in. I would hate to see the entire enterprise under a restraining order while the lawyers accumulate even more billable hours into the next decades.

The facile dismissal of Google as a money machine is one of the biases Prof. Grafton brings to his view of the effort of large-scale digitization, and it puts him in line with mainstream journalism. In my own view, it discredits his opinion of Google's work.

There is some irony that this comes from the great moneybag institution sitting in the swamplands of New Jersey. One could suspect a certain insularity in a university without a Med School, or a Law School, or many of the other things that bring modernity crashing through the gates. To my great surprise, Firestone has been scanning for Google since 2007.

Prof. Grafton is also very correctly concerned with the poorest societies and non-Western texts. He is concerned with the lack of balance between population and library books in India and the UK: (in millions) 1100 pop./36 bks. and 60 pop./116 bks. respectively. He is appropriately concerned with the rights of the authors of out-of-print books. No one should accuse modern humanists of a narrow focus.

Clearly, a *New Yorker* article has limited possibilities: one cannot get too technical, or too long-winded, and one cannot afford to lose the up-scale literate readership. But for all its limitation, a *New Yorker* article can define the direction of an argument and thus trump more specialized and substantial publications. *The New Yorker* text has been vetted by editors with their fingers on the pulse of acceptable opinion. It is acceptable to be excited about Google projects; hence, Toobin gets his six pages, lest opinion be formed by the guy from *Wired* in the *Sunday Times*. But it is also imperative that the enthusiasm of all is appropriately curbed, so the captious Princeton professor gets six pages to put out any brush fires of the imagination, and that should do it for Google in *The New Yorker* for a while.

Professor Grafton does not believe in the promise of a trend towards universally accessible knowledge representation (I hope this is a neutral characterization that does not raise ire; if it does, twitter something). He knows the raw materials of such a project too well. He seems to abhor the trend, if there is such a trend.

> "The rush to digitize the written record is one of a number of critical moments in the long saga of our drive to accumulate, store, and retrieve information efficiently." [Grafton, 2007-1]

Prof. Grafton thus does grant some legitimacy to the effort, even if it is "rushed" and by innuendo unprofessional, and even if the "moment," through its criticality could go pear-shaped and produce rubbish, one could exegete.

> "It will result not in the infotopia that the prophets conjure up, but one in a long series of new information ecologies, all of them challenging, in which readers, writers, and producers of text have learned to survive." [Grafton, 2007-1]

I personally would have used the word "thrive" in place of "survive." "Survive" in the context of "challenging ecologies" implies a precarious existence. It seems the only endangered ones are those who do not find their way into the electronic medium.

The new methodologies are challenging, Grafton says. Indeed, they will challenge and sweep aside much of the scholarly procedures that were taught as rock-solid as late as the seventies, such as the system of citation and referencing that could not imagine the mouse click or the hyperlink. Another such system would be that of the scholarly transcription of early modern texts that becomes extremely questionable in a digital world where high-resolution images of the pages of a sixteenth-century book are a mouse click away. The obsolescence of these systems will become increasingly apparent.

It may be possible to interpret the concept of information ecologies as discrete database designs and discrete interfaces. It may be, however, that this analogy emanates from the somewhat recent past, when departments such as History, English, and Philosophy were closed eco-systems; they are still considered as such by those who long for the good old days. Computers have contributed significantly to building two-way bridges between departments, and they have enabled interdisciplinary work. If "information ecologies" is read as discrete electronic environments, we can expect data integration to bridge specific data sets for sharing. At the very least, each record of items in a database of historical fact or fiction will have at least an estimated date. This process of chronological ordering of seemingly disparate things on a large scale should not be spurned.

Alas, Professor Grafton does not dwell long on the new ecologies; his attention immediately fixes on the past. Neither the present nor the future can hold his interest—the lessons to be learned from the cataloging techniques of Babylonian custodians of clay tablets have ever so much to tell us: alphabetization! He is more interested in the canon tables of Eusebius than in the dozens electronic tools and interactive canon tables for the study of the bible available for free on the Web that unmask Eusebius as a scholar working abjectly without a computer.

The notion that the acquisition techniques of the Alexandria library, apocryphal or not, has any remote connection to the work of Google can only find play in the imagination of the extremely learned.

Since Prof. Grafton can demonstrate an encyclopedic knowledge of the handling of information in the past and can enumerate and document problems, which he is not loath to share in detail, we can assume that he sees only problems and no solutions in Google's efforts. Of course Professor Grafton's work in the history of scholarship is first rate, and so is his involvement with high profile digital projects. The problem is one of *past versus future*.

A highly trained humanist familiar with the development of the text tradition and working with texts in Latin, Greek, Hebrew, and Arabic will not succumb to hyped vaporware. One caveat: not unless that scholar is at work in wrenching some esoteric field not only into digital media, but also into data structures that allow advanced forms of analysis, and who can see the promise of the effort, even if perfection has not yet been attained. Another caveat: one should not assume that the scholarly efforts of the past had attained perfection; one need only remember Ernst Diehl's lament about the lack of a *Thesaurus Linguae Graecae* in the 1920's and not forget that all he wanted was a complete list of titles, authors and dates of Greek texts; had he seen TLG in *Project Perseus*, not just the titles but the actual texts, he would have thought he had died and gone to classical philologist heaven. Were we to look into Diehl's study and examine his sources, we would wonder that he achieved what he did. We would also be thankful for David Packard's work and be confident that splendid productivity tools can compensate the lack of Greek in the modern professoriate, for those who can work in that tradition.

Obviously we must train people to study the past, and we must get a handle on all the material that has been hidden away by zealous custodians. The loss of widespread expertise in Latin and Greek will make this task ever so much harder. But we should not expect that we would find all that much that has not been found in the last two hundred years when positivistic exploration of the past was the only game to be played. Certainly all the archives and anything else covered with the dust of the ages should be photographed, described, transcribed, translated, and entered into a database. Who can be against that? I personally would like to see the various Hapsburg archives digitized, and of course the Ottoman archives, although I do not see any light at the end of those tunnels. The very mass of materials will be a problem for the non-Google.

Our understanding of what has gone on in history and in scholarship has lurched from generation to generation based on what information was available. Neither more artisanal reading nor large-scale digitization will explain away the cataclysms of history and the machinations of rulers and the cohorts of those departed before their time—any secrets hidden in the archives of the Kremlin, Topkapi, Florence, Venice, Vienna, or Rome will not make much difference except to the career of the scholar who unearths them. The argument for digital resources is not that secrets will be uncovered or new insights will be gleaned, rather we must ramp up for global mass education, and technology is our only path. We need wide avenues; do not point us to narrow, steep stairs. It will be the new cohorts working with the digital sources who will glean new insights, discover any secrets, and, as a matter of course, find the steep, narrow stairs in a link table.

Prof. Grafton correctly alludes to the democratization of reading; reading privileges will be extended. If there is to be a new wave of work on the past, it will be aided, perhaps even driven by the analysis tools, multifaceted software, database innovations, AI routines, and statistical tools being developed by Google and others, as well as by new source material coming online. Skeptics should not stand in the way.

Computer scientists, who are not encumbered, as are the humanists, with stewardship of the past will attempt to make vapor coalesce into an alpha version at the low end of functionality. The future, after all, stretches before us, and alphas become betas become Version 3.0. The highly trained humanist will appreciate improvements on specific, high-quality digital humanities projects; however, we cannot expect unqualified support or encouragement for tentative beginnings. Let us hope that future generations of scholars will embrace the tools developed by the technical disciplines. The actual skins of dead animals will be involved only peripherally.

It is not unlike trying to persuade a New York traffic cop from the turn of the last century that electric signals will replace his function.

Electronic Texts Demand Informed Users

Yet there are some minor chinks in Professor Grafton's armor, not in his stories from the annals of humanisms or his history of printing—if there are chinks there, I would be the last to know—but in his demonstration of familiarity with electronic methods and workflow there are some problems. Hands-on familiarity with electronic files would have affected his discussion of questionable (read: faulty, incorrect) OCR. Grafton does echo some points made in the Townsend blog and by many others. Yet, we do not chuck the manuscripts copied at St. Gall because some monk misspelled "approbrium [sic]" or skipped five lines per page. When working with OCR text over extended time, especially with badly printed source texts, one becomes as attuned to faulty OCR as a scholar of old text becomes attuned to ligatures or to scribal errors. There are always the same mistakes - rn for m - m for rn etc. Consequently, one does not type random words into a one-line query window, as do the clueless Web vagabonds. Instead, one inspects the wordlist sorted by frequency, corrects the misspellings which are generally found in the lower frequencies and if necessary creates a query containing correctly spelled words and incorrectly spelled words, using an alphabetical list.

Thus, if one were to present an informed critique, one should not present faulty OCR as noteworthy, but instead remark that the search function of GBS is at the absolute lowest level of functionality for the good scans and unusable for the bad scans. One would suggest that the publishing of alphabetical and frequency word-lists might be one way to bring some correction to the situation. It could be done automatically and could be the beginning of a clean-up effort and add significant value to the PDFs. I trust that the Google techies will figure this out on their own.

The Mormons knew that in the late seventies when they developed the first really useful interactive search environment on a personal computer; I learned it from them some time later. [NB: *WordCruncher*, formerly known as the BYU Concordance, this was a truly artisanal experience, and it is still used today by the same people, metaphorically, who drive restored 1929 BMWs.]

In most search environments, any search that yields several thousand hits must be pared down; either the number of texts must be decreased, the date range narrowed, or the search term must be adjusted. The unusual thing about Google general queries is that they yield an infinite number of hits. It is dipping into the stream of indexed data and retrieving likely references ordered by a measure of relevance. Depending on the previous use of the term in the system, it may be very good or it may be spurious because of a lack of use. The results for Chopin will be very good; the calculations for technical terms from medieval philosophy may still be looking for more instances of queries. The system will mature because the users are generally not random actors—their behavior after the query will inform the system. In the meantime, as we will explain further below, set "Full View" on and pretend you are in a magnificent bookstore.

Let me embroider and add some technical detail: in working with electronic texts one works with wordlists of single or multiple texts, 10 to 20 thousand words or much more - two thirds of that is in the low frequencies where the errors are; there are no errors in the high frequencies. Unfortunately there are more low frequencies than high frequencies. Errors can hide in running text like tapir can hide in the jungle. Errors, especially OCR errors, cannot hide in word lists. OCR errors are misread letters (c for e) and thus are different from human errors that substitute words, both spelled correctly (king for kind). Running a spell-checker on a word-list, is, in fact, a trivial task, misspellings can be added to a blank supplemental dictionary producing a list of all faulty OCR instances in a few minutes. Relatively simple programs can then be written to ferret out common OCR errors and can be turned into general text filters. Some virtuosity is required, but the work can go on. One might add that Google has a deep understanding of misspelling since a proportion of Google queries and proportion of its source material on the Web is spelled incorrectly in many languages. I feel confident that the problem of misspelling in GBS is tractable with technology.

Work with electronic texts is a large and complex field. The Google people have come to the party brashly and uninvited, but they have brought so much beer and pretzels and money that they must be welcome even if they trash our manicured lawns. Bad

OCR is not the exclusive province of Google, although I suspect they may have underestimated the logistics of large-scale digitization. I suspect they are dealing with the problem by means of statistics, which is what they do with everything else. They calculate what percentage error rate will still give acceptable results. Perhaps they will also calculate the percentage of bad scans and procedures to redo them. Certainly they must create algorithms that will filter OCR text, make actual corrections, and produce files acceptable to error-averse academics. But a corporation that deals with Web pages from around the world is not afraid of a few billion misspelled words.

Google does not cause the shallowness of contemporary society. If it is not in the eye of the beholder, then at least, let us not lay blame where it is not deserved. Speak and Spell devices are not the problem; computers are not the problem; Xerox machines are not the problem; electronic texts are not the problem. Perhaps our age is no shallower than the thirties—at the very least some of the more overt prejudices can no longer be paraded in public.

Text search methodologies are routine, and it is not really worth discussing any pros and cons. Text search methodologies exist and Google indexing has propelled the field to the kind of prominence that Erasmus and Voltaire might once have enjoyed. The insights gained from definitive well-conceived queries of electronic texts are generally worth the bother making them; this includes putting the text into electronic form and doing all the preparation and evaluation of word lists. Google does not find things by accident; it finds things because there are lists of lists of lists.

Glossing and note-taking and slow reading are valuable tasks not to be neglected. However, scanning through the paragraphs with the naked eye in the hope of finding something specific is clearly a hit-and-miss methodology and must be replaced by searching electronically. That problem is especially acute with texts that have been read but were not glossed. Even if the thing is found, one cannot be sure how many instances of the same thing are lurking elsewhere in the text, and thus, one is tempted to commit one of the 640 cardinal sins of scholarship, give or take a few. That particular sin (365) is a compound one: attributing significance to a single casual reference, not mentioning other references of the same kind, not doing a thorough semantic analysis of a given text to find all persistent technical vocabulary before even thinking about descriptive analysis. Time is invested in creating electronic files because it is assumed that searching and studying a particular set of texts should be done seriously— not as a random actor might, winging interpretation by means of a few impressions, some favorite ideologies, and some rhetorical flourishes.

We shall grant the extremely learned an exception, a *get-out-of-subjective-bias-free card.* For most of us, the minimally learned, technology is a promising technique to test our bias by confronting semantic content head-on in lists and links to passages, not one word at a time over several hundred pages. I am speaking generally here and not casting aspersions at all of scholarship or at anyone specific; it is instructive, however, to take monographs or articles and follow some of the citations that support descriptive analysis with an advanced search environment.

One can consider the question, is it possible to support the conclusions based on a thorough semantic inventory? A complex picture emerges.

Experience with text files would also not have let Grafton refer to *Gutenberg* texts as hand-keyboarded when, in fact, most represent cleaned OCR. It may be possible that *Gutenberg* texts are now prepared by offshore typing services as was the digitization of long runs of journals, or that a brand new version of human is power typing *Middlemarch.* Maybe legions of 160-wpm typists have risen from the grave. I scanned *Middlemarch* at Hopkins on Sunday afternoons in 1989 while watching the NFL games, and *Daniel Deronda*, and the rest of them. The texts were immediately dragged off by someone from Chadwyck-Healey behind their toll barrier; thank you very much indeed.

In its artisanal past, submissions to *Gutenberg*, as were the first files of *Intelex*, were generally OCR done on kitchen tables and cleaned in *WordStar*. To this day, cleaning OCR is the main task before us—as Google shows us so persuasively. Much benefit will derive from clean electronic texts. The history of scholarship cannot be considered complete if the main problem of electronic representation of text is not recognized as the main task before us, today. There was a time when producing copies of Aristotle or inputting catalog cards was the main task.

Hyperbole is a respectable rhetorical device that I assert.

Wrapping Up "Future Reading"

Nevertheless, projects are mentioned, and the balance between skepticism and informed critique is maintained.

Prof. Grafton's point about the volume of printed books available for scanning is more serious. It is not really an argument for or against anything, as much as it is a warning that there are forces in play that do not augur well for large-scale digitization. According to his calculations, perhaps 75 percent of all books that were ever printed fall into the current copyright protection period. It is clear that there are many high-minded advocates of various rights that are not going to cede that pile of potential profit to Google or will at least negotiate a cut. That is clearly a problem, not because there are legitimate claims for compensation for most of the books in question, but because the orphans have suddenly found uncounted parents who want to deny custody to the uncles from Google. Only time will heal this problem, and at some point, all the greats and near-greats of the twentieth century that have had a cottage industry of toll collectors grow up around their works will be indexed with all the other great works of humanity in a free database of ideas and supported by links to the actual texts. Help me Jesus.

Another warning from Prof. Grafton that casts doubts on a universal infotopia is his point that a universal history would have "to include both literary works and archival documents never meant for publication." [Grafton, 2007-1] The point, though true, is a strange one to make, since the digitization of "documents never meant for publication" is one of the major undertakings of digital humanities, as everybody knows. Perhaps the extremely learned, in their pre-digital epistemology, adhere to some natural hierarchy of the published and the unpublished—different libraries, different reference works, different gatekeepers. In the digital humanities, technology has penetrated both areas with equal force, and I should add that the representation of non-textual artifact, whether artistic, historical, or utilitarian, has also been the target of large-scale digitization and concomitant representation in database format. Given that we are all aware of this, one wonders what rhetorical significance such a warning might have.

Professor Grafton's notion that the road through the digital is easy and the road through books is narrow and hard seems weak and contrived, although I suspect it is intended to be inspirational. Perhaps it is aimed at a younger generation that is all digital, perhaps he knows the readers of *The New Yorker* well—fair enough—but there are many laborers in the field of digital humanities that have been trying to widen the access to texts and to take away some of the boulders in the road left by generations of pedants who became the stewards of our textual heritage. This is a task worth accomplishing.

Reading a Positive Future

I believe that the Google founders, who have benefited from the best American universities had to offer and who optimized their educational experience and that of their co-workers, are simply not willing to see humanists disappear down a rabbit hole to perform mysterious rites with their texts. With very few exceptions, the high-resolution color image of a medieval manuscript on a laptop is a superior resource to the vellum lying on a varnished table. Electronic transcriptions of a manuscript tradition side-by-side in table format are superior to a printed text with variant readings in the footnotes. Photographing a sixteenth-century folio and working with the color images of the five hundred pages is far superior to trying to prop open the book on foam rubber wedges and hold down the pages with velvet bags of marbles. The time invested in the photography can easily be recouped by reducing the time spent in the archive, no contest, with oceans of time left over. Scanning millions of books is a great optimistic venture with no clear and easy path to completion; it is like designing the Duomo in Florence and building the foundations without having the engineering in hand to cap the dome.

We can, with confidence, expect libraries to keep busy and digitize their holdings and let us work with the images, OCR the text and clean it and develop data structures and statistical routines to organize textual communication. The smell of the parchment can be an entry in the metadata provided by the archivist if must be; I suspect it smelled differently in the sixteenth century. What is so bad about dragging all this stuff out into the open for a few minutes, taking a picture, and putting it back in its box? We can do no systematic work unless we get all the items of a particular tradition into a database.

One illustration is the digital collection and database of relevant data for the study of Persian book illustrations from the Persian Book of Kings undertaken at Cambridge University with funding from the Research Board and others. Many copies of the Book of Kings were cut apart, the handwritten text discarded and the illustrations sold to tourists in the nineteenth century and later. In some instances individual pages were cut apart and mutilated in an attempt to separate recto and verso images on the same leaf. The task was to photograph illustrations (or buy slides where possible) of intact manuscripts and cut illustrations dispersed from Europe to India to America so the manuscripts can be reconstructed virtually. Nobody said, "well, there are many images, let us think about this." In a thousand years, digitization will have progressed to the point that even the texts of the handwritten copies of the Shahnameh will be digitized and analyzed for variant readings. That should keep some robot going for a couple of months.

Someone with a digital camera was sent to Turkistan and points east, to Iran and India; the pictures were taken in the most unlikely places; some items were in advanced stages of decay. Now some six thousand images are neatly ordered in a database, the scenes identified and linked to the location in the text, ready for the scholars of the field to seize the opportunity for comprehensive descriptions and synthetic analysis to borrow a concept. Another five thousand have been described, but the images have not yet been acquired.

Not everyone is rushing forward. One must remember that digital efforts may be as much as one generation ahead of what the working scholars trained twenty or thirty years ago are willing to incorporate into research and publication plans. This is especially true of a field where description of a single manuscript is the measure of success—even if that description is demonstrably incomplete. Yes, it will have to be redone, all of it, in good time. Some future students will find that database in some years, and they will make the connections that continue to elude the current luminaries in the field; they will do it just to spite their elders. But I digress.

I am sure we can look forward to more star humanists entering the lists urged by the increased functionality of the hyper-vapor; to quote Professor Grafton:

> "It is hard to exaggerate what is already becoming possible month by month and what will become possible in the next few years." [Grafton, 2007-1]

One might respond humbly: "It is hard to know what that means, Professor Grafton, but we assume you also google."

Grafton's essay is a short, off-the-cuff reaction to the trends in digital humanities; of course, the bulk of his discussion, from clay tablets to microfilm, has nothing whatever to do with digital humanities but comes from his field of expertise. However, since this reaction comes from a respected scholar, teacher, editor, and multifaceted belletrist, it can be seen as a welcome antidote to the harmlessly virulent enthusiasm that some writers from technological circles (e.g. Kelley, Toobin, Khale) have tried to spread in the pages of *The New Yorker* and elsewhere. We hope for answers from Grafton to the questions: "Is this stuff any good?" "What good is it really?" "Is it help or hindrance?" I am not sure we get the answers.

The 2007 essay tells a simple story, one I am sure he has told many times to his students and technologically infected colleagues: "Please, boys and girls, do not stay in the shallow end of the pool, go deep, seek depth." In Grafton's formulation, book equals depth; at first sight, without nostalgia, in the face of fifteen million PDFs, it seems an empty formalism. The essay is essentially a pedagogic effort, and as a teaching effort, it is not so much unassailable apodictic truth for the ages, but an excellent bit of rhetoric drawing on the trope of exaggeration and the subsequent slaying of the straw dog. Because Grafton is a high priest of humanities, he performs such rituals routinely to strengthen the faith or renew the faith in the slouching novitiate gathered at his feet.

Yet high priests hold tenure only till they are recalled by their deities and their altars are broken and their rituals forgotten. The message "go deep" is a general one and a timeless one; however, the ritual sacrifice of the computer as a straw dog will lose all credibility in the next decade—if it has not already become untenable. Even the learned and the fashionable can burn their fingers with that one.

At the height of his scholarly, editorial, and belletristic powers, Professor Grafton has chosen to indulge nostalgia. He indulges nostalgia for his own path from bookish alienation to the top of his profession. By alluding to his own apprenticeship with fondness, we can only surmise he would like to see himself, Kazin, and several dozen others cloned for the benefit of humanities studies. Imagine a team of Graftons, drawing deep drafts of stinky, possibly putrid, vellum, working in Graftonian manner; that is what professors do, they build students in their image, at least till they get swept aside by shifts in focus.

Before we move on, perhaps another word should be spent on the online "Adventure in Wonderland." It is a list of links that might as well have been collected by an intern of the magazine. There are no recognizable paw prints of the extremely learned, and so we should not spend much time trying to divine significance of picking one site over the other, or the parsing of the significance of one descriptive phrase here or there. It would be fascinating were one of these commentators to try to do that and really weave a tight tapestry of links for us.

I don't mean to be unfair to the extremely learned. Prof. Grafton's ability to publish anything anywhere, freshly cooked or warmed up, his ability to influence what gets published, his ability to influence colleagues, decision makers, and the readers of *The New Yorker* (and googling Web vagabonds around the world) must be a heavy burden. A cheerful acceptance of the morphing of the past into the future does not seem to be integral to the rites unveiled in the recent revision of the 2007 *New Yorker* piece [*Worlds Made by Words*, 2009, "Codex in Crisis"].

Worlds Made by Words

Worlds Made by Words is a wide-ranging series of essays on various topics that range from Trithemius to Lovett. It also includes more recent topics such as Hannah Arendt's book on Eichmann and the ensuing controversy, which allows Prof. Grafton to indulge an entire separate wave of nostalgia for the discussions at the family dining table. All essays were previously published and now revised. The only real common focus is Anthony Grafton, traveler through disparate textual landscapes. The tone is essentially non-optimistic: "Times have been, and are, dark" [WMW, p. 8].

"Codex in Crisis" is a reworking of the original *New Yorker* piece into a serious sixty-page essay with copious notes. The enlarged essay was published in a limited run of four hundred copies by Crumpled Press, in 2008. We will cite the 2009 version in *Worlds Made by Words*.

If the *New Yorker* piece was a signpost, a direction-giving cameo, "Codex in Crisis" is a full-blown review of digital humanities and the tangential field of electronic publishing. It represents both the strengths and weaknesses of the extremely learned scholars. As the author reads the 2007 "Future Reading," the author sees nothing but lacunae, things that obviously exist and were not alluded to, things that have been found to exist but received no reference, things that should have been mentioned but were not. That diagnosis may also be aided by editors at *The New Yorker* and the uncounted e-mails offering counsel. A rereading of "Adventures in Wonderland" can only lead to wonder at the gaffes under the author's name.

So we can speculate: did the writing of the *New Yorker* piece bring forth a serious research effort which led to the quintupling of the text, or was this store of knowledge already present in 2007? There are no aspersions cast in suspecting energetic research; the field is moving fast, and the time from 2007 to 2008 was an excellent time to go deep into digitization and figure out what is going on. Or was the whole thing cribbed from the Internet? The publication of "Codex in Crisis" in a limited print run in 2008 suggests a continuous writing project, and "Future Reading" was just an initial attempt on the subject.

"Future Reading" remains a puzzle for me; it tries to be programmatic, yet the finger is always pointing into the past. The list of projects in "Adventures in Wonderland" muddies the issue since it is a mere listing of items without any substantial discussion. The tone of "Future Reading" cannot hold out much encouragement even to the most sanguine of enthusiasts of digitization. The fact is that just about everybody, including Prof. Grafton, works with digital projects. Is the task he sets himself to debunk Google for straying off its turf? Is the task merely to tone down the rhetoric of semi-literate techies? Or is the task simply to bring a sampler of genuine scholarship to *The New Yorker*, and is the Google discussion just a teaser? Perhaps he is just venting his measured disdain for those who do not do as he does.

If the 2008 essay involved an intellectual ramp up, possibly inspired by much feedback to the 2007 effort, which is my hypothesis, then it is both to be welcomed and to be treated with care. It is to be welcomed in that one of the extremely learned of our time should stoop to gather information on digital humanities. It is to be treated with care because a quick ramp up cannot lead to a mature judgment.

2007 Rewritten in 2009

One wonders why any of the text from the 2007 essay was kept. I go with Anthony Trollope when it comes to rewriting, although I don't always follow his advice in other arenas; he holds that the clearness of the voice is lost in rewriting; he suggests facing a clean sheet and starting over. Whether that principle holds for a rushing to the aid of the codex being gradually strangled by digital humanities can be argued. However that may be, Grafton forces us to look at the text of the 2007 *New Yorker* and compare it to the 2009 piece, an unwholesome task that brings up all sorts of doubts in the reader. For example:

> 2007: "Still, it is hard to exaggerate what is already becoming possible month by month and what will become possible in the next few years." [Grafton, 2007-1]

> 2009: "It is hard to exaggerate how much material is becoming accessible month by month and what will become accessible in the next few years, for those who study the distant past or the Third World as well as those concerned primarily with the present" [WMW, p. 300]. [NB: The page numbers are the 2009 version.]

The 2007 sentence is an enigma enveloped by a conundrum. People obviously have asked what that sentence may mean, especially since the usual turn is: "it is easy to exaggerate..." for example: "... the value of scholarship on dead white men." So, the original sentence implies that it is OK to say any old thing touting the useful glories of digital humanities, and it will probably hit truth more than exaggeration. In any case, the thing to be avoided at all costs in the normal course of writing, the most obvious trap to fall in, exaggeration, is hard in this particular field but really nowhere else. In addition we are given two time frames: "month by month" and "next few years."

The 2009 sentence tries to be more precise, obviously, letters have been received from directors of projects feeling hurt, confused, and betrayed by not being mentioned. The additions of "distant past," "Third World" and "present," in no way lessens the abdication of judgment—which is replaced by a reflexive skepticism—or else—by irony, the last defense of the over-whelmed. Including this sentence in the 2009 piece, which does present some withering judgments, seems an attempt to balance linguistically that which cannot be balanced substantively without much more work.

I do distrust the topos of the tsunami of information. High quality digital humanities project do not multiply like fruit flies, nor do publications by the Harvard University Press. It is not that hard to get a work-study student to stay on top of digital humanities projects in a given era or in a given language, should one care to do so. Much of the new projects are the digitization of sources that have been at a particular institution for years, to the general indifference of the profession. Having them in digital form is not more remarkable than had they stayed in their dust covering. But it might be possible to spend some time rummaging in a database rather than flying to Duluth to look through the papers of the Smaland Emigrant Association, disbanded in 1936. Individual papers, Web pages of assistant professors, or pages of small local research teams can be ignored as safely as ignoring most of the papers read at the MLA or AHA every year. The veritable tsunami of large-scale digitization is essentially irrelevant since no new knowledge is being created, yet; only existing volumes are being scanned and presented in an evolving environment. Only when that project attains critical mass, when OCR improves and when sufficient user statistics can be processed, will any of the important possibilities be opened.

However, we should not wonder that a scholar of the Renaissance, who has spent several decades assimilating the array of sources in all that field or fields may cover, is irritated and dismayed by all the digital sources of indeterminate quality that keep popping up. Are there not people to protect us from all that? Since one cannot do today what an extremely learned would have done a hundred years ago and simply label it tendentious, popular trash, and then turn to the vellum, some grudging respect must be granted:

> 2007: It has become impossible for ordinary scholars to keep abreast of what's available in this age of electronic abundance - though D-Lib Magazine, an online publication, helps by HIGHLIGHTING NEW DIGITAL SOURCES AND COLLECTIONS, rather as material libraries used to advertise their acquisition of a writer's papers or a collection of books with fine bindings [emphasis mine]. [Grafton, 2007-1]

> 2009: highlighting library Web pages that do an especially good job of organizing digital sources and collections … [changes only].[WMW, p. 301]

The emendation is instructive; I can imagine a call from an editor at D-lib.

2007: "highlighting digital sources and collections."

2009: "highlighting library Web pages that do an especially good job of organizing digital sources and collections."

The reference to "material libraries" is a curious one that harks back to another time. Today it is hard to find a material library that is not trying to get into the digitization field.

Fine Bindings

The curious attempt to compare "D-lib" with acquisition announcements of yore is also instructive; here is a scholar who understands fine bindings. If I am permitted a small aside on fine bindings: I cannot conjure up dozens of examples, or even one, where the bindings, especially fine bindings, play a pivotal exegetical role. I can however bring forth two examples from my personal content-obsessed world where fine bindings have become irrelevant.

I spent some considerable money (you can check ZVAB for the going price today), for a second edition of von Hammer's *History of the Ottoman Empire* published in the 1830s in German. The binding was beautifully embossed red leather, and I was enthralled by my purchase. When I got home with my prize, I realized that it was practically impossible to read, mostly because of the binding, and I should have spent a quarter of the money on a reprint of the first edition with a flexible cloth binding. I photographed the first thirty pages and printed them out on my A3 printer only to realize that although the pages were quite readable in A3, the whole thing was a futile undertaking. To this day the red leather mocks me from my bookshelf.

Along come Brin and Page to crash on my couch during a bike trip through the mountains around Salzburg, and I show them my useless treasure. "Dude," they say in unison, "that is sooooo artisanal. We have PDFs of all that, dude. Dude, just download the files." And off they went to the Salzkammergut texting Mountain View on their fully integrated, eye-blink driven 3G multimedia mountain-bikes. Little did the dudes know that their multivolume retrieval code was not working and their data on volume sets was rubbish. However, with a little ingenuity and a couple of e-mails to Google, I was able to get the three volumes

I needed, and thanks to the Google PDFs, I am able to clean up the electronic version of Hammer that I am working on when not worrying about what other people think about digital humanities. Since then, four first editions, all ten volumes of each, scanned at Michigan, Harvard, Oxford, and Lausanne have come online. Boy, user support really works. Lausanne is the best—Swiss precision. Then I said to Brin and Page, "Hey dudes, please back off the von Hammer thing, dudes."

In my two copies of Leunclavius' *Neuwe Chronica Türckischer nationen ...*, 1590, the text is identical, page by page; one is in its original whitewash wood binding, with a leather spine with metal clasps fashioned at a time unknown to me, possibly at the Capuccin monastery in Brünn. The other was trimmed and rebound in fine leather for a nobleman's library, possibly as late as the nineteenth century. The spine is broken on one side of the front cover, and it was badly trimmed, which explains why it only cost four thousand euros. The vendors of the two volumes were not forthcoming on the provenance, only assuring me they were not looted in the second quarter of the twentieth century; to date, I have concentrated on working with the text and have let my interest in the clues hidden in the binding and the various collection markings lapse. Is that bad? I am fashioning a transcription in modern German and English translation and supplying the early German only through page images. Is that bad?

In order to reach the infotopia on which the extremely learned can smile their pitying smiles, we cannot concentrate exclusively on unimportant minutiae. The argument that all the minutiae of old texts is crucially important does not hold water—at least not with early printed books that are surprisingly easy to photograph. I am of the opinion, lonely but not alone, that it is a dog that will no longer hunt. It is a dog that has been sitting by the fire, arthritic, for a decade although atavistic encoding professionals are mixing Advil in his or her dog food.

In a world where the original manuscript viewed at 5x magnification is a mouse-click away, any transcribed/translated sentence can be verified quickly by someone trained in the tradition. More important than to track each ligature and each abbreviation, is to take Leunclavius' collection of sentences, specifically the information content of each sentence, from different parts of the book and unite them in a common chronology in order to start comparing that chronology to Ottoman sources and to European epigones like Hammer and Zinkeisen.

Someone else will have to make the arguments for other parts of the textual heritage. However, the principle that the original, with magnification, is delivered with the transcription/translation should inform the arguments. Let us try to extend the work of Karl Lachmann and not cling to his procedures. We must try to think what he would have done had he had a laptop and a scanner. This principle will change the equation in the direction of *content over form*. Infotopia here we come; can a database be far behind?

Given that Lewenklaw is the first to publish a serious, reliable, and scientifically historical (in the German sense) chronology of Ottoman history, one wonders why I have not been able to google a detailed examination of his Turkish chronicles; part of the answer is that the historians and handbook writers of the seventeenth through the nineteenth centuries did not document their sources exhaustively. Another answer is that Lewenklaw's work in Roman law and Greek texts was of greater interest than his work on the Turks. Perhaps someone has been sitting in an archive for years pushing bags of marbles around in slow motion. The other answer is that we did not have the intellectual tool of the *data structure* and the retrieval technology of SQL and the display technology of HTML available until recently so that such an undertaking would appear remotely reasonable. Nor is there the people-power in the field of Ottoman studies that such work would be routine. The Europeans are still working through Hammer, perfecting his work on Ottoman sources, and the Anatolians are still working on a bibliography of extant chronicles, trying to determine dating and authorship. A sixteenth century source based on a translation of a lost Ottoman chronicle surrounded by a grab bag of data from that time is hardly on the A-list at publisher's parties. But I digress.

"Codex in Crisis" is Divided Into Three Parts

The storyline in "Codex in Crisis" is not as clear as in the shorter earlier piece. The essay is divided into three main parts: "The Universal Library," "The Google Empire," and "Publishing without Paper." The three parts are preceded by a short introduction, similar to the beginning of "Future Reading" but bulked up. The conclusion, also entitled "Future Reading," is functionally equivalent to the last paragraphs of the 2007 *New Yorker* piece of the same name.

In the introduction we read:

> "Instinct and experience predispose me to find substance in critiques of the new textual world" [WMW, p. 290].

At first, I completely misread this sentence to say that Prof. Grafton would offer a "substantial critique" of the new textual world based on his "instinct and experience." I got very excited and started scanning for the critique in the rest of the introduction. When I returned to discover my mistake, I realized to my horror that despite an explicit disavowal later on, Grafton is finding substance in Jeanneney's piece (reviewed below) and not presenting a critique himself. All we get is an apprenticeship novella on the glories of the libraries of thirties years ago.

And I find myself agreeing; permit a digression. I discovered libraries in the sixties as a refuge from my tutors of limited horizon. That the real action is not in the classroom but in the stacks was my insight, not unusual for a kid from a North Carolina high school with impecunious but extremely literate parents. The library also paid my rent. I worked in circulation shelving books, after graduation and before graduate school I was stack supervisor and led a major shift of books to make some room for the LC classifications that were growing dramatically as new acquisitions and reclassified Dewey's arrived by the cartful. While working on my dissertation, I was weekend supervisor and had my own key to the front door, Wilson Library, UNC. Alas, we did not have any seventeenth-century books in my stacks. I learned much in those stacks, but not enough to propel me to extremely learned status; I acquired little Latin and less Greek; I had sympathies with the Palookas and hung out at the gym coaching the saber team.

I can still experience and understand nostalgia for that time, even though I discovered I would rather have a key to the computer center, which was not necessary since it was open 24/7 except for systems backup at 4 AM. I found more genuine mind-to-mind interaction in front of the I/O window at the computer center than I ever found in the circumspect posturing in my literature department. At the computer you could find people who would actually help each other with difficult problems in their code that would take hours to resolve. I found the intellectual atmosphere so intoxicating that I decided to remodel my mind into a suitable space for programming—a hard task for an ABD in German. I now have experience with several dead programming languages. We were the few, the bleary eyed, the novice programmers; the year: 1975.

I got fired from the library, finished my dissertation, the first word processed at my institution, and left Chapel Hill for greener pastures. Yet my nostalgia for those dark stacks, especially the 100s, which I personally shifted to the lowest level and still see clearly in my mind's eye, does not affect my analysis of Google. Those stacks have been superseded by much larger stacks, with windows all around, and all the old German Hegel and Kant editions in the 100s are now in storage and available only on request. I tried to browse them through the OPAC; that was not the experience I wanted. They could have been discarded.

But I am getting verklemmt, talk amongst each other.

When I realized my mistake in reading the sentence quoted above, probably because I was thinking about what Grafton had said about Jeanneney in the sentence before and reflexively resisted the actual logic of the communication, I started a serious search of the introduction. I believe that is called acquisitive reading, an attempt to try to find out what is being said, looking for content: nostalgia, nostalgia, list of libraries in Europe, nostalgia, the importance of knowing the history of collections, the more you know about that, the greater your scholarship.

I am beginning to regret having bought *Worlds Made by Words*, but I launch another expedition into the introduction. I see only someone bragging about his career; after a long quote about weird characters in the Bodleian, which makes me want to reread *The Stranger*, I read:

> "To have known reading in its artisanal form is to distrust any plan that treats books as interchangeable and aims—as does Google—at universality" [WMW, p. 292].

Books are made interchangeable; is that Google's failing? Google has a plan that does that. Do libraries do that when they have multiple copies? Is that bad? It aims at universality with that plan. Have I missed a definition of interchangeable? I wish I had indexed this text. Is it that a certain book can only be read at the Bodleian? What to do with the copy at the Lumberton-Satterwhite College Library in Cambridge? Why will my spell-checker not accept "artisanal" and keep insisting on "artisnal?"

I did the slow read; I don't follow. Believe me I am stuck on stupid here. Is someone shooting from the hip? And finally there is "[artisnal], artisanal, whatever, reading," a new concept. Let us spill some of that and see if the cat licks it up. I like artisanal bread, better than Wonder Bread. Artisanal reading is the craft of reading in a small shop, by an artisan, with craftsmanship, like Hans Sachs, making shoes that really fit well for dancing on Johannitag, writing artisanal poems on the side. Artisanal reading must follow artisanal writing. Is this artisanal writing? Am I wrong to expect information? Am I to be unhappy with global new media? Can one read artisanally on a computer; can you see Hans Sachs with a cobbling machine? The hammer must keep time to the music... The mind wanders. The inquiring minds still want to know.

And I don't know about "aims [...] at universality." Perhaps the Google people are not that good with words, perhaps they think that universality is a good thing, they have let the u-word slip one time too many. Perhaps others think that one could shove some "aims at universality" into their shoes without doing them harm. Obviously, they have not considered Jeanneney and, it pains me to say it, Prof. Grafton [see, WMW, pp. 290–292].

NOW, FOR SOMETHING ENTIRELY DIFFERENT: OTHER VOICES

Before we look at the three main sections of "Codex in Crisis," let us reprise the discussion about the Google Project from 2005 to 2007. Of course we shall be extremely selective; there is no hope to cover all of the reactions in the various forms of print. I will mention just half a dozen pieces, liberally interspersed with personal observations about the direction of certain backwaters of digitization in which I have developed an interest. In this age it is getting harder to stake a claim as the once wide-open prairies are increasingly being fenced in.

Four years ago, the discussion about Google digitization centered on the legal ramifications. There is even a bibliography of the main pieces on the Web. (Google "Google Book Search Bibliography" and poke around in archives going back to 2005.) This was the time of Phase I, before the proposed "Settlement" in 2008 and the clamorous challenges to the settlement ushered in Phase II.

One should not be surprised at legal wrangling, that is where the money is—not for Google, but for all those who hope to make money from Google initiatives. When things of no recognized value such as library books become the focus of Google, a crowd gathers. Remember we are talking about out-of-print books, which can be bought for a quarter at a flea market with no percentage to the author. The discussion in Phase I was carried on by various advocates of various interests with no interest in the use or usefulness of the project and no interest at all in the older books. Their great interest was to blur issues to make redress of wrongs only vaguely plausible. The discussion in Phase II has gotten more specific as to who will pay what to whom. This gives it some legitimacy at least in the eyes of the beneficiaries. Let us hope this too will subside with one last wave of post-game analysis where all sides can declare victory. The legal wrangling could well lead to Phase III and the phases beyond.

A *New Yorker* essay about the legal aspects of GBS, ["Google's Moon Shot. The quest for the universal library." Jeffrey Toobin, *New Yorker*, Feb. 5, 2007] nevertheless gives some revealing background information on the motivation of the founders to pursue the scanning of old books. This was published some seven months before Prof. Grafton's corrective. Toobin cites the little known fact, little known to those who don't read celebrity biographies, that both Brin and Page, the founders of Google, worked for the Stanford University Digital Library Technologies Project, one of many projects at American universities and around the globe in the nineties that were organized to see what digital collections of a medium scale would look like.

Even more interesting is a quote from Toobin's interview with the Google founders, in which the notion of information writ large is touched. To paraphrase, the Google founders seem to understand the qualitative difference between the information their algorithms can deliver from the "indexable" Web pages of the surface Web, and something called "high quality information" which is stored in the written material collected over the ages in books. Their goal seems to be to bring that high quality information to readers via the screen by means of algorithms modeled on the current page ranking or code not yet written. This means they could be way ahead of most of us who simply want free PDFs of our primary sources. It could also mean that they have not seen through the smoke-and-mirror routines with which humanities professors dazzle their own graduate students and any Computer Science graduate student assistants they can lure into their departmental cost-sharing nets.

Toobin goes on to give a very readable account of the history of the Google project and of who is suing whom and some even-handed speculation about everyone's struggle to come to terms with the brave new digital world. All seems to depend on the predicted lethargy of the federal courts, or that some epic agreement among the parties will be reached and everyone will finally get paid.

Whatever the case, it seems highly suspect to accuse the Google founders of rapacious profit making and make fun of their corporate motto, just because they are throwing big money at a very legitimate problem. We must consider that they may actually have a vision of information beyond Web pages and contemporary publishing; this is certainly something that cannot be said of contemporary publishing. As long as the publishers and their lawyers dominate the discussion and spin it in the direction of their position, we need not waste time on it. It is time to find new channels for the discussion.

In this context one should take a look at Kevin Kelley's enthusiastic piece on book digitization—which earned him an acutely arched eyebrow from Prof. Grafton. Since I have a long-standing involvement in scanning, I am not as sanguine as some of the cheerleaders that the great throng of Internet users will know what to do with vast amounts of antiquarian e-books, searchable or not. I am not afraid that the unsanitized thoughts of yesteryear might inspire unsophisticated people to mischief; there is enough unsanitized thought in contemporary media. I do feel that the vision of universal education is half-baked; but there could be a number of people with training and education distributed around the planet who are lacking resources—and they could be helped; I certainly have been helped by these resources.

Kevin Kelley, in his New York Times Sunday Magazine article, "Scan This Book!" May 14, 2006—quotes Brewster Khale: "We can provide all the works of humankind to all the people of the world." Khale, the head of the Open Book initiative (the force behind IA), is a great visionary and philanthropist in the Open Source world and compares this project with the moon landing. He says it is something that will allow us, the moderns, to finally one-up the Greeks, the ancient ones.

I find enthusiastic pieces of journalism harmless and uplifting; I am not going to ridicule careless use of concepts like universal; the vision of something comprehensive, even if a bit blurry, is basically to be embraced. It is important to inspire people; once they get down to work, cleaning up the OCR for a volume of Ottoman history, they will get a clearer idea of their relation to the universal.

Kevin Kelley, clearly sympathetic and enthusiastic, goes on to give considerable background to the efforts of Google and others in scanning, and he sketches a bright digital future as everyone links arms and skips down an electronic yellow brick road; the yellow bricks, ironically, provided by scanning factories in China. What is not to like about this Technicolor future?

The Libraries

Libraries and Google [ed. Miller and Pellen, Hawforth Press, 2005, available online] despite its promising title, is really too old to have an impact on the current discussion. It has been widely reviewed and presents a collection of short essays by a number of librarians of various ranks and importance, giving their take on GBS and Google Scholar. It is of some interest to browse through the various problems as libraries conceived them at the dawn of this new age of Google. Michigan wonders if libraries will no longer deal in printed materials in the future and advocates close contact with the proverbial eight-hundred-pound gorilla. Predictably we have concerns from Oxford about damage to their non-acid-free books of the nineteenth century, which are oxidizing on their own sitting untouched by human hands, thank you very much indeed. There are moans of despair, shouts of defiance, and technical analyses of this that and the other. In sum, there seems to have been an encouraging move toward re-engineering in response to the announcement of GBS. However, there is little in this volume that will survive beyond its utility as an eye-witness account; it is a snapshot, as is this presentation, of one frame in time of an evolving phenomenon—and for that, it is valuable.

A voluminous discussion of GBS has proliferated on the Web. Despite the considerable bibliography on the legal aspect of the project, predictably, there is nothing of real interest to users or humanists that has come of the discussion. Attempts to stop it have failed, the prophecies of doom have fallen on deaf ears, and the echoes of European bellyaching on American cultural hegemony have subsided and moved on to other more heinously grievous examples than "La Google"; the paranoids, of course, still lock their doors to keep world domination from starting at their house. The chief librarians with few exceptions are manically waving their pompoms, and no markets concerned with books have collapsed because of Google. The ongoing complaints of copyright defenders have largely been addressed— to my satisfaction if not theirs.

Of course, in today's world of blogs, blogs of blogs, and counter-blogs, it is hard to frame any topic in terms of a bibliography. A bibliography supposes some ordered dis-cussion—collected, organized, and possibly annotated some years later. Today, every random thought is immediately blogged, creating an illusion of publishing and organized discourse. Thus, originality of thought, once achieved through the systematic assimilation of the relevant literature and the subsequent extension of the discussion, can no longer be taken for granted and may no longer be achievable.

A Voice from Paris

As an example of strikingly original thought, which has found both a strong echo and some considerable skepticism in Europe, are the torrents of themes and variations around La Google by the former head of the French National Library. This could be of interest to any antiquarian humanist who has ever tried to pry a copy of something from the BNF. [*Google and the Myth of Universal Knowledge*, JN. Jeanneney, U of Chicago, 2007 (Original French 2005). (For a serious review, of the original

French, see or google David Berman, *D-Lib Magazine*, Dec. 2006)].

I will not be able to deliver even a cursory discussion of this thin volume without diving at least ankle-deep into the cultural warfare as it is still practiced in la belle France. I hope to do that with humor and irony halting this side of derision.

There is really one overarching reason why it is safe not to take this philippic against Google too seriously. It is an analysis based on the mere announcement of the GBS initiative. It has nothing to say about the actual digitization project and any failings of the initiative, but it has everything to do with elite French bureaucrats' attitudes about activities outside their marble and glass palaces. It seems motivated by a primal fear that can strike only a high-placed French bureaucrat who realizes one morning while scanning *Le Monde* over croissant and cafe au lait that the Americans are doing something the French should have done a long time ago. So, having finished the coffee, and after four months of encouragement by his exalted peers and his fawning entourage, JN declares war, with an editorial in *Le Monde*, which then morphs into a book. This story is narrated in the book in great detail, lest you think I exaggerate.

For le directeur, the attack mode amounts to denouncing everything that has ever happened from west of Calais to the Pacific since before the Battle of Agincourt, all the while attempting to appear a venerable European statesman and the protector of legitimate "non-Anglophone" culture; perpetually under siege. Concomitantly, he declares himself guardian of the interests of all the disenfranchised of the world.

At best, it is a laundry list of complaints going back to the De Gaulle administration. His argument contains a lengthy indictment of advertising, a justification of an exemption for advertisement in French print media, an indictment of the American administration for not signing the Kyoto Protocols, a strange narrative about saving French cinema (that I have heard somewhere before), and the imagined deleterious influence of Google page ranking on French schoolchildren's understanding of the French Revolution. Actually, Google has to stand in for considerable anti-British/American spleen although Google had nothing to do with pulling the rug out from under the great, lost and mostly unlamented Napoleonic projects such as conquering Europe. Many elite French institutions see their organizational provenance in that time. On n'oublie jamais, mon Empereur!

Jeanneney displays a fairly knee-jerk anti-Americanism, which he sees an important part of his role as the former chief steward of the jealously guarded treasures of the BNF. His cultural jingoism is, however, tempered by a genuine embrace of technology and a grudging admission, that "Le Web" (actually invented at CERN just over the French border, by Europeans - well a Brit actually, but well inside Francophone territory and thus a cause for great pride) and "La Google" are Americanisms that are to be embraced as long as La France, l'Europe, and a long list of minor players in the realm of global information management, in that order, get a significant piece of the action, or at least, the BNF can set up a competing project with EU Euros. Thus we can ignore his swipes across the Atlantic and concentrate on some substantive elements of his critique.

The chief failing of his little book is that it does not differentiate between "American or global popular culture," "Google, the international search engine," and "Google's library digitization project." It should be possible to separate university libraries from mega-malls, as it must be possible to separate the Comedie Francaise from the Moulin Rouge. From an American point of view the two serve separate functions and only mischief can come from obscuring the difference.

Jeanneney sees a conflict between the profit motive, which infects everything American, and Francophone public institutions, which he characterizes as financially disinterested. Long live the Francophone taxpayer. In a passage that will make Americans laugh heartedly, he calls on government regulation to insure the "proliferation of creativity." Should this not come about, through the exclusion of any hint of profit motive and anything American, he sees threats to the common interest and "the global scales, in this realm and others, tip toward the hyper power of a dominant civilization" [Jeanneney, 2007 p. 33]. One must suspect he believes France would not be covered and that the civilization in question is exclusively Franco phobic. Hence, allons enfants de la patrie!

Some of his arguments have been overtaken by subsequent developments; some of his arguments have been, in fact, proven prophetic after observing the function of the beta of GBS for some years. The argument that only English language books will be selected has proven to be unfounded. Of course, Jeanneney makes the point, strangely quoting Churchill talking to De Gaulle, that Oxford is not really part of Europe, and that England cannot be counted on in patriotic pan-European projects that are initiated by France and cheered by its EU vassal states, like the fight against American popular culture and Oxford's partnership with Google. This may have been a swipe at Tony Blair.

That the preponderance of books in GBS is in English cannot be disputed, but it also varies with the subjects searched. Granted, there are a good deal more books in English in American and British libraries. The cause for this deplorable state of affairs can be found, not exclusively, in the international publishing demographics and book buying patterns, the American emphasis on universal and international education and the outcome of the Battle of Waterloo, and not in a sinister anti-francophone plot hatched in Silicon Valley.

From all indications, there is no committee that decides what to scan and what not to scan at Google partner libraries, (with the exception of Harvard which scans nothing past 1923), as there is at the BNF—no doubt devouring many hours of afternoons away from mistresses and causing many a black eye and ripped silk cravat. Indications are that the books in Google partner libraries have simply been taken from the shelf and scanned, so we can shelve the Anglo script bias argument. Since libraries in Europe have since joined the project, Jeanneney must be doubly pleased that the Public Library in Lyon, second only to the BNF in

France, as well as the Bavarian State Library, the University of Madrid among others have let the Google barbarians in.

A quick look around the BNF's electronic backyard showed some interesting numbers (subject to change):

BNF queries	"histoire" - 30,643,
	"history" - 1,826
	"Geschichte" - 1,185
Google queries	"history" - 154,115
	"Geschichte" - 50,822
	"histoire" - 45,923

BNF queries for Hammer-Purgstall, the author of a ten-volume history of the Ottoman Empire published in German in the nineteenth century yielded not a single non-French volume in fifty-seven hits.

There are no real conclusions to be drawn from either the BNF Franco script vs. non-Franco script ratio of 16:1, or the Google ratio 3:1, that would make someone a demon and someone else the savior. Let the French scan their French books and *brava, bravo.* At some future date, after untold person hours, all the various online editions can be sorted out. Until that happy day, the naysayers shall not trouble us. If the Europeans want to opt out of the settlement on orphans, good for them, let them cool their heels as spectators at the local *Bet and Win* as the real game continues.

Perhaps we should mention the introduction to the English translation of Jeanneney's slim volume by the current chief Canadian Librarian who brings some heavy international bureaucratic firepower to bear in the UNESCO Universal Declaration on Cultural Diversity. Alas, this UNESCO declaration laying out principles of cultural diversity, inadvertently trod on and otherwise ignored systematically by American techies just being techies, can be forgotten as yet another weapon to be trained on Google. The five principles "d'honneur" of the librarians of "francophonie" of the declaration make sense only against the backdrop of the Brussles-Strassbourg-Geneva (Montreal) bureaucratic axis that the French especially are treating with resounding skepticism. Thus it seems strange that the chief librarian of Canada, no doubt in a frenzy of omniphonical correctness, should parade this red herring in his otherwise heart-warming introduction.

The consensus of technology pundits on this subject, led by Brewster Khale, seems to throw its preponderance in the opposite direction. Access to the Web via Google, et alia, for the UNESCO charges around the world and any Francophone refugees awash in an English-speaking world will cause a bootstrap effect as one user at a time finds access to the modern information marketplace. They will have access to free HTML manuals and to the great libraries of American and European universities and the BNF for former French colonials. Third World users will start as consumers and evolve into providers. Thus, Google will be part of the solution and is clearly not the problem. This may not be believed in France, whose past efforts in the third world need not be enumerated, and it may not fit into the agenda of UNESCO, whether political or humanitarian. What possible benefit could there be in casting doubt on the Google scanning initiative? Frankly, I have no patience with arguments that try to denigrate significant contributions to the work of the humanities by advocating global openness in one breath and empowering the stewards of elitist exclusivity in the next. I suspect it may be as simple as protecting turf against those not anointed by *Sciences Po*. [This can be googled]

More trenchant are Jeanneney's arguments about the organization of knowledge and Google's efforts in that area. Jeanneney breaks a lance for the importance of informed contextualization. He detects a danger in the dissemination of uncontextualized information and the subsequent dangerous con-clusions drawn by the uninitiated operating without the guidance of librarians. Here he touches a crucial problem in the Google digitization project, but it's too late to protect humanity from books. The more subtle point about ranking "pages" rather than providing "books," could not come under discussion and would only worsen the apoplexy. It might have moved him to direct his staff to google all day to make sure French sources on the French Revolution stay at the top of the hits.

In his fury at Google, Jeanneney does not differentiate between Google's search engine that fields millions of queries every day, and the "library digitization project." He should rest easy, book digitization is a tiny subset of Google, a pro bono gesture, really a decentralized consortium—not the end of the BNF, the French way of life, or research in the humanities by qualified professionals with the able assistance of librarians. It may be some time before page ranking will emerge as a powerful technology that will affect everyone's relationship to what was once the printed page.

To put this in context: Google is a marketing tool. That is how it pays its bills. No argument. Google has a feature in its general search screen called "I'm feeling lucky." That button takes the user to the first item on the list of hits. It has been calculated by someone who cares to calculate such things that this feature, which is used in about 1 percent of the queries, costs Google over one hundred million dollars per year in lost advertising revenue.

OK, one may believe it or not, but one could do the arithmetic—Google's budget for the GBS for six years is rumored to be one hundred million dollars. A small step for Google, a huge step for the humanities. Given the efforts to increase budgets for digitization by Jeanneney and others, it would seem that the impulse of Google has been positive, even should they decide the whole thing has been a mistake and pull the plug tomorrow—as has done Microsoft.

It seems it is not possible to avoid nationalistic perspectives when engaging in culture war. Is seems sad that the man formerly sitting in the first chair at the BNF should lend himself to these perspectives. There must be other ways to motivate library technologies in Europe. Be that as it may, European cultural insecurities are of little interest unless they can be leveraged so money is made available for digitization. Then, there is still the big hurdle that the resulting scans are actually made available to the public for free—where they can no doubt do untold harm. This is not a given in the old world, including the UK—but it is still early in the game.

Books of Europe Unite

There is one voice from Europe that should be mentioned for sake of completeness: Ioanna Mamali, author of *The European Library*.

Mamali's slim volume should have been available on limited preview so I would not have parted with sixty euros to buy the pamphlet and spent the money instead on a weighty volume of Ottoman historiography. Mamali offers a Cook's tour through the EU efforts to coordinate electronic resources. Curiously, Google plays a significant role since it seems to have seriously scared the blankety-blank out of them, leading to a five-page analysis and spurring furious activity. Jeanneney's arguments are recapitulated including the touching concern for French students in danger of receiving their French identity from the Anglophonic milk at Google's breast.

The arguments against Google are enumerated: commercial interest, cultural hegemony, non-contextualization, and unprofessionalism. I find none of these arguments compelling. The Miller & Pellin volume shows that a good deal of thought has gone into the shepherding professional librarians have undertaken at the start of this project. American libraries see this initiative as a source of empowerment, not exploitation, and their involvement is ongoing.

Mamali goes on to argue that the notion of a universal library has been discredited. I would be emboldened to ask by whom? By a Princeton professor? By European National Libraries unwilling and unable to share turf? By the BNF who fears its holdings will be swamped by larger language groups So the vision is, correct me if I am wrong, everyone in their own backyard, dancing their own folk dances, wearing picturesque costumes passed down from their agrarian past, when they were lopping each other's heads off?

It is then only a small step for Mamali, happily taken, to affirm that the content of national libraries is the property of the respective state, to be administered by the state and only the state. I am merely paraphrasing the arguments offered.

Mamali does show a screen of the Google text search. She uses the word "Archimedes" as a search term in the Works of Archimedes, an enlightening example showing deep familiarity with the concept. One wonders how often Archimedes used his own name in his essays. I think I can sense a subtext of profound concern, if not fear of a level of technological achievement not common in the old world, but there is also a determination not to leave a good hair standing on Google. She throws out the notion of universality in order to follow Jeanneney's arguments against Google, despite being an advocate of a pan-European project. She mentions killer features in GBS, that are years ahead of current thinking at European libraries, in passing, in order to show Europeans are not easily impressed, and she fully expects tenured bureaucrats in Vienna, Bratislava, Riga and elsewhere to do local digitization.

Mamali tries to spin GBS as eager for publisher contacts but throws cold water on the idea that more libraries will join the effort for the discredited universal library. Fortunately, that prediction has proven wrong.

The last several pages show screens of a Web site called "The European Library," the latest incarnation of some decades of effort by various national libraries of Europe to work together to create a common Internet portal. On the opening screen there are quite a few items to be selected and checked; this requires some initiation. There are, after all more than twenty institutions hooked to the portal. It seems that trying to search over too many collections leads to interminable waiting times. The good news is that the system does not time out, even after fifteen minutes!

The comparison to GBS is instructive. If you say "Boo" to Google, it cranks up and spits out reams of PDFs and recent books with some relevance real or imagined to "Boo." You can then spend profitable hours going through your results. You say "Boo" to TEL, you get a five-minute wait followed by nothing. An attempt to find something in Gallica (BNF) that you know is there could well hang because of failure to exclude various other national libraries that drag down the system. I would just as soon use Google to get to the BNF. Some notion of universalism, some central facility and unifying principle like that in Google, may well be the destiny of European efforts, may they like it or not.

I don't want to deride the effort to create a pan-European library portal, although connecting twenty servers is never an easy proposition. The temptation of designers is to cover all the bases and overcomplicate the choices. First, you have to set the switches on the TEL opening screen, then you put in the query. What could I be looking for that would require looking in Bucharest and Copenhagen and stations between, logging on to each national server one at a time? Why not hire some techies from Palo Alto to merge the catalogs of the European National Libraries, design an update strategy and deliver queries world-wide?

No doubt one can learn to wring information from TEL. At this writing I prefer to go to the individual libraries to try my luck. Instant gratification and positive experiences with electronic archives and libraries, even to the patently unqualified or the merely uninitiated, is still an absolutely American vice, incomprehensible to Europeans.

Wrap Up

Google has no need to protect privilege, it certainly has no interest in denying access to the unqualified, access is universal and the material by necessity requires a universal perspective. Google has conquered the Web in dramatic fashion, with a simple idea: let all those with a question come before me, let them type it into my search window in telegraph style, and I will give them a statistically defensible answer. Its world is made of the surface Web and the deep Web. The surface Web is all indexed and purring like a kitten, advertising is reaching eyeballs, and queries are being handled. The ongoing challenge for Google is the deep Web, with all its proprietary information locked away from indexing engines.

The final frontier, the wilds, the brambles, the undiscovered country, is the non-electronic Web—alphanumerics printed on dead trees, and in some cases, on dead animals. Google is at least on the right track; let's get some people into those libraries; let's wave thousands of books at high speed cameras and run some OCR, and let's give away the PDFs and link in any features and algorithms we have working. They have run it up the flagpole, and this one is saluting.

Brin in the New York Times

In 2008, around the time of the unveiling of the settlement, Sergey Brin published a few paragraphs in the NYT. After a clever but unimportant introductory paragraph, there is a sentence that takes my breath away:

> "Larry Page, the co-founder of Google, first proposed that we digitize all books."

A true word spoken. Page indeed was the first, ever in time, to propose that "we digitize all books." There is a *thunk* that I hear in my head at the phrase "all books." What a sentence: "Let us digitize all books." A sentence later, we read:

> "Today, they number over 10 million and counting."

Brin then goes on to sketch the legal challenges and makes a case for the settlement. From his arguments it is clear that he feels confident that the books before 1923 will be done and finished in the near future. He is concerned with "saving and making available the works of the 20th century." The argument is simple: without digitization more and more orphaned books will be lost due to a variety of causes ranging from indifference to old junk to earthquakes, floods and fires.

The essay is disarming in its simple plainness. It is a bit discouraging to read some of the negative reaction that follow in the ninety reader's comments. I liked the world better when the thoughts, mine included, that one entertains while reading editorials remained private clouds passing through the mindscape and were not immortalized in print. Clearly we live in a polarized society; perhaps we have always lived in a polarized society; yet I have no fear that Brin and Page, having achieved the ten million mark a year ago from this writing will carry through to a conclusion—and that they will rescan the pages with finger hats.

In conclusion he mentions the three things that are receiving special attention: "...improving (1) bibliographic information and (2) categorization, and further (3) detailing our privacy policy." I would not bet against them.

MEANWHILE, BACK AT THE TRESTLE:
THE CODEX HANGS...

Let us return to our stake-out of Prof. Grafton's revised and enlarged essay. It is difficult to know if it is helpful to do a précis of Prof. Grafton's "Codex in Crisis." Perhaps it would be better just to characterize each of the three sections. (1) "The Universal Library," forget about it. (2) "The Google Empire," clearly an intimation of "evil empire," but it is better than microfilm and makes vast amounts of material available, more material than any organization before it. (3) "Publishing without Paper," don't even think about parking here.

I am heartened that now in the improved version of "Future Reading," one cannot just survive, but also thrive in the new "information ecologies" [WMW, p. 293].

The section on the "Universal Library" is a mixture of *it's been tried and failed* and *it's nothing new*. Prof. Grafton dips into the history of scholarship, again, to bring forth many handfuls of information that may or may not be relevant. How profit driven has the academic publishing industry been in the last three hundred years? More than Elsevier today? Are libraries really making a dent in the field, or are they merely rescuing unprofitable but important activities? Have there really been characters in the Middle Ages or in Babylonia that can be seen as precursors of computing? Are we given a typological interpretation of Google and its aim at universality that tries to find prefiguration in the past? Was Trithemius a prefiguration of Horst Feistel? Let me be obscure since I can't be extremely learned. Of course, with Google, obscurity is not what it used to be. I admit I don't know much about failed attempts at universalism in the past or if that is relevant to Google today. I can't really ask the right questions. One must stay with the assigned topic. I am tempted to give no marks to this section, so sorry.

The Google Empire

The section on Google's empire does point to a dynamic future; yet, Prof. Grafton emphasizes the limitations; I am not sure Google would see this problem. I will refrain from a detailed examination; I mean, who knows what will happen, let's just keep working and pretend everything will be all right and invite Cassandra to stay in the guest house for a month, to cheer her up, get her to relax, by the heated pool, stop worrying, have some Tequila Sunrise. I shall just flip through some of the themes touched.

The TLG, although mentioned only by association with *Perseus*, only gets oblique praise in this early section of Grafton's argument, but more will come later. The uninitiated might get the idea that it is some sort of remedial tool for those who flunked Latin 101.

> "Perseus, … an incredibly useful site based at Tufts, began with Greek and Latin texts and now embraces works from the English Renaissance. Readers can make direct online use of dictionaries, grammars, and commentaries as they struggle through the originals" [WNW, p. 301].

I would have asked around if mainstream classicists who do not struggle through the originals may have found more substantial uses of *Perseus*.

No amount of editing will save the section on world poverty [WMW, pp. 301–302]. The nostalgia for the New York intelligentsia and its socialist past is clear:

> "Capitalism, of all things, is democratizing access to books at an unprecedented pace."

Of course, many practitioners of thirties ideologies followed Sidney Hook into Neo-Conservatism and its consequences.

A dominant metaphor used in these discussions is the *flood of information* and its associated problems. Imagine a kid from Boston standing in front of Widener, it would take many thousands of dollars in tuition and fees and many years of hard work before that kid would know his way around that temple of learning. Is that a problem? Not for the extremely learned.

> "The Internet's technologies, moreover, are continually developing, and many of the changes make it easier for a user to take a stand in the flood of information and fish out exactly the right book or article from the foam" [WMW, p. 303].

The discussion goes on to describe the necessity of "focused searches" to get information out of JSTOR as though this were some problem. I was trained on journal runs thirty years ago, and I must say, I don't miss going through volumes of indexes to make sure one had not missed anything. For those in graduate school taking "Research Methods", the lessons on journals have been cut by 80%. There is no "foam."

The intense research is paying off, however, as Prof. Grafton skates perilously close to actual data-mining techniques:

> "One of my favorites is Amazon's list of "statistically improbable phrases," or SIPS, in any given book. Click on one of them and Amazon whisks you off to a list of other books in which the same highly unusual combination of words appears - a fast and simple way to find connections that previous buyers have not already made. Your local reference librarian still knows a lot more tricks than you do for finding information, in books or on the Web. But the powers of search keep growing, and it is hard to imagine what they will be in ten or twenty years" [WMW, pp. 303–304].

I have a problem with "a fast and simple way to find connections that previous buyers have not already made" No matter how I parse this phrase, I cannot get past "have not already made." Let me start over and try to explain the concept of SIPS.

It is not a matter of "highly unusual phrases" but unique technical vocabulary as it is used in the humanities; most recently the label appears as "key phrases." For example: "New Traditionalism" is one of these SIPS for Kazin's "On Native Ground." Unfortunately this well has been polluted from the perspective of literary studies, it seems that "New Traditionalism" also refers to elaborate McMansions in the Tampa Bay area. Awards are given for designs. There are however, several literary criticism texts in the SIPS link in Google Books that mention "New Traditionalism." The trail is hot. Try it: go to Amazon, find a SIP on some book you know well and use that phrase as a query in Google Books.

Amazon has done its homework; along with the SIPS, they provide the first sentence. Traditionally, a topic sentence contains the semantic clues to the rest of the piece, which can then be searched.

An interesting paragraph begins on p. 309 [WMW] and shows Prof. Grafton bubbling over with excitement for the future. He mentions Google and other collections of books, music, and film, "more massive than anything the world has ever known." He lets himself be swept into the future of data mining, a future that will be achieved when the "material emerges from protection." Ironically, he mentions the data mining algorithms of the NSA, when there are at least a hundred more likely sources for data mining code in universities around the world; just wander across Harrison Street, two blocks. But this tells a good story, from the violation of all the fundamental rights we hold dear to untold knowledge about our culture.

Grafton's main point is that "we shall still need our libraries," and I agree. I am also willing to apologize for all the digitization enthusiasts who have lamented the brick and mortar libraries. I am sorry about what they said, but you must understand, if Google Book Search does become the new Library of Congress, if they do clean their data and their images completely, I will have to retract my apology and invest in a project that will turn the lower levels of Firestone into a combination bowling alley and skating rink for the kids from Matawan.

Prof. Grafton buttresses his argument for geographically distributed storage by asserting:

> "Neither Google nor anyone else will fuse the proprietary collections of early books and local systems created by individual archives into a single accessible mass of information." [WMW, p. 310]

Let me say that I would like to try. The only cause for failure would be that someone is standing at the front door of the archive with a shotgun to keep the integration team out. Any data in a relational database can be linked to other tables if they have common fields and some common connection that makes integration sensible. If we are talking about books and cataloging data, many potential links are inevitable. Any data in weird legacy systems can be dumped into text files and reformatted for SQL and run on a cheap laptop.

The use of the concept of a "mass of information" or "flood of information" is already the wrong way of thinking about the problem. There is another way. I am sitting at my desk, I am thinking about a book; I do not know which of eight *proprietary collections* or the eighteen *individual archives with local systems* that I know exist in Rome and Lazio might have that book. I go to my computer and type in part of the title and a PDF of that book comes up. I download the PDF, start reading, and print six pages. I book a flight to Rome on my computer, send an e-mail to the curator, and the next morning I am sitting on a flight to Rome reading the PDF on my laptop to prepare myself for the artisanal experience of visiting the collection. Now was that so hard?

There are no technical impediments to unified catalogs; there are no technical impediments to photographing pages of books, no matter how old; there are strong imperatives to get this work done. Lets call Silvio.

One could contemplate weirder problems, and I do this only to horrify the skeptics; no votes there not already lost. Linking Persian Miniatures with Japanese Rock Gardens might at first seem nonsensical till one notices that in many miniatures the rocks and boulders have facial expressions; I think I could design a link-table or find someone who could, not entirely unserious, but let me see some Japanese rocks or scroll paintings and let's see if we can make data-points for facial expressions. If artists have seen faces in rocks then we can have fields that could link that data. If Japanese Rocks are indeed expressionless, my bad, let's look at rocks in South-East Asia or Latin America. There might be some pushing piles around here and there, but if there is a plan for merging data, it can be done. Graduate students in the future will do this kind of work to get degrees.

And finally:

> "Though the distant past will also be more accessible than ever before, in a technical sense, once it is captured in a vast, disjointed mosaic, it may actually recede ever more rapidly from our collective attention" [WMW, p. 310].

Although it is carefully formulated, this is a red herring that will embolden an informed reader to drop the book.

Is the past to be honored only through solitary contemplation of a manageable piece portioned for one or at most for the ten that will fit around the table at a seminar?

The distant past may well recede from our attention, but it will not be because of data integration [google this if you must]. Data integration will not yield a disjointed mosaic any more than mosaic makers make a disjointed mosaic if they know what they are doing. The experience of Persians and others may not be so diametrically disjointed. If not the faces on rocks, let's find data points for court scenes; the Persians were masters of court scenes as were the Europeans. The concept of disjointed mosaic does not serve this sentence well. Far from it, there will be many linked data tables and a printout of the link structure will look more like a bowl of spaghetti at the table of the victim of a gangland slaying of the 30's. But an interface or a series of nested query screens can be designed to support the workflow of different scholars to give them an artisanally satisfying experience. In the history of artisanship, there is nothing more beautiful than a great interface to complex data, in the eye of this beholder.

A few phone calls would bring a small patrol of Oracle jocks to Prof. Grafton's office to talk data, strategy, and tactics. There are extremely competent people dedicated to supporting the extremely learned in universities everywhere. Let us not get stuck on the idea of only one true mantra: "We will still need our material libraries and archives."

e-Publishing

The section on publishing draws on Prof. Grafton's experience as an editor. Clearly we must be protected from unripe first impressions masquerading as vetted descriptive analysis in a proportional spaced font—the editors at Harvard University Press and *The New Yorker* are protecting the public.

[Since this includes me I will have to pack my caboodle and be gone. Please stop reading! But I will finish writing, without the approval of an editor, to assert a timeless privilege: to have an essay sit unread in the drawer. Today the mutation is to put it on a Website or publish it for a couple hundred euros with an "on demand" service and let it languish there, undemanded, except by family and friends, unread, but lurking in hopes of poking someone in the eye, with all due respect. But I digress.]

The love of the printed page is enduring in Prof. Grafton, so we can be sure that JHI will serve as a fire starter in Vermont cabins for the foreseeable future. Electronic subscriptions will continue to subsidize (and enable) print.

Clearly there are problems with electronic text resources. One positive feature is that it is possible to trace the use down to how much time specific users spend on individual pages. The news Grafton brings is bad but hardly unexpected: students generally skim information and spend woefully inadequate time on any given article. But what about the user statistics of a motivated serious researcher, or the combined data of a group of highly competent researchers? This is the kind of data Google is collecting. Can anyone in universities be bothered to do this kind of study? So Grafton uses technology to reinforce his vision of a generally disintegrating intellectual situation. He chronically misses opportunities to gather positive insight.

This section culminates in a series of paragraphs where an academic in ancient philosophy ridicules the use of the TLG by charlatans. He does so in a really mean-spirited, shocking tone. People with little Latin and less Greek have learned enough to query the TLG and embellish their papers with quotes in Greek from authors they have not even looked up in Wiki. Is that bad? That is very bad, unless it is a red herring! As bad as it is, if it is true and widespread, what is the implication for digital resources? I must admit, I don't get it; I really don't get it. Is bad scholarship caused by the TLG? Was there ever grotesquely bad scholarship before today?

I quote the entire section in hopes that my outrage at intermixing serious digital resources with examples of sophomoric use will be shared.

> "Listen, for example, to Jonathan Barnes, a specialist on ancient philosophy, describe what the computer database of the Thesaurus Linguae Graecae (TLG)—a searchable, full-text archive of ancient Greek texts—has done for his field:

"Load it into your laptop, and you have instant access to virtually the whole of Greek literature. You cut and paste snippets from authors whose very names mean nothing to you. You affirm—and you're right—that a particular word used here by Plato occurs 43 times elsewhere in Greek literature. And you can write an article—or a book—stuffed with prodigious learning. (There are similar things available for Latin.) ... The TLG is a lovely little resource (I think that's the word) and I use her all the time. But she's strumpet-tongued: she flatters and she deceives. "What an enormous knowledge you have, my young cock—why not let me make a real scholar of you?" And the young cock crows on his dung-hill: he can cite anything and construe nothing."

> Barnes's description of the siren song of the TLG will bring no pleasure to anyone who spends time, for example, grading papers or evaluating the work of young writers. The 200,000 titles compiled by a single entrepreneur, Philip Parker, with the aid of algorithms and a staff of programmers, offer a preview of an ugly future."
> [WMW, p 322]

Grafton's arguments in no way detract from the fantastic achievement of the TLG and the *Perseus* environment of tools for the study of antiquity. The extremely learned should know better and do appropriate penance in future publications.

On close examination, the 2009 essay seems to be bulked up with steroids; there is less there than meets the eye.

There are several more 2007-2009 quote pairs that could be culled out; yet the result would be the same, an attempt has been made to be more precise, mention more sources and deflect potential criticism. Perhaps one last example is instructive; the 2007 piece contains the sentence:

"The computer and the Internet have transformed reading more dramatically than any technology since the printing press..."

The 2007 sentence continues to announce "Google Book Search" and continues on to describe it as a projected "comprehensive index of all the world's books."

In the 2009 extension, the sentence cited above becomes the location of a major insertion:

"...since the printing press. In the great libraries from Stanford to Oxford, pages turn, scanners hum, databases grow—and the world of books, of copyrighted information and repositories of individual copies tremble" [WMW, p. 289].

This is the story of the expanded version: books are in danger, libraries tremble, and rights are being abridged.

Grafton continues with a mention of the apocalypse from Revelation 6:14:

"And the heaven departed as a scroll when it is rolled together."

The quote seems to be informed more from a Hollywood image in support of pseudoecclesiasticism, than any theological significance. A mention of the apocalypse in the context of work done currently in libraries from Stanford to Oxford sets a tone that I refuse to comprehend; something is askew in the rhetoric. Excitement about a technological future is characterized as "millenarian prophecies" which inevitably are associated with the apocalypse. Perhaps the apocalypse will only apply to dusty books and the laptops will be fine. Perhaps the logic of the extremely learned is beyond my understanding. However the quote does set the stage for an ideological test: books are good, and "liquid fabric of interconnected words and ideas" are bad.

He presents us with a bonfire of technological believers. He also shows us an honor roll of dogged information managers working with clay tablets, papyrus, slips of papers, and microfiche to solve the problems of their day. The first to be sacrificed to the flames for invoking millennial prospects is Kevin Kelley. The most prominent victim is Greg Crane, whose work has been reduced to a snippet about an experiment in scholarly communication, doubtlessly informed by Crane's expertise in database design. Instead of honoring Crane's work on the TLG and his work on the tools integrated in *Perseus*, he is dismissed because he thinks critically about scholarly communication.

Cultural Pessimism

I find this hard to explain and will have to delve into the personal sphere for an explanation—I am sharing about my own experience here and not presuming to speak about anyone but me and one or two close friends. I have noticed a corrosive effect creeping in with age, in my own attitude and the attitude of my aging friends in the academy. In the past I have identified this as cultural pessimism and dismissed as something that will never happen to me. Cultural pessimism is not always successfully resisted as the young grow older because it is not recognized for what it really is: personal pessimism. The corrosion is brought on, among other things, by the instinctive resistance of the young to the old; consequently, it hits teachers especially hard.

The young learning system will defer to the teaching system, but it will find myriad ways of showing callous disregard for the timeless lessons of the ages, dredged up by the teaching system. This continues until the young begin formulating their own timeless wisdom. No doubt it hurt my own father when I categorically refused to share his love for Dickens as I began to graduate from the Hardy Boys to literature. I would read anything and everything, but I was careful to leave Dickens to the side. I think the accumulated carelessness of students and sons (and the world at large) with cherished ideas and practice, over time, wears down the pedagogue. This careless lack of respect for hard won expertise and deserved authority—disrespect in modern usage—lets the pessimism seep in, brings forth dreams of early retirement and leads to a souring of textual communication.

Were it not for the vast gap in learning, understanding, and vision between the learners and the teachers, one might still hope; yet, it will be a long and winding road before one of today's gamers becomes the extremely learned of his or her generation. We will still have the texts that were produced to be read and understood. Our savior may be someone who can play *Civilization III* at the Sid level and give up the game for sandals.

I speak generally here, from the laments of friends who teach in the humanities, and not from experience (teaching about computers is different). I have been told that you can lead the students to the water, but you can't make them ever go deep enough in your favorite places. Those that have an inkling what you are trying to do will think they have found their own places to dive, the teacher can only warn them of the shallows and disappear in the depths to gnaw on the personal liver in private. The fact is that, to paraphrase Heidegger, everyone must make their own science. The extreme scholar is by definition alone and no amount of editing by clever UP staff will communicate the true experience to the unanointed.

Not all teachers succumb, but the infection is pandemic. Clearly, more interesting to the young, to the *New Yorker* reader and to the ages a-coming than veiled warnings of the effect of technology and the subtext of praise for Alfred Kazan's note cards and yellow pads and the privileging of Underwood typewriter technology, and the threat of vigilant bouncers patrolling the velvet ropes at the club of publishable ideas, would have been some witnessing of the positive effect of technology on Prof. Grafton's own career and present work-flow. We live in a let it hang out age and opinions are given credibility through personal sharing.

This lack of connection to the experience of the present is painfully obvious in the six pages of his 2007 *New Yorker* essay. The first two illustrations retrieved from the Graftonian depths are the problems of Mesopotamian librarians with the sort-order of those pesky clay tablets and the acquisition practices of the library at Alexandria. Curiously, the Cook's tour continues ominously in the sixteenth century with the bankruptcy of publishing entrepreneurs in Rome overestimating their market.

More interesting for us, the young and the young at heart, would have been Prof. Grafton discussing the development of twentieth-century libraries and the effect on research of digitizing library catalogs. The OPAC is no straw dog to be shooed or slaughtered, it is cast in titanium; its only potential predator is Google, and that danger will be some years off and will likely be a cooperation—not a fight to death. So what is it like to be in the first generation of your species to use a union of the library catalogs from around the world? What is it like to watch hundreds of workers, in the US, Mexico, and Europe photographing out-of-print books? What is it like to see the smartest and most motivated workforce in history deliver these images to Africa and around the world? Is that scary? Please, where is the worry?

More interesting would have been showing the difference between copying out references from the card catalog and spending hours tracking down wrong page numbers, which I remember well from my time as a graduate student. The example might seem banal, more banal than a sentence about Babylonia, but there is banality in innovation. Are we to argue that this kind of bibliographic drudgery that did not obviate errata sheets in even the most prestigious publications is to be missed because it reinforced detailed knowledge of the text editions of a tradition? Can we let WorldCat take care of that for us?

There are no aspersions to be cast in that direction that would convince; much was gained, little was lost. Such pedestrian examples would have led to some mention of positive improvements in text research, text preparation, editing and communication and the freeing of time for reading and writing.

The notion that people start writing too early, contributing to a glut of half-baked ideas in immature prose, seems a strange argument in an age where preschoolers send e-mails. [WMW, p315] Perhaps we should look for a silver lining in pre-school literacy. Let us grant that there will always be Bozos that write, but let us not despair that great writers will emerge from practice. Many great writers! If the submissions to JHI are really so bad that they have to be rewritten by the editors, then let's talk to Prof. Crane and see if we can fix the problem with a data-table that excludes style.

Some respect will have had to be granted to the pioneering work of digital humanities of the last forty years that has integrated rapidly developing technology in addressing the tasks universities set themselves, not too much to ask from the expert in scholarship. I personally am pleased. For pity's sake, we have not all been tearing down the city wall so the barbarians can pillage.

We have no need of unsmiling faces and long or stubby fingers gesturing toward repositories of priceless treasures accessible to the privileged few with a high gag threshold, when it is clear that all professors at Princeton and elsewhere, save a handful, will gladly admit that computers have been good to them and even transformative to their work. There are privileges to high priesthood purchased with the responsibility to be mouthpiece of the eternal one, the one who will accept sacrifices over the next fifty decades. It is not enough to bask in the warm glow of the fellowship of scholars in a "dark, dark time" [WNW, p. 8]. The pursuit of truth, the task Prof. Grafton sets himself, requires that the stones cast at technology be recognized as a temporary expedient in a limited horizon—more as a plea for moderation in times of turmoil, and not as a final judgment. The truth content in a final judgment will be determined, as truth has always been determined in conflicts of will, by the energy of the advocates. I believe no harm will come to books.

But the future will not be held up, even in the ominous, measured prose of the extremely learned. In one of the rare single sentences where Prof. Grafton gives us some insight into his personal use we read:

> "It is an amazing experience to teach literary texts that you know well, but not perfectly, with the Google Book text up and searchable on your laptop" [WMW, p. 305].

It is possible, on reflection, that this was related to him second hand. Let me cast a jaundiced eye anyway.

We have made the point and will explain further that the Google search in the present release is below entry level. I would rank the "mark all" feature in Text Pad, my weapon of choice with text, much superior, but only in the sense that it too is below entry level. One should not use Google Books when other tools are better or other archives bring more predictable results. Look first on *Gutenberg*, especially in order to search text, and resort to Google Books only if all else fails, or if it becomes important to inspect an antiquarian edition. Look first on Internet Archive to look for a specific edition, then dig through Google Books, but allow plenty of time for browsing, you have just gone into a bookstore with millions of old books.

One short call to the University computer center would mobilize someone who could install a real text search environment, loaded with the texts for next semester, on Prof. Grafton's laptop. It is hard to exaggerate what insight might be gained were the extreme scholars to become actual power users.

Let us end on an up-beat note. I don't think we can learn much about digital humanities from Prof. Grafton; he does not really try to teach us; he merely tries to warn us and worry about us and show us all the amazing stuff he has culled from the mists of time. We can learn much about scholarship from him, not in these essays, but we can be inspired to follow some of his footnotes and stray into other chapters of *Worlds Made by Words*.

We shall not learn much about paperless publishing from him; he plans to be the last one standing. We cannot gag the enthusiastic advocates for digitization so the enterprise will appear more legitimate under a jaundiced gaze. We may get some fresh wind in rear-guard skepticism about digital humanities, but retreating armies fight rear guard actions. We need not worry about books, or about libraries, or our schools of library science—they are up to the task of re-engineering and are leading the effort of digitization and utilizing it for their purpose, and Google is merely following their lead.

We can accept Prof. Grafton's judgment:

> "Like Erasmus, Google is both a generous and a fallible guide to the universe of books" [WMW, pp. 305].

Again it is hard to know exactly what that might mean (Pandora's Box meets the "Black Jar" of Google?). There is a postscript that will shed more light on Prof. Grafton's continuing involvement with Google.

Grafton Live

In February of 2009, Prof. Grafton lectured for an hour at Google (*largo*, no, *andante moderato*). We see a different persona in the practiced lecturer. He is obviously at ease and able to connect with his audience. He seems to speak extemporaneously but fluidly without hesitation, repetition, pauses, and in well-formed sentences with a slight monotone. His gestures are minimal, confined to a stork-like spreading of the wings—the gestures of a man who does not need cheap rhetorical tricks to simulate charisma. One gets the idea that years of practice lecturing and leading discussions have left their mark and honed his delivery.

In this instance his presentation is distinctly low key—he establishes his credentials as a user of Google, although it would have been more helpful had he given them a piece of his mind.

Clearly the Google people in the room will never understand what harm they are doing books. The founders have met skepticism from other quarters; let us hope they do not tire of ankle biting. When he overtly praises the dimension of their effort, they do not realize that he is mocking gigantism, the pituitary condition here used metaphorically, and alluding to gigantomachia, and we know how badly that went for the giants.

When he takes them on a Cook's tour of the history of publishing and archiving, they do not realize that these are his only wares; he has no substantive thing to tell them about how to do the task they set themselves. The Google workers in the audience should be disappointed; they invite a luminary, a renowned expert on books, and all he can do is tell them that he mostly worries about Princeton undergraduates—a demographic least deserving worry. If we could do a wordlist of the talk, the semantic category of worry would get the most hits. I have resisted digitizing "Codex in Crisis," indexing the texts and playing semantic games out of respect for copyright law. But someone who will watch the lecture might want to count the instances of worry.

He reads from the essay "Codex in Crisis." First he reads the last paragraph to demonstrate that he sees a balance between computer use and book use. He admits that he goes fifty-fifty between book and computer. What he does not say and only implies is that "book use on the computer does not count." I think it is only fair to tell the Google people that. Reading books on the computer is superficial, it is the acquisition of information, and not reading; the better you are at it, the more superficial you become. Seems I remember similar things said about writing on the computer, but my memory is selectively expunging the nonsense ideas of the past.

In these discussions we should lay cards on the table. In most texts there is rhetorical posturing, obscurantism, irrelevancies, temporal bias, limitation of horizon—and the list goes on. The ideal of sequential slow reading can be accepted only for certain works of art, where, in the hand of a great artist, it is really important to attune to each nuance. Making a transcription of an old codex will teach you nothing if not how many words and how many repeated formulaic phrases are wasted to make a few little points. Reading Husserl teaches nothing if not that each sentence is made tentative through once uncounted parenthetical phrases. I would embolden Google to not let Prof. Grafton depress them and make them unsure of their mission through some subtle Socratic stratagem. Assert that there is a new way of reading and that the future of the polis depends on learning how to do it. Devil takes the hindermost!

Prof. Grafton also reads them the persiflage of the TLG. I do hope the audience averted their eyes as I did. It is not unlikely that the Google text people in the audience have heard of the TLG, possibly as an important resource, perhaps as a model for other philologies—stranger things have happened. The near lascivious, borderline insensitively incorrect and professionally untenable, as a lone characterization presented to laymen, makes me wonder [a southern expression]. I think Prof. Grafton was himself shocked by the shocked expression on the faces of his audience—though we can only intimate this from his reaction after reading the quote. That was a piece of work, a real piece of work [another southern expression].

Predictably the questions were few and stuttering. Someone asked has he any worries about book preservation; he curiously misunderstood the question which was admittedly badly asked and answered that he was worried indeed about losing millions of electronic book files, but he was somewhat sure they were properly backed up. He continued by reminding Google of their responsibility as the soon-to-be greatest library on the planet. Beware of gigantomachia.

Someone asked about Kindle and was told that the current version is not mature, which is somewhat true, but certainly more could be said by someone who had actually used one for a few hours. Someone worried about the reading pedagogy in his daughter's school; well, he should worry.

In summary, the message was less precisely formulated than the written text, but was unmistakable. It is time to worry about books, about their physical survival, and about whether their content can be adequately absorbed by the new generations of readers. It does not seem that Prof. Grafton has trained a large cadre of highly motivated go-getters who will carry on his work, else we would see more optimism. That could be the fault of Princeton's emphasis on undergraduate education that seems to wear down the extremely learned without producing worthy successors in abnegation, only heavy hitters in finance; who would get a PhD in history with a BA from Princeton? Let us hope there are other graduate schools where the torch is passed with enthusiasm for the new electronic tools.

Grafton's lecture can be seen in full and is easily located with Google.

The Blog

The last *coda* to date (*capriccio, andante moderato,* and *allegro furioso*) of the performance by Prof. Grafton in the arena of digitization is "Google Books and the Judge." It is a short two-page blog occasioned by, among other things, Google's deal with *On Demand.* Personally, I find the *Espresso Book Machine* a rather atavistic device, a sling blade in a world of weed-eaters. It is possible that the market is big enough and that the overhead on the Espresso gadget is low enough that this company can survive. The Google endorsement is certainly a big thing for *On Demand.* I hope Prof. Grafton's endorsement of the principle of on-demand publishing in his Google lecture did not motivate some lesser novice visionary at Google to think that this is a good idea. I would prefer people learn to read PDFs on their laptop, the notion of several million old books printed for $8.99 each, possibly from bad scans, does not warm my environmental cockles, undeveloped as they are. The real nuisance with on demand publishing is that these outfits are listing their potential offerings on Abe Books and Amazon, and to a lesser degree, on ZVAB. Thus I have had to wade through dozens of on demand wannabe rare editions to find an actual book that I want to buy. Not pleased!

The second part of the final *coda* is a reading of some of the positions in the proposed settlement. My own interest in the settlement is negligible; it will not impact my own work as long as I don't waste time reading about who is doing what to whom. I am satisfied for now with the PDFs of the nineteenth century; they have not yet occasioned a fistfight. There is enough there that we can now experiment on how to use this technology.

Prof. Grafton, as an owner of out-of-print copyright, does have all the right to be concerned; yet I cannot see an extremely learned one take sixty dollars and a nickel per download for a book his publishers will not reissue. Such a person would be the first of that species to make the cash register ring; that should make an interesting footnote in a hundred years. I would be mortified. He tries to spin the issue as one of cost to the user resulting in profit to the corporation in a "monetized" situation. Monetized by whom? I think that is a curve ball in the dirt that only Michael Jordan would swing at. When it comes to business law, all bets are off with the American justice system.

I really dislike blogs; they are good for technical discussions among birds of a feather, but there is a careless quality to the medium, even when the blog is in *The New Yorker*. Writing for the magazine used to mean something before they went digital and published short paragraphs laden with innuendo. It devalues the readership that becomes victim to a self-fulfilling prophecy, "let me manipulate the morons by dashing off a few phrases." And the morons will respond.

The just punishment is that no one of stature takes the bait, and the text and responses will be associated with your name forever. It would be mortifying to have to read the lame responses of the devalued readers who devalue the original by adding their one last rusty kopek. Or else, it is even worse to have someone, as in this case, blow in with technical jargon that is completely out of place and should not be seen in public, not realizing this blogger is just trying on the medium, better to have stayed with the genre essay and let the editors give legitimacy.

The last section is instructive since it is the first substantial, technical, and valid criticism about Google books in Prof. Grafton's writing, save a complaint about misspelling. Prof. Grafton is being very generous when he says that Google has misdated hundreds of books, I think it is more in the thousands, but this will be fixed.

Prof. Grafton makes a valid complaint about not being able to find all volumes in a set. In this case, he cannot find the pieces of a multivolume first edition of *Middlemarch* using the GBS advanced search feature. Actual adepts and adept votaries have failed at coaxing individual volumes out of the mists of Google, so no one should feel like the Lone Ranger. Admittedly, one really has to have worked with large databases and learned how to whip data into shape before one can really understand and forgive GBS in its present form.

The complaint about multivolume sets is a serious one, one that has been in the blogs for years. It is based on a misperception of the relative value of the general query window and the *advanced book search* panel. The academics coming from the OPAC want a specific book, all the books by an author, or all the volumes of a set. By habituation, they are used to filling in such queries in their local library and getting what they requested. They are frustrated when they get inconsistent results and end up trashing GBS after they have downloaded some neat stuff they were not looking for.

It is also hard to explain to non-Google people just how deeply the notion of page ranking has informed Google's work with books. The vision is "ranking pages" not "delivering books." It takes some time to process this; it is not slow reading, but slow understanding.

The monadal bit of information that will be ranked and retrieved is the page, not the multivolume set, not one volume of a multivolume set, although one volume will be retrieved based on the page(s) it contains. Based on the search term, pages of books will be retrieved, and the book itself will be opened to the page. This is good and bad. It is good because if you have the book in your hand or on your screen, it does not mean that you can find the page with the reference. It is good because it would be no good for Google to point to an edition of Eliot's collected works. It is bad because bad OCR makes the open page just one of many with the same term.

One must remember that antiquarian books are riding piggyback on the software developed for the marketing of new books. It will take some time for the commercial retrieval algorithms to morph into the best antiquarian practices. Until that time, much data will have to be cleaned.

Perhaps the techniques of listing new books can be informed by the work with old books. We, in the sense of a communal effort of users (the eyeballs on the screen) and developers (huddled in the black box), are trying to evolve solutions and not insist on being right or having information organized this way or drop dead. Closer examination will unmask page ranking as a quite clever stratagem that will get us out of some of the expediencies perpetrated by publishers in binding together disparate items. It may also unmask authors who mix the disparate in their texts. It is also the only solution to dealing with multivolume sets of history that will treat Spain and the Levant in one volume and France in another. The love with Google books in its current form can blossom only if you can accept and profit from where Google leads you.

This does not mean that we are not impatient that the advanced search feature works as advertised. Dates must be checked. A single title in identical spelling must cover all volumes of a set. Secondary titles must be input for individual volumes. Volume numbers must be retrofitted or else chuck the whole advanced search feature and let WorldCat link your holdings. Make people sit at the screens till every book file has found its OCLC mark record. Get volunteers from around the world to do the work. Give everyone a hundred records and see how many they can match up in a dummy WorldCat dump. Give

OCLC a billion dollars, give them faster computers, and promise them that you will fix their metadata as well. But why did Google not do that in the beginning? Did someone miss a meeting? Were important people biking in the mountains? It would have been so easy; these are circulating libraries; each book has a bar code, for crying out loud.

Remember, Google wants to rank pages; they think they can pick relevant pieces out of the text, and they think they would not serve the user well just to hand over the book and say ciao— although they will give you the book if it is old enough.

It makes no sense to expect Google to be a well-organized library with all the dates in place, or an OPAC of a smallish collection that has been massaged by catalogers for thirty years. One look at the speed with which work was done should be enough to put that to rest. Do not go to Google if you want a library environment. Go to Internet Archive. There you will find the Blackwood first edition of *Middlemarch* from the Robarts with three clicks, or go to HOLLIS, search for George Eliot, reverse the date order and click on the link under *Middlemarch* 1871 and you will see the first American edition, scanned by Harvard for Google. Ask Prof. Darnton for his Harvard login and password so you can download the file. To try to beat Google with the stick of "you are now the library of Congress, act your part" is futile and should be ignored after being answered in some detail.

If, however, if you want to be taken into the middle of the some nineteenth-century periodicals, or old library catalogs, or biographical dictionaries long forgotten, you will land there with the page open, a difficult task in material libraries. This applies only to the part of the collection given the "Full View." The rest is fairly useless as the snippets have gotten ever smaller under the pressure of the madding crowd of defenders of rights. For the experience, query "von Hammer" at Google Books and select "Full View" and browse the beginnings of Ottoman studies in Europe. Or query Anthony Trollope and browse through his testimony for a commission on copyright or download the St.

Paul's Magazine; if you can find all the volumes, that would cost a pretty penny at the booksellers.

Google presents many legitimate research paths for scholars who also work in material libraries. When you query Google Books you will be astonished at what you find—that is unless you have to pretend you already know where everything is. It will take a generation of the extremely learned who are not pining for the thirties to take full advantage of this and explain it to the rest of us.

Forget the *author, title, advanced search*, it works well enough that you can download treasure. Experiment with the basic search and follow the first few pages in Full View mode. You will have, in fact, been taken to the stacks of a great library, and some helpful acolyte has even opened the books for you. See what you can do with them. If you feel you must supplement that experience using the materials in a material library, who is stopping you? See you in a couple of days.

Let me sumarize: after a few years of writing on Google in the highbrow press and after a fifty-page article published as part of small genre collected works of Prof. Anthony Grafton, we can make a line at the bottom and add up. It is positive that a recognized scholar takes the time to produce sixty pages on digital humanities. That shows real engagement. Unfortunately, Google has gotten in the way of Grafton's critique of the current intellectual situation and has had to take the heat for all sorts of modern phenomena—bad reading and bad writing being the worst. The advocates of the project have been dismissed and the project itself has been found wanting. The arguments behind those conclusions seem to center on a selective reading taken out of the tales of humanism that delights, informs, and deflects the real question.

The arguments essentially promote pessimism towards the contemporary scene and towards many who have put a magnificent resource into the world. Prof. Grafton will not let himself be drawn by this siren's call; he clearly is above serendipity in dealing with electronic sources. He gives the novices in the field only limited license to learn from digital resources; else his pages would seem patently absurd. He does, however, sow enough doubt so that the detractors can quote him. That is certainly his right, but I do not grant that it is his responsibility.

If and When

I can only lament that as his last word he takes sides in the legal dispute in the settlement, no doubt in the belief that his voice wants to be heard. Having heard the voice, let me quote the last two paragraphs of the 2009 *New Yorker* blog:

> "Google excels at listening to users, identifying complaints, and fixing them. They'll correct mistakes users bring to their attention and will continually improve the system as a whole. But it's utopian to believe that the company could or would repair the millions of errors already built into the system-or that new problems won't continue to crop up, as Google vacuums up more millions of books without finding out in advance what book professionals know about how best to identify and organize them.
>
> Will the juggernaut keep rolling? We'll know later this year. But should it? It may be too late if and when we find out." [Grafton, 2009-2]

The implication is that only existing errors would be lost and future errors avoided if the project would be stopped. The "could and would" is a dangerous formulation that flows trippingly from the fingertips but has serious consequences; it implies both "inability" and "unwillingness" in one fell swoop. I think that is a minority opinion. Not enough information has been assimilated by Prof. Grafton to evaluate the Google project. The attempt to balance some lukewarm praise with some devastating blow below the belt is rhetorical street fighting. The chaos here is in the mind of the beholder.

I have tried to show that it may be possible to correct many errors in the Google scans. It may well be possible to fix the problems with the author-title search. An exploration of the "Full View" listings as an adventure in serendipity is not possible for Prof. Grafton—too bad. There is the notion that Google is run by the uninformed, perhaps he could glance at: *Libraries and Google* [ed. Miller and Pellen, Hawforth Press, 2005—available online], which shows some of the discussion that went on early in the project, and which has been ongoing for the last four years. The insistence on the recreation of the OPAC with alphabetical and chronological listings is an *idée fixe*.

Is it only the implication of unprofessionalism and the fantastic gigantism that allow him to imply the juggernaut should be stopped? OK, one expects the author of serious books to say all sorts of unpublishable things at a party. Blogs encourage such unreflected impulse. It would be better if writers of reputation did not give in to impulse. People could read and wonder what is meant.

What was implied is: Google could not repair its errors and would not if it could; to believe otherwise is to be utopian. In Prof. Grafton's vocabulary "utopian" is ranged at dim just this side of stupid. That is the judgment of the "Fellow of the American Academy" (since 2002) blogged to the world. One does not expect the run after the hansom of the extremely learned scooping up metaphoric horse apples in print. I fear this is what happens when one mixes learned authority on one hand with opinion building in trendy genres on the other.

I almost fear to ask: "Is there twitter to be parsed as well?" When one has to chase after high-profile blogs, there are no more rules—the name no longer offers any guarantee.

Time for Some Ripe Tomatoes

This brings us to the last sentence:

> "It may be too late if and when we find out."

With that dire warning Grafton sends the blog reader on the way.

"It may be too late if we find out" does not make much sense; something is missing. The publishers will not abandon their suit, Google will not delete the files, and the District Court will not close up shop. "It may be too late when we find out" seems to work in the paragraph, but it is hard to know what action agenda is implied. Is it just to smear Google as arrogant in the face of the District Court shown impotent to affect Google's actions? Is it just an extension of the "juggernaut" metaphor? Or do we just have loose words careening around in *blogorama*?

So how does "if and when" help us to divine the meaning of the last sentence. I offer this little aside as an example of how quickly one can gather up some verbal eggs and ripe tomatoes from GBS to hurl at extremely careless bloggers.

We could go to Fowler's 1908 edition [H. W. Fowler, *The King's English*, 2nd ed.], which quotes Gladstone as a plausible use of the phrase should the writer have sufficient reason:

> "If and when it was done, it was done so to speak judicially."

Yet Fowler does have to reach:

> "[…] 'when' with a past tense, unqualified by 'if', would make an admission that the writer does not choose to make; on the other hand, the time reference given by 'when' is essential; 'on the

occasion on which it was done (if it really was done) it was done judicially'."

Gladstone has just invented plausible deniability.

I prefer to go to the 1994 *A Dictionary of Modern English Usage* [H. W. Fowler, Wordsworth Edition, 1994].

> "Any writer who uses this formula lays himself open to entirely reasonable suspicions on the part of his readers. There is the suspicion that he is a mere parrot, who cannot say part of what he has often heard without saying the rest also. There is the suspicion that he likes verbiage for its own sake. There is the suspicion that he is a timid swordsman who thinks he will be safer with a second sword in his left hand. There is the suspicion that he has merely been too lazy to make up his mind between if and when."

Of course we harbor no such suspicion that would apply only to semi-literate netbook owners who have started writing too early and bloggers who type without thinking.

In our case we must use another exemption for the learned editor, professor, and Fellow since 2002, courtesy of H. W. Fowler:

> "Only when the reader is sure enough of his author to know that in his writing none of these probabilities can be true does he turn to the extreme improbability that here at last is a sentence in which if and when is really better than if or when by itself."

We spend all this time on that last short and meaningless sentence, which is intended merely to manipulate the debased reader, to show how quickly one can plummet from the heights of renowned Renaissance scholarship into the silliness of the blogger.

The Phoenix Rises

I am weary of the small genres. I am weary of reading blogs, and I am weary of essays that promise gloom and doom and condemn technological development in a few pithy paragraphs. In that weariness, Prof. Grafton's latest piece, "Apocalypse in the Stacks?" *Daedalus*, Winter 2009, seems a breath of fresh air. The essay is a pleasant read, a bit breathless, but a good short tour of the lay of libraries, electronic resources, and scholarly methodologies. The agenda is still focused on the past, and there is not much that can be taken home. The twelve-dollar fee to download seems excessive; I would say that a good percentage of that should be considered an involuntary contribution on my part.

Once the reading is done and the rhetorical glow has dissipated we wonder what we have been told. That is the time to muck about in the text. I generally like doing an outline. This time we have 12 pages divided into seven short sections. 1. Libraries described, all kinds. 2. Electronic resources described, all kinds (with a tone of frisky loathing.) 3. Library collections grow, we know. 4. Back to the old sources and celebrate failed digitization at Stanford. See! 5. Two full pages on research trends starting with the sciences and the admission that productivity has increased since the 50's. Really? 6. Nostalgia for the students of the 50's. Modern students careless and sloppy. Not buying it. 7. Lets form a committee.

One wonders what the point could be of two columns on the university libraries of today. Would it be better just to hang out a sign: "Please go to the following eight library association Web sites to experience the struggle of libraries with modernity first hand. The professor is in Italy." I fear I have become too involved in the message and have lost the capacity to enjoy elevated prose. I am thinking dark thoughts: have so many negative e-mails come in that we can look forward to further demonstrations of an encyclopedic grasp of the present? Or is the point to lard all this verbal Filet Mignon with enough skeptical asides to keep the agenda of "Future Reading" alive. Would Twitter help?

In Section 5, Prof. Grafton sketches the work flow in an unnamed science department at Princeton: First thing: after brushing teeth, check the new articles posted from around the world; second thing: over coffee, discuss postings with col-leagues; third thing: dive into electronic work space and crunch some data. Prof. Grafton does not draw any conclusions from this workflow other than it leaves the library to the side. He is glad to pick it up and dust it off in the name of humanities and social science. He does not ask himself the question how the physicists or the biochemists have come from publishing papers in heavy journals fifteen years ago to posting their day's work for colleagues and collaborators around the world. Are there any lessons here for the study of humanities? I would like to think that the studies of text, images, and thought could trace a similar trajectory.

Alas, I am glad that I am no longer on campus. In my world there are many opportunities to stay in touch with trends, to communicate ideas through innumerable platforms, and to get enough of bellyaching and exciting research rolled together— even with the Alps surrounding me as I look out my windows. But most of all, I get to work with sources and to indulge whims for information that I have never had before—even though I have spent my life at great American universities. I have tried to understand Prof. Grafton's beef, and I have come upon a telling clue. On page 91, col 2, last paragraph of "Apocalypse in the Stacks?" we read:

> "The vast American open-stack collections functioned, historically, not only as repositories, but as memory theaters for advanced graduate students and faculty."

In the next paragraph he laments the passing of the theater:

> "Nowadays the spacial organization of books and journals shifts so often that easy browsing has itself passed into memory."

The loss of the memory theater is a serious blow. Alas, Prof. Grafton does not elaborate and follows with a non sequitur.

Perhaps because I have been chasing after computers since 1975, I have not noticed just how dislocating the world has become to those heavily invested in the past. Not just in the materials and sources of the past, but the methods and procedures of the past. My greatest joy was to see the computer become ever more adept at handling the past—from printing Amharic to indexing phenomenology to designing queries for Persian Miniatures. I can understand dislocation, but I cannot wish to roll back all that has been done for the last forty years. Who would? I also have no patience for researchers today who will not come to terms with the electronic sources in their field. We must move on, and we must drag the wounded with us.

I would have enjoyed more on the memory theater, but especially in how we might get beyond the memory theater. Can we make a virtual memory theater.

I remember the memory theater well. Before I entered graduate studies I was Stack Supervisor at Wilson Library, UNC, and I personally was involved, sleeves rolled up, in shifting every book in those stacks. I developed techniques of picking up an entire shelf of books and neatly depositing those books up to fifty yards from where I picked them up. I could even deposit on a shelf that was half full, half here, half below, in one motion. I still have those skills forty years later to my own amazement when I putter around in my own library. But more to the point, I have personally shelved hundreds of carts and paged thousands of books and shelf-read miles. I became the ultimate tracer because I knew how books were misshelved. I could smell out of sequence cutter numbers.

I also internalized the location of all kinds of subjects. I stopped bothering with call numbers eventually, and I would just get the book. I was weak in the 300's and the H's, great in the 100's, 800's, 900's, the B's, D's, K's and P's. When I worked on my dissertation this skill became invaluable. I developed similar skills at the Duke library. I did have some suspicion that, while my memory theater was a magnificent stage, there were theaters greater than mine.

I also developed a critical stance towards some of the members of my troupe of millions. Clearly the computer did have something to contribute to texts, something that had never been seen before on the intellectual stage. Kids with printouts from the catalog could do well in the memory theater without any memory. Finding books was not the real challenge, the real problem was figuring out what was written in them. I suspected it was easier to work with old texts since the problems of subjectivity were not so pressing. Fewer sources, fewer choices, clearer analysis, fewer expectations.

Yet I decided that computers could mediate between the mind and the text. The computer could present lexical material that would keep my mind from making dishonest jumps. My own path became clear: head them up, move them out, digital humanities.

Here we also have to say goodbye to Prof. Grafton. I have no confidence that working with the actual originals rather than digital copies of sources will help anyone but the select few. Let us bid him farewell with a quote from his favorite area of study, "material texts." In this case he refers to a new area of study which we have learned to know as "Bibliographical Scholarship" from Prof. Darnton:

> "Practitioners of this new form of scholarship [examining actual manuscripts and editions] have taught us how books took shape in scriptoria and printing houses, traced the network of agents and booksellers … and recreated, from marginal

annotations and other traces of many kinds, the ways in which readers responded to the books before them" [AS, p. 92].

Prof. Grafton goes on to make the case that each early book becomes unique through the marginalia. Point taken. I have no problem with all sorts of special work groups examining all ancient marks and glosses on any scrap they can find. I can only advise they queue up and take a substantial database course.

What we have here is a fork in the road: we can have a material scholar in suitable garb surrounded by piles of material artifacts copying out notes on marginalia. This fork has been closed for some time; there are no more piles; they have all been put away in archive boxes to be requested one at a time. So we are left with the second fork: scholar in archive with the material artifact in question affixed to foam rubber on one side, the laptop with SQL up on the other. This scholar is filling out records on a particular fifteenth-century book: page number, text of gloss. Back at the office, a techie is merging the data from eighteen such scholars so that we can finally find out who was marking up all those books in the fifteenth century and send out a summons. A third tine will emerge; pages will be photographed and glosses will be found at high magnification back at the office. The image of the gloss may well be copied out automatically as will the paragraph glossed. That is how my team would do it.

The advice "get thee to a database" is informed by the decades of work of the Duke Papyrology Project, where it was possible to match up torn papyrus fragments, one piece in St. Petersburg, one piece in Frankfurt through splicing digital representations of letter fragments. It is also informed by the work on the Documentary Geniza where wordlists of the Arabic vocabulary in Hebrew letters is the only real hope of evaluating communications in that corpus—and finally by the work on Persian book illustrations where a database of illustrations indexed to their location in text can finally sort out hundreds of battle scenes, court scenes, and garden scenes. Other examples abound.

The truth is: this work will go on—as will cultural pessimism. Much good work will be done before the current generation turns pessimist and hands off to the next. Many books will be printed—with or without UP imprimatur. Vast amounts of text and descriptive analysis will appear on the Web. It may well be that, among all the textual flotsam and jetsam, the carefully constructed database of humanistic artifact will be worth keeping.

PART TWO: THERE IS SOMETHING ABOUT
GOOGLE BOOK SEARCH

Jump right in!

What is it about old books? Why are we still talking about them? And even more puzzling: why are we spending millions to turn them into electronic data? Well, for example, Charles Dickens knew how to start an item of prose data: "It was the best of times, it was the worst of times, it was the age of wisdom, it was the age of foolishness," and so on.

Not only has every age since recognized itself immediately, but also, psychology is at work. The series of contrasts force (or allow) the mind to expand in order to process multiple, seemingly mutually exclusive scenarios. This can bring about a doubling or even quintupling of the mind space available for the prose data—a brilliant beginning for Dickens and an aspiration of this essay.

If we can expand the mind, literally, effortlessly, by reading just part of one old sentence, let us try to free up some mind space in order to consider Google's plans for electronic scans of old books. Let us do this as a gesture of intellectual generosity and as an exploration into the unfamiliar.

And let us forget all our conflicted or outright negative judgments of Google and remember that the emphasis is on really old books. They are the ones you can get for free; nobody is fighting about them. Here we are not concerned with the previously mentioned orphans, although they will come up; we are not concerned with the settlement and whether or not Google is a monopoly of library books. Giving away several million e-books of the eighteenth and nineteenth centuries for free is the kind of monopoly I like. We shall not concern ourselves with all the other manifestations of Google.

And let us not succumb to the imagined implications of Ted Nelson's hyper-snippet: "Google now owns all of literature" [T. H. Nelson, *Geeks Bearing Gifts*. Mindful Press, 2008., p. 179].

The Judgment of a Founding Father, Declined.

Ted Nelson's snippet is convenient because he says in five words what everyone else is saying in five hundred. We shall discuss only three words: *literature*, *owns*, and *Google*.

From T. Nelson's jibe, which is not buttressed by systematic analysis—something chronically lacking in his factoid-based hypertext universe—we can glean that literature has value and that it can be owned. For the term *literature* we must substitute a more precise formulation: "electronic texts scanned from actual books in libraries and presented in PDF format. There are pictures or graphic representation of all the individual pages, along with the electronic text, the actual letters and punctuation, the words and sentences in ASCII or some other representation." Actually, *Gutenberg* and the print-on-demand shops who have appropriated free files own all of literature. Google "owns" only the books no one could hope to sell.

We must also substitute a more precise explication for the term *owns*. Google has spent some considerable resources to organize the scanning of library books, old and newish. The number of items scanned has moved over the fifteen million mark. Google reserves non-exclusive rights for the items scanned and keeps archival copies of every bit and byte. As I understand it, some of the non-exclusivity resides with the institutions doing the scanning, correct me if I am wrong. Thus, in a very loose sense, Google can be said to own the texts or, from an uncharitable perspective, it has taken ownership of electronic files, many still protected, that will eventually age out of copyright.

Since we are only concerned in this essay with books out of copyright, any file that I have downloaded can be said to belong to me. That includes first editions of Dickens and Trollope, as well as editions with fabulous illustrations. That also includes sets of nineteenth-century Ottoman history that can be magnified so that the tiniest footnotes, the printed marginalia, and even the kerning can be examined. That compares to printed editions selling for three to four thousand euros for badly deteriorated print, difficult or impossible to read without a glass. That includes an 1860 monograph by Konstantin Schlottmann on von Hammer-Purgstall that cannot be found in any library in all of Austria, now sitting on my laptop.

There is some language of guidelines on the first two pages of the Google book files, but that is framed in the form of a request. These files are actually being sold on the Internet along with all sorts of files from other archives, but that has nothing to do with Google. The picture is quite complicated, as should have been clear from the discussion before, but it is not a case of *owning* in any traditional sense. Everyone who has ever worked on texts from the nineteenth century will find wonderful treasure. The most amazing thing is that items generally unaffordable to the average researcher are now available at no charge in a most convenient medium for study. This means that the collectors can still collect and inflate the market; but those who actually want to work with antiquarian texts have a wide open avenue.

Finally, we should look at the proper noun *Google* in Ted Nelson's snippet. In this context, *Google* refers to a broad consortium of partners from the libraries of American and European research universities, as well as public libraries, private collections, publishers as well as individuals who self-publish one or more texts. So we must grant that *Google* really serves as a place holder for any number of actors from Stanford to Michigan, from Harvard to Oxford, from the Bavarian State Library to the Public Library of Lyon. Beg pardon from all the distinguished consortium members not mentioned.

[Digression on Public Discourse]

Let me digress. We have lavished a couple of sentences on Ted Nelson's cryptic and possibly ironic remark in order to illustrate the kinds of judgments about Google Books flitting about in the modern, media-driven collective mind. Not a month goes by that the "serious" international press does not publish a bit of nonsense about Google's scanning project. The problem is that it does take some considerable experience with scanning projects to be able to appreciate the dimensions of Google's effort, something the news departments of the *Times*, the *Herald Tribune*, or *Die Zeit*, with the odd exception, do not seem to be able to muster. The complex issues, technical, intellectual and scholarly are collapsed into "Google owns the Bible," "Google now sells old books," or "Google cheats the heirs of renowned Elizabethan dramatist." I hope to counteract the smudges such prevailing judgments are leaving on modernity, or, at the least, I will try to form ideas based on the experience I have gathered since I installed a Kurzweil scanner in the early eighties and watched in amazement as a printed page became editable, searchable, indexable, and reprintable electronic text.

Great value is given today to grievances, both real and imagined, and the pairing of villains and victims, both arbitrarily and sometimes deserved. Even the extremely learned humanists are bringing their centuries of baggage to the discussion. Rational argument and even-handed perspective are not unknown. They are, in fact wide-spread and prevalent in the modern collective mind-like organ, but alas, they are consigned to oblivion on the heap of the non-squeaky wheels.

Outrage seems to be the dominant tenor in much of the public dialogue. However, outrage is also poison for the mind that pulls the discussion into inescapable pessimism, revolution being an option for only a handful of the completely disenfranchised. This is not to say that outrage is inimical to creativity - our contemporary art belies that notion. Nor is it inimical to science; as we see, ever more resources are assigned to visualizing the ultimate and final end of life as we know it - in the somewhat distant middle of the current century. The past century fought two world wars, weathered a pandemic and a full-scale depression in the time allotted us by the disaster scientists. Of course the demise of the Internet is brought into the immediate future for those who want to experience global catastrophe before Visa finally pulls their card out of circulation.

Yet there must be a division of labor; one should reserve part of the spectrum of thought for ideas predicated on the continued existence of society even without glaciers and polar ice caps. Someone should have a scenario, however unlikely, based on the continued existence of the Internet, on the development of new ideas, on innovation, on exploration and on predictable serendipitous resolution of problems. The fall of Constantinople was not the end of that city, far from it, to mention just one example of the many worst-case scenarios that actually have happened. Even if the worst case breaks all the eggs in the basket, it will mean omelets for someone, and the chickens will lay eggs under new management.

I realize that in our age of superlative crisis consciousness, school children are taught to say, "But there will be no more chickens and no more eggs." Thus putting one of the most vexing questions that has perplexed humanity to rest, finally. And they are taught to believe it, no doubt in the concomitant hope of not having to learn the multiplication tables and to learn to spell all those awkaward [sic] English words. Part of that curriculum is also to calculate how many Google queries it takes to kill a polar bear, admittedly a complex calculation, based on the amount of electricity used by Google in a day divided by the number of queries and the percentage of polar habitat thereby destroyed. So the bar for discussion has been set quite high.

There have always been end of the world scenarios. Several hundred years of science cannot protect us from the need to visualize a grisly end. On the contrary, one could say it took several hundred years for science to discover the comfort of the apocalypse. Those who emphasized the moment, the now, have seen their moment pass, and the *Zeitgeist* was returned to the worriers. I will not engage in worry, but rather will think *out loud* about the future of texts. I plan to do this until the oceans of melted ice lap at my doorstep or not. That particular future will revolve around my personal relationship to texts and will not be swayed by the current dire imperatives. I ride my bike even in winter, recycle even organic matter and my flat is heated by the steam from the municipal waste-burning facility. So let us consider electronic texts.

There was a time when one had to visit a bookstore or to a library to acquire a text. That is no longer the case. There was a time when getting the collected works of Trollope was a problem: either spend some money on a set, if there was one to be found, or spend several years in bookstores assembling the texts. Now the texts can be downloaded for free in minutes. Even first editions of rare parts of Trollope's works—the travels to America, Jamaica, and Australia—are available. And that is just one example of a series with no end visible.

In the previous section I have shown some puzzlement with famous professors who feel they must defend an old order that made texts rare and exclusive. The crucial point is that for the anointed acolytes in the academy all sources are relatively easy to acquire. As one of the acolytes myself, I had my study full of library books. But now I have my laptops and my indexing programs full of texts that will not have to be returned by a specific date. Not only do I have physical possession, but I also have methodological possibilities far beyond what I had with the stacks of books. This question is really one that separates the generations, not the generations of age, but the generations of imagination in the most general sense.

The Web indexers, Google and others, do not have an ideal of sequential reading. I would think they can read, but they do not base their work on reading. Their work is based on bags of words of individual pages, Web pages or book pages. Their work is based on indexing. Indexing brings information to the individual user. As the individual user accumulates information, that user will also create indexes, unless the Google indexes are good enough to obviate that step. One should differentiate old indexing from new indexing. Old style indexes were a selection of names and concepts with page numbers published in the back of a book. Each book had its own index. New indexing involves a database that can point to the location of every word in a series of books, in the case of Google, a series of ten million books.

The notion that careful reading, supported by a lifetime of systematically assimilating sources and augmented by brilliant understanding of the past and presented in polished prose, is the measure of all things will eventually age out of the system. Of course all our great thinkers, scholars and critics have worked this way and have produced a textual record that can be examined. Generally that record will be found wanting over time. The human interaction with automated processes, be they databases, or indexes, or pattern searches give new opportunities to the human mind.

One should be careful to maintain the proper borders, although they may appear arbitrary to some. We shall bracket out those questions of the existential that do not deal with cultural artifacts and thus are outside academic "learnedness." The techniques mentioned above help only with texts and other artifacts of human culture. These techniques intend to describe and classify artifacts. The human brain is confronted with artifacts that have to be brought to awareness and subjected to methods that yield some sense of understanding. Several thousand books on Shakespeare for example, the letters of Voltaire, whatever. That is the perspective of epistemological waifs, which I happily join on the low road skirting all the theory of the field. Of course brilliant reading and writing are of great value; they are both the target and the result. Brilliant reading and writing supplemented by a textbase or database of the items under discussion is even more interesting. Methodologies are in flux.

We would like to pursue a line of argument that is unimpeachably objective, of unquestioned authority and apodictically true and unassailably valid and universally hailed. With contentious questions of contemporary culture, any recourse to argument by authority can only appear hopelessly atavistic and irredeemably gigantomachic. So we are prepared to mix it up; we are prepared to blog and to twitter, but only about antiquarian books and their new life and their new potential as electronic entities and the resulting implications for the study of the textual tradition in the humanities. That should lose all of the twitterers and the most grievous bloggers.

[End of Digression.]

Why Old Books?

OK, ready? So granted, Dickens's *A Tale of Two Cities* is a bestseller to this day; thus it is not really an old book.

So the question persists, why physically old books? Certainly the canon of classics is available in newer and better editions with introductions, scholarly apparatus, and warning labels. Certainly the writers of diverse ethnicity and gender who have been passed over for generations in favor of the canon are appearing in new editions, both electronic and print. We obviously can't find them in antiquarian editions. So the question of *why old books?* is not an easy one to answer. Somehow people feel inexplicably good about the idea that old books are scanned and made available to people in Peru or Sri Lanka or Korea; it has a feel of universality and inclusivity, and it seems to justify having kept them all these years, unread on the shelf.

Or is this finally the revenge of dead white men? Are we rolling back the idea that progress has been made in humanistic research? What shall we do with all the nationalistic blather, grotesque prejudices, and inadequate understanding of the workings of the world and of society that was the stock in trade of eighteenth-century publishing. What will scientists do with the Google scans of physics and chemistry books from the 1820s? Will they simply drop into the laps of astonished and perplexed historians?

I will adopt the Dickensian strategy to open minds for this difficult question and the accompanying tentative analysis of that part of the Google phenomenon concerned with the digitization of one-hundred-year-old library books:

"Google is the best of search engines, Google is the worst of search engines."

"We had everything before us, we had nothing before us."

The Moving Target

Before we can start, we must emphasize that anything with Google is a moving target. It is the proverbial river that you can't step in twice. The same holds for the Internet as a whole. Even worse, the book digitization project is a coalition of various universities and libraries that have their own agenda and are developing their piece of the project to meet the needs and desires of their own students and staff. The Google partners are not going lock-step down any garden path, be it technically in developing a delivery strategy, or be it legally in reserving their own rights versus the publishers' and other interested parties' liberal demands.

Even worse, there are uncounted loose cannons on the decks of the SS Internet— actors with the technical skills and the access to scanned book files through the distributed nature of the project that allows them to place their vision of things into the infinitely hackable world.

Events promise to overtake this presentation; the preparation of a manuscript, even with the latest productivity tools, cannot keep up with events that require a 24/7 news channel.

Thus it is with the outrage of a writer about electronic book files (and not with the glee of a user of electronic book files) that I discovered in 2008 someone had loaded a quantity of Google Books (all out of copyright) into the Internet Archive, in multiples of a hundred thousand. It is as if you were writing about the difference between the NY Public Library and the Sterling Memorial Library at Yale when over the weekend all the books from New Haven show up on Fifth Avenue and Forty-second Street. Unfathomable.

Of course, loading the Google books that are clearly out of copyright into the Internet Archive assures that Google cannot close access. Or rather, should it close access, there will be a free copy in IA. I see this as a cybernetic event. By that I mean that all of us involved in the Web and in things like digitizing books form a gargantuan organism. That organism is composed of all the computers, software, electronic pathways, human minds, and fingers at the keyboards that interact over the Internet. Thus, if some undergraduate at Michigan gets the thought, "oh my God, Google is going to pull the plug on free access to old books," and if that person is competent enough to launch net bots to copy all the books to IA and, just to be sure, to the personal disk array, then the cyber-organism will have changed. As a part of that cyber-organism—I will have changed as well—as surely as had I acquired some new collection, or some new software, or learned some new programming technique." It is possible to extrapolate something similar in the past; let us say that the library acquires some set of volumes thus allowing me to acquire new information. However, in the cybernetic model, the connection between the computer network and the human mind are too constant and reciprocal—and thus different than anything we have ever experienced before.

Upon reflection one can see some silver lining in the absorption of Google holdings into IA. IA is clearly not commercial, and there are no tirades in the generally available media against the commercialism of IA, that is not to say that there are not anti-IA tirades for a multitude of sins of commissions and omissions to be found in a digital world that holds all perspectives and encourages expression before reflection. However, in contrast to widespread suspicion that Google intends to charge millions for its scans once a market emerges, there is only a relatively small fringe that claims IA is infringing systematically on rights by not tracking down copyright holders aggressively.

One can accept IA's arguments that it is underfunded and without necessary staff to investigate copyright status of antiquarian books exhaustively. And who cares anyway? No one is accusing IA of a profit motive—concern for absentee authors notwithstanding. Why not go after lending libraries or photocopiers.

So moving the Google holdings to IA is a preemptive strike aimed at all the blogs and all the journalists that keep insisting Google is scanning books for the money. Those arguments will have to be modified, although there is no indication this event has registered except in a tiny subset of bloggers. Assuming that Google, with its considerable resources, can add killer features to the electronic antiquarian books, and assuming that augmenting this added value requires regular maintenance, then that enhanced electronic resource should generate revenue as every other "deep Web" resource that generates revenue. But the texts will still be on IA for free, and they would not be there had Google not had them scanned.

I will argue for my person, that we should understand Google, and, perish the thought, trust Google and support its effort, even if that means paying a reasonable user fee once the project matures and provides significant value. We certainly should pay a reasonable fee to any owners or heirs of orphans legally entitled, or else we should change copyright law and bring it more in line with the perceived value of old books. There are myriad examples of Web resources that charge—some a pretty penny— without generating outrage.

So it is hard to know how to think or write about this mass file migration. We are accustomed to the movement of millions of dollars through electronic channels every day. So why not copy several hundred thousand books into some other archive? I could think of several good reasons, but perhaps I have lived long enough that I still get dizzy. This could be an elegant move, indicating cooperation, consolidation, and expansion if it represents corporate policy. It could an amazing bit of vandalism if it is not policy. It could be a sign of the disintegration of the Google project if all the guards who should prevent such a thing have fled into the hills. At the least Google should have sent out a posse to recover the loot.

My outrage is confined to the frustration of a writer trying to describe something that will not hold still—this is exacerbated by the fact that much that goes on, goes on inside the *black box*. Of course, as a user, I am delighted at the increased access, especially to the index files (some of which I managed to download before that feature disappeared in IA).

But what about the chapter, mentioned above, making a big point about the differences of the IA and Google Book Search?

By necessity, I will take a middle course. I will try to present the interests of humanities scholars, or at least, I will present what I imagine these interests could be. In that sense this essay is independent of any one actor, rogue, or visionary in the field, and I will sketch out sensible directions for the project even when unanticipated developments occur.

There is an important, obviously transformative, even cross-culturally epic, dimension to large-scale digitization that will find its proper place, irrespective of the hormonal urges of Web-savvy undergraduates to shake thing up by hacking Google and IA. This episode is a reflection of the distributed nature of the project and shows that it is the university libraries, even individual researchers more than the imagined corporate monolith that are determining direction. The work is, after all, going on at their campuses; they are solving local academic and library problems, and their staff and students will be the first beneficiaries of the fruits of their considerable labor.

So we will ignore the inevitable foam that is churned by all the people with too much time on their hands making thing go *blip blip blip* on their screens. We shall steer this presentation on toward the inevitable promised land of the universally accessible universal library, past the shoals of terrible scans and worse OCR, past the bad metadata and the non-metadata, past the ire of publishers and booksellers, past the jeering Europeans who want to run high-tech projects but don't want to part with their thirty-five-hour work week and six-week vacations in Thailand, past the uncertainties of corporate policies and fortunes—and onward, to the humanist sitting in her study with an amazing library of electronic primary and secondary sources on her laptop. Men also welcome. Only as a last resort shall we keep an obituary for the project, for the Internet, and for life as we know it at the ready.

Setting the Stage

The topic is Google's library digitization project, here specifically concentrating on the scans of books a hundred years and older. It is done in the context of text scholarship in the humanities and for the benefit of humanities scholars. So what precisely is the attitude that one takes when holding a book from the 1820s; I mean a book that actually stayed in the 1820s—not one of those that have been reissued decade after decade to this very day (e.g., books by Goethe, Austen, Hugo, and Dickens.)

So what about all these old books that were never reissued because they were sitting too securely within their temporal horizon—can we breathe life into them? Do they have a life? Will we have to undo the industrial revolution and two world wars, the waning of the power of aristocracies and various emancipations, to go back to that time and the texts of that time? It turns out old books become a problem as soon as they are taken off their dusty places on the shelves and we try to internalize equally dusty idea content.

Because Google is not the only player in the game of digitization, we have to take great care to define just what it is we would like to discuss.

First, we must separate the new book versus old book question. Throughout this essay, we shall remind the reader periodically that it is old books, books hundred years old and older, books that are completely out of copyright, that are at issue here. But let us start with the *new books*: for clarity sake, we must also separate out the recent publications that are actively participating in the market as best-sellers, as so-so sellers, or as non-sellers, from books that are out-of-print but still within the generous copyright period, despite being published before the advent of the movies called talkies. The first group obviously needs protection so the authors and publishers can get their well-deserved rewards. The second group, the eighty-year-old orphans, needs help. They can no longer be purchased, but the books are still of interest, to a select few at least, because they obviously sold out their last print run.

Technology can have a considerable impact on both sets of *new* books by facilitating the sale and marketing and revenue stream of the currently published offerings and by reviving a limited revenue stream from the out-of-print. The most unfortunate consequence of the system of copyright adopted ten years ago from the European model, is that the classics of the twentieth century will not participate in the electronic future as long as teams of lawyers are engaged to protect the revenue stream from print editions. Equally unfortunate is keeping electronic versions locked in proprietary systems. This may become increasingly obvious with time. Many questions will have to be settled before these markets come to terms with the technological solutions that academic text mining and companies like Google, Amazon, and Sony have placed into the world. We would like to set these questions aside, as fascinating as they are, in favor of considering the really and legally old books.

The reason is simple: we can concentrate fully on the questions of use and usefulness without any interference from questions of the commercial interests of ownership. In addition, we can concentrate on the functionality of the "Full View" function in Google Book Search which is reserved for items clearly in the public domain.

Of course, the wary and the cynical of this world will deny that anything Google and other successful corporations do could possibly be without commercial interest, and there is some truth in that. However, before any commercial interest can be realized, a market will have to be created, and to date, the market for coherent and effective used of PDFs and spotty underlying OCR of antiquarian books is still in the blue sky of visionaries.

The lack of a market appears strange only to those of us who realize that we are talking about nothing less than our collective heritage of ideas.

This essay will attempt to contribute to the realm of potential scholarly usefulness of antiquarian editions—a realm covered with real dust. Thus, this essay is happy to be free of the more contentious parts of the market of electronic publications and will focus fully on the emerging market for electronic antiquarian books.

THE ARCHIVES

Finally, we must separate the many existing archives from the Google archive of antiquarian books. The Internet Archive and various other players have a different vision than Google. In fact, Google's vision is quite unique, else it would not be Google. We can also predict that there will be a confluence of vision over time.

Without doing a survey of the dozens of archives on the Web, let us begin with the Internet Archive. I suggest gooling the archives and poking around. Screenshots with explanations can be found at:

[http://www.humancomp.org/batke/sagbs].

Archive Example No. 1. [http://archive.com]

The **Internet Archive** has a pleasing, library-like interface; it delivers many different media types, including archived Web pages. For the querying and delivery of texts, it behaves like a well-maintained electronic catalog.

The Internet Archive has enjoyed a reputation of careful work, good metadata, and it has a group of dedicated volunteers and staff to keep the house in order. I mean, if you are spending an hour scanning an eight-hundred-page book, why not take two minutes to find someone who can fill out a metadata sheet, evaluate the scan, give the date and the place of the scan, and link to the relevant OPAC or WorldCat record. That has been the practice of scans at Robards in Toronto. The Internet Archive seems a serious commune, but its relaxed rules that allow indiscriminate uploads have already strained the illusion of order and tidiness.

It will have to be seen how the IA will absorb several hundred thousand Google scans without metadata and many pages showing the fingers of the operators. The advanced query function in IA does allow the exclusion of specific strings, so it is possible not to see the new uploads. Yet, it is one thing to accept chaos inside the black box—it is another thing for chaos to crash in through the door. Latest indications are that some cleanup is in progress at IA to deal with the Google influx. It seems that querying virtuosity will become increasingly important to pick through the mounting debris at IA.

There is no indication that IA will offer searching of texts. Of course, OCR'd text can be downloaded and searched locally. Thus there is no index of the corpus. IA behaves like a library, it hands out PDFs and electronic text, but it will not presume to open the book for you.

Let us consider three more archives picked somewhat randomly from dozens of candidates, Austrian Literature Online, Gallica from the Bibliothèque nationale de France, and *Project Gutenberg*. The three archives illustrate the range possible in the delivery of electronic material.

Archive Example No. 2. [http://www.literature.at]

Austrian Literature Online is an example of a *local market* for e-texts at a regional university in Austria that is trying to leverage technical expertise to become a national Austrian resource by offering first editions from the Austrian National Library and other archives of Austraica. Of course, it also wants to become an international resource, hence its English language interface. In that ambition it is not alone. The archive has a sparse, minimalist look, that has been redesigned in the last year.

Some features such as building PDFs for downloading run very slowly. One wonders why PDF's have to be built for each request. Even if a user may want only 40 pages out of 300 it seems strange to build the files for each request. There may be European bandwidth issues that I don't grasp fully. These problems are not fatal and are shared by many local market Web sites without the computing power of Google, Amazon, or the Internet Archive. There are however some problems with the Innsbruck site; the files can be sent to a print-on-demand service. Given the opportunities for downloading PDFs, it seems an atavistic enterprise to send antiquarian books to a POD service. Questions arise: is this a minor revenue stream designed to take euros out of the pockets of locals who have not grasped that they can get the files for free? Is this some misplaced social awareness trying to make hay out of the fact that not everyone can afford a laptop? Are they hoping that someone will buy "first editions" at bargain prices thinking they had finally scored on e-commerce? Generally, there seems to be a disconnect between the technical capability to set up a quite elegant archive site and the administrative myopia to insist on such a questionable revenue stream. Print-on-demand clearly has its place in universities, but not for antiquarian books. I hope that this perspective will win out and POD will pass on.

An additional problem with Austrian Literature Online is that it has listed its holdings as a multivolume set to be bought on Amazon one volume at a time. On its face this is not a problem; anyone can sell whatever they think someone else will buy. However, the Austrians have discovered a trick to spam Amazon. A list of several dozen Austrian authors is printed quite aesthetically on the title page of each of the POD volumes. Thus, for example, a search for Hammer-Purgstall, the Austrian orientalist, will yield the entire catalog of the POD books but no work by Hammer-Purgstall is actually in the series. This is vexing.

This site is an example of entrepreneurship gone wrong in the e-text world, whether through excessive cleverness or through abject cluelessness.

Though quite clever, I think this skirts close to deceptive advertising when a site has "optimized" its Amazon listings by printing an alphabetical list of authors on its title page. When balancing the potential world domination of Google versus thousands of entrepreneurs spamming the market, I'll go with Google.

So consolidation of efforts could be crucial to save technology from itself. Multiply the Austrians by every other country, state, county, municipality or university or private collection that wants to set up a server with its holdings, and the archives are multiplying like the brooms in the *Sorcerer's Apprentice*. It has already begun.

Archive Example No. 3. [http://gallica.bnf.fr]

The French National Library, BNF (or BnF) has ambitious plans for electronic texts and is furiously at work digitizing its vast holdings. The interface is solidly library-like. Unlike the Austrians who are bilingual English/German on all screens, with the BNF, even on the opening screens, you are digging out the undergraduate French, which is no great help further into the site with crucial decisions on action panels. Even the Google page translator balks at the BNF opening screen, the English version. The name Gallica indicates a national agenda, an unquestioned matter of course in France. Lets let the French be French. The interface has changed considerably over the last few years. The interface has become uncomplicated and elegant. The metadata seems to be excellent, with each volume of a set described in some detail. The interface has been honed in the last year, the full-screen mode for reading is excellent as is the thumbnail browser. Front and center are statistics on the collection which seems to hover around the one million mark.

Both the Austrian and the French display system have changed dramatically in the last two years. The trend is toward look-alike; it seems that there is only one way to display full screen page images. Yet, each archive will insist on designing its own look. I find that the vanilla Adobe PDF reader leads to easy habituation. The habituation leads to increased productivity. As a general point, I prefer to work offline with the latest Adobe PDF reader. I see no reason to keep an active Internet connection open to read antiquarian books, especially from archives like the BNF that offer only the texts. Let's optimize the downloading channels, encourage users to get the texts onto their local storage, and get offline to work. The notion of having huge reading rooms where hundreds of terminals are used to read the holdings of the library is at best a temporary solution to the universal access problem. Libraries can rest secure in the thought that they will continue to be important institutions, even if a growing percentage of users will prefer to work at home or read on their phone.

**[Three Digressions: Privacy, the Non-material,
the Text Search]**

1. The problems of privacy in intellectual work versus the potential of insight to be gleaned from archived browsing behavior in the digital age.
2. The shared universe of libraries of physical books and the non-material electronic representations of texts.
3. The text search feature.

Libraries will continue to be repositories of printed materials; they will also be the agent of delivery for electronic materials. It is no longer necessary to go to the library to find a call number; increasingly, it will not be necessary to find a call number at all;

one will simply find and download the item, book, article, or image.

However, our attempt to understand the processing of information into knowledge cannot rest with the delivery of texts, printed or electronic, to library patrons. Many librarians, especially librarians in the old world, are certain their job is to protect the materials in their collections. That is, in fact, a serious business and it is shocking to learn how much vandalism and theft involves printed books. But libraries are also privy to much information about borrowing habits. Librarians have gone on the barricades to protect that information with strict confidentiality. Since valuable materials pass into the hands of users, identities must be established with great accuracy.

In collecting user statistics on the Web, Google has shown that it is possible to get reliable and useful user information without identity checks. I realize that not everyone will grant that, and many suspect nefarious processes scheming in the black box. However, Web sites have links on them, everyone can see that; counting the links provides valuable information for indexing and improves the function of querying without invading privacy. The same is true of queries, browsing behavior and downloads of texts. The methodologies of marketing and analysis of consumer behavior have not been suspended just because one is working on Charles Dickens. There is no need to pretend that intellectual behavior is immune to recognizable pattern that, if analyzed well, can actually be pedagogically valuable. We are engaged in mass education, but we are barely keeping up and cannot allow ourselves elitist luxuries of hiding behind thick hedges in the name of intellectual privacy, statistically speaking.

Google's attempt to rank text pages in a meaningful manner, if it is to be successful, requires the collection of comprehensive data and sophisticated processing. Certainly downloading statistics of place and time are valuable, as are the queries and the subsequent browsing patterns generated by the queries. Even more valuable is to observe the actual reading of a text, not for world domination, not for privacy violation, not to smoke out an individual working on Stalin or something worse, but in order to discover how a reader, preferably an expert in a specific field, uses a text or a sequence of texts.

Page turning can be tracked, as can the non-sequential access to paragraphs through word searching. The Google text search feature was designed to work online, by means of login to a personal account, which can be established with a pseudonym, as every undergraduate knows, with a little sleight of hand, if that is thought important. The behavior of the expert reader will contribute to the improvement of indexing, even if the identity of the reader is not known and the reader is not even identified as expert.

The search feature allows a simple string search that will bring up all the text passages with that string—the OCR gods willing. To get the full benefit of the feature, the reader must create a Google account. I see it as a mutual benefit, I get free indexing, browsing, and downloads, all a major boon for me. Google will even keep a list of pointers to electronic books for me to obviate resubmitting queries or downloading everything. In exchange I would be happy to let statistics be collected on my use patterns so the next user can benefit from my experience, such as it is, statistically speaking.

Lightning in an open field scares me, quicksand scares me, caves with millions of spiders scare me, single issue activists scare me—analysis of my reading patterns does not scare me. Upon sign-in, it is possible to submit a query string and see the resulting hits in a small window with the page number and a few words of context. Clicking on the page number will take the reader to the page. No fooling. The page can be read as a graphic with the query string marked in yellow or in text mode, so it is possible to see just how good or bad the underlying OCR is. We shall have more to say on this below.

Most commentators on the GBS phenomenon rarely go deep enough into the system to describe the implications of the text search feature. They either retreat behind privacy issues or rail against ranking in general without appreciating that there could be a coherent methodology behind it. The text search is used by the reader (scholar, baker, candlestick-maker) to extract information from a book not easily acquired from sequential reading.

To be honest, the text search feature in GBS at present is very much low-end, well below entry-level. There are quite sophisticated text research environments that are programmed to learn, that deliver semantic inventories, lemmatization, word counts, statistical tests, and graphical output. One can only hope that somewhere in the ten-year plan for GBS there is a budget for prototyping delivery of advanced environments.

But even with a simple system, if it can be determined that ten readers picked the same string to search on a particular book, then the index on that item can be improved dramatically. By the same token, if a student can discover that ten Kant scholars searched for "xyz," then "xyz" has to be examined in detail. Of course to get such expert user information would mean teaching a generation of scholars how to use a text search feature, a process already well under way.

There are many unexamined assumptions about reading and about the encounter with texts that have profound effects on the understanding of our textual heritage. Many of the unexamined assumptions hail from the "learning" phase in our education. Phase strategies have been developed to teach careful reading to novices. In the encounter with texts, the novitiate can be quite long, extending well beyond university. Although this opinion may be greeted with incredulity, help is available only to those who realize they need it. The problem under discussion is what to do after a text has been read the first time: how can the certainty, the tyranny of the first impressions be escaped? How can the continuing involvement with the text lead to new and different ideas? How can the collection of supporting evidence avoid falling into chronic blind spots and how can descriptive analyses explore new perspectives? How can we avoid seeing only our own favorite ideas in a text and avoid ignoring unfamiliar ideas? Remember, we are considering multiple readings of a text, texts from different cultures and from different ages, and the involvement with the same text over a number of years.

Obviously, passages have to be assembled based on the thematic structure of the text, passages from different parts of the text. As long as sequential reading remains the only approach to text that readers can imagine, despite all the cognitive problems with that proposition, especially the problem of a second or third sequential reading, the potential of text search will not be understood. As soon as one realizes that text search is not unlike an extremely complete and convenient index, one can forget the questionable ideal of subsequent sequential readings from cover to cover; one can escape the limits of short-term memory, escape built-in biases of whatever description that determine memory, and find the entry points into the text that actually are germane to adequate interpretation. This is especially important in dispelling impressions gathered during the initial sequential reading and in verifying interpretive strategies found in the secondary literature, which are testaments from sequential readings not one's own. From there it is just a small step to being able to read graphical output of semantic and thematic patterns and to understanding the standard deviation.

In fact, one does have to acquire some considerable experience; first, with interpreting literature (or texts) in general, and secondly, with electronic text methodologies, somewhere short of having to get a degree in multivariate analysis, before text search features can be fully appreciated in their amazing power. Electronic texts are not just a delivery channel for random downloads by clueless Web vagabonds, but a serious methodological avenue of approach to difficult interpretive questions to be dug out of texts by scholars willing to become familiar with new methods and a new way of looking at texts. An example might be to track vocabulary use that points to cognitive dysfunctions or personality mutations. The point is not to create new meaning but rather to apply finely tuned linguistic instruments that can quantify impressions gathered during reading. These new methods require a serious encounter with a specific set of texts and not impatient clicking around with the mouse. Reading the text in question would be a first step in such an encounter. Absent serious informed encounter with a specific text, we are wandering in random cluelessness. This applies also for literature experts evaluating research on texts with which they are unfamiliar (e.g., material outside their field). I fear that the general belletristic form of much humanities research has given the illusion that all fields are open to all comers. This illusion of homogeneous accessibility is not more than either a dumbing down of the research problems or an arrogance of committed ideologues who will find grist for their mill in everything. Unless we become aware of the structural weaknesses of our institutionalized knowledge fashions, we will not do justice to new tools. Time for a deep breath. Time for the uninitiated to fill out that application to graduate school and the rest to return to their texts.

Archive Example No. 4. [http://www.gutenberg.org]

Project Gutenberg was founded with a clear understanding that processing of electronic primary sources can inform the reading process; the service is old enough to remember when philology was still philology. *Project Gutenberg*, despite its ironic name, (it should really be called Project Unicode) seems to be the best adjustment to the technology; it does not have to carry all the baggage of a library, and in addition, its emphasis from the start was on clean plain text. Thus, the *Gutenberg* files are immediately useful for all sorts of data mining and statistical and semantic analysis, and also for reading from cover to cover on an e-book reader. In contrast, the PDF's from the partner libraries, and by extension, from Google, are merely a preliminary step—a first effort at bringing dormant books into the electronic world. Subsequent steps will have to lead to nearly clean electronic text behind the images (as are the *Gutenberg* files).

It is easy to browse through the *Gutenberg* holdings. Most author entries have a Wikipedia link. Since *Gutenberg* does not pretend to be a library, it uses Wikipedia liberally and without shame. The electronic text files are trivial downloads. The text can then be loaded into a local indexing engine. And all is quite wonderful.

There is some problem surrounding the provenance of the texts. An electronic humanist tends to treat an ASCII file of a work of art or a work of history with some suspicion. With PDF files, these concerns do not exist. If pages are damaged or missing, reading will reveal that. However, one simply cannot know what weirdness could lurk at byte 13,573 of an 800k text file of a Dickens novel. It is also possible for electronic files that were once clean to degrade through careless local processing. Personally, I would spend considerable time tracking down the original and checking each page and reestablishing the original pagination, even the original line endings, before putting it on the electronic workbench. In addition one must design a solid system of storing archival copies securely.

So the irony is that electronic files open methodological avenues that are forever closed to print editions. Absent universally accepted standards for electronic files, citations will still have to fall back on the printed editions. That means we can use inferior public domain electronic editions to improve interpretive productivity, but when quoting research results in print we shall have to use proprietary printed editions restricted through copyright law. This qualifies as irony.

The fact is that with printed editions one can only use reading, marking the text, excerpting, and using printed indexes or in rare cases printed concordances. Of course the whole notion of authoritative editions is a bit of a fiction left over from the early days of philology. The editorial process is an ongoing event that starts with the drafts of the author, through the editorial process leading to a first edition. And this is under optimal conditions, where the original text can be brought into question only by corrected subsequent editions or unincorporated drafts or chapters discovered after an author's death. In texts obscured by time, a text can only be pieced together from fragments often with no direct link to the author. The practice of scholarship to anoint temporarily an edition as authoritative is merely an expedient to bring everyone to the same page and avoid unnecessary squabbles over usage and word order. Yet the practice of decade-long editorial projects with huge production costs has already yielded to electronic editions in many areas of study. We have to accept that each area of text studies, be it single author or period or topic will have its text stewards who will work with varying degrees of effectiveness.

The standards for textual sources for Ottoman historiography are quite different than the standards for sources of Immanuel Kant. In the former, the work consists of establishing chronologies, establishing the dates of writers and manuscripts, and taking the initial steps toward printed editions and translations of texts. In the latter case, the full power of electronic methodologies can be unleashed on several editions of electronic texts in advanced research environments. Kant's texts have produced several distinct schools of thought over the last two centuries. In the case of Kant several distinct electronic list-based editions are available. It is hard to know which task is more difficult, to cull chronologies from the mists of time or to make sense of two centuries of explanation, argument, dialectic, commentary, refutation, and counter-refutation of a well-established corpus of electronic texts.

Of course, working with texts involves a good many people, some beginners, some productive, some brilliant, some looking to make their own mark. Thus eyeballs of varying competence and varying agenda will run over text. Some of these eyeballs will also have fingertips attached and thus will add to the corpus. Much of this activity goes on in environments of varying economic comfort, and the perpetuation of comfort can easily become an end of its own. The idealism of Lovejoy and the AAUP early in the previous century have generally advanced academic professionalism, but not everything that goes on in academia, be it today or before the AAUP, is necessarily worthwhile. The only real imperative seems to be to accept helpful tools when they are developed. Microscopes are helpful to study microscopic things. Telescopes are helpful for studying things far away. Computers are helpful for studying things that must be ordered, sorted, counted, plugged into equations that are iteratively executed and the results graphed. While academic freedom allows each scholar to pick the area of study—within the parameters of political correctness and fashion—academic freedom and the autonomy of the researches should not be a shield from technological innovation. Text scholars who do not use computer indexing should end up in the same drawer with contemporaries of Leeuwenhoek who thought microscopes to be a passing fad in biology.

A GOOGLE RHAPSODY

Google's approach is qualitatively and quantitatively different from any archives on the Web (although one could argue that at present, *Gutenberg* is the most useful for the implementation of electronic methodologies). Nevertheless, Google is operating on a different scale, exponentially projecting a path into the uncharted distance. Here we have not a well-maintained electronic card catalog, but a piling up of various diverse things. The distinction between searching the catalog and searching the content has been obscured deliberately in the general search screen. Ultimately that is OK since one can always get to a title page and find a MARC record from the Stanford or Michigan catalog in another window, if that is desired.

So, the first difference between Google and the Internet Archive is that Google tolerates chaos within its ranks. Their attitude seems to be: *our ranking algorithms are clean and operate equally well with good indexed data or with bad OCR.* Chaos in output becomes a matter of degree, not something to be avoided. This could be one of the main strengths of Google going forward with its projects.

The scale is important since the very mass of the statistically reduced chaos that Google presents increases the chance of either finding exactly what you are looking for or finding something you did not know you wanted. This is the serendipity effect. Serendipity is important in humanistic research because the questions are rarely straight forward, often obscured through time, and under the best circumstances, don't admit simple answers.

The serendipity has been taken out of the surface Web—you get what you asked for—serendipity comes only if you don't really know what you are looking for or change your mind while looking. With Google books, serendipity is routine, not unlike browsing in a used book store (of several million volumes with advanced query functions and text search).

Let us say, like a good humanist, you approach the Google window intent to find a particular set of volumes of Ottoman history published in Pest in 1832. In the list of things Google throws up, you find four contemporary reviews of said work from publications in Jena, Berlin, Heidelberg, and Prague, as well as a reference from an 1850 German biographical dictionary (with the pages open to the relevant passages). In addition you find three copies of the set of volumes in question, as well as an English abridged edition and one volume of the French translation. All in all, a good moment's work done with a few mouse clicks. In the Internet Archive you would have found all ten volumes of the set and no serendipity. In a real library you would have been on the hoof for a couple of hours.

Before we continue, it is important to reiterate one point. Because of all that Google does and the vast numbers of users it accommodates every day, Google has become a symbol or icon for much of modernity. People from all walks of life tend to hang whatever concern they have on this symbol. Here we would like to separate out this iconic role in popular culture that Google holds and cultivates, from its scanning of old books. There will be those not willing to concede the distinction because Google does this and Google does that, and it all melds into vague spleen of the helpless facing the all powerful. Granted, the new book scans and the surface Web are already melded into a marketing strategy, but they are not at issue here.

However, it will be humanities scholars that are really the only market that could have interest in books older than a century; let me be clear, I mean books actually and physically older than one hundred years. We should inject some realism into the future scenarios—for a dose of realism, try to read the first English translation of *Don Quixote* by Thomas Shelton (1606), or the 1898 reprinting, or try to read the early editions of Hamlet and see how fast you scurry back to the Penguin Classic. Try to enter a query string for these texts or their contemporaries and discover the wonder of non-standardized spellings.

Working with antiquarian books requires special skills, not a given for all humanities scholars, akin to extreme sports, that require skills not available to the average athlete. Antiquarian books are not the next fashion wave that will sweep the world. Let me repeat, it takes special skills to read Richard Knolles's seventeenth-century *History of the Ottoman Empire*, and only a few specialist would be up to the task. So let us temper our enthusiasms for the bright, old book future with an understanding of just what level of training, what level of literacy, and what level of cultural tolerance is required to read into the past. The current cohorts of students and teachers who are quick to find incorrect thinking a pervasive problem had better stay way away from, among other things, historiography of the seventeenth century. Nevertheless, I love a parade, and I will not make it rain.

To bring this initial examination of the prerequisites for this discussion to a close, I will touch on some of the physical dimensions of GBS.

A Brief Discussion of Nuts and Bolts

Rumor has it that the Elphel 323 camera, Google's weapon of choice scans at 1,000 pages per hour. A respectable output but nothing spectacular. One hour has 3,600 seconds, two pages per scan gives the people with the latex finger hats 7 seconds to turn the page, if we count 0.2 sec for the actual exposure. I achieve roughly one third that with my Canon 8800F flatbed, that has a travel time, forward and back, of roughly 12 seconds, depending on the image size, giving me 6 seconds to turn and set the page, and I have yet to scan my fingertips. My flatbed also represents a capital investment of 124 euros.

I could imagine that a project with more generous capitalization than my study and plans to scan millions of books would come up with some designs, short of automatic page turning, that could cut the scan rate in half, or, even better, increase the time per page slightly and increase the fidelity of the images dramatically, or at least make it so we don't see the finger hats.

To date over ten million items have been scanned. There is some indication that as new partner libraies are added, the scans are getting better than in the initial ramp up.

So I think those of us working with old editions can safely stop ignoring the elephant, softly blowing bubbles in the deep end of the pool, and start talking sensibly about the implications of what Google has wrought. And, incidentally jump to using and learning to use the new tools and the vast amount of source material Google and others have given us.

The look of GBS has changed over time. What you see today you may not see tomorrow. This makes it difficult to discuss the actual nuts and bolts that Google is showing to us at present. It will be brief because in its modesty, GBS is not showing much that might arouse the technically salacious. It will be brief also, since there is no reason to dwell on "undocumented features" [read: bugs] that will disappear over time. In addition, given the secrecy toward the general public of the mechanics of the scanning and the delivery strategies going forward, much of this analysis is on shaky ground. Yet several years of use have made GBS part of my repertoire of electronic tools. I have seen the output change over time, alas, without logging the changes, confident at some point something recognizably sensible would emerge. There are encouraging signs that progress is being made. The screens seem neater. New features appear, map links relevant to the text or links to other books, but only with some books. However, it is still difficult to predict what a query will present, or to be confident that you will be able to reproduce a certain set of query results. It requires some relinquishing of control and the willingness to work with what appears before you. Chaos is reduced by small increments; the actual degree of chaos is no doubt a well guarded secret. I have corresponded with the Google support people on various points and am generally satisfied with the explanation—the only explanation—that GBS is a beta and we are working on it.

There is some technical discussion in snippet form in various library journals and Web forums that deals with the functionality of GBS. Some are brief anecdotal histories, some are a curious misunderstanding of the role of older and newer scans, some are a clichéd embrace of the future, some are emphatic clichéd rejections of the present and future, some are devastating critiques of the quality of the scans. Most numerous are laments about the grotesque state of the metadata that GBS shows to the user at present in what must really be the longest beta-test without dramatic improvement in the history of Silicon Valley. (Oh, I forgot Windows 1, 2, 3) Any scholar of even shallow experience will be able to find the metadata for any scanned book in twenty seconds, given a legible title page.

Each of these textual complaint snippets are surrounded by blogs and counter blogs that cover all the bases. One gets the impression that there are lots of people going to work each morning that worry about the functionality of GBS enough to fire off a quick three sentences to their favorite blog every couple of months. So the temptation is not so much to discover some worthwhile perspective, than to summarize the "obvious" problems and the "obvious" solutions shouted out in the blogs. However, I suspect that these blog voices, even though some come from the very institutions that are actually involved in the scans, are too thin and too weak and too scattered and thus allow problems to continue unaddressed—I assume—or it may simply take some more time. Some problems may also arise from the fact that essentially clueless people are wandering through the holdings of GBS; they would be clueless if they were to wander through the stacks of Firestone, picking books from the shelf and wondering where the metadata is.

In addition, the detailed technical discussion of things Google seems to concentrate on the search engine part of Google and is driven by the implementers and their local modifications. I get the impression that the Google blog on GBS is more a marketing tool, not unlike the new online libraries, where some marketing assistant is tasked every other day to generate some discussion—usually in vain.

This essay is not written with an eye to the ubiquitous blogosphere, although clearly the active discussion is going on there, with paper publishing lagging behind. One of the insights that we can get from following the electronic media is that it is still the reasoned, carefully crafted, text piece, which is given some time to mature and which is given the luxury of editing that trumps the spontaneous *blogous* outpouring, no matter how close the blog may be to technical detail. However, I have no intention to worry about applying scholarly methods to this ephemeral medium or to quote every two-sentence blog that happens to say something clever and true.

In addition, it is important to reach outside the blog discussions. To be successful, GBS needs to find new users. The professional bloggers will not spend long hours digging through antiquarian books with the text search feature. By the same token, the scholar working on old texts will not have exhaustively plumbed the depths of Google blogs. If the metadata improves, if people begin to understand what they should query, and the ranking of the first ten hits becomes sensible, they will come. All the users who expect an OPAC will have to age out of the system.

So, all the four hundred people who have blogged the fairly obvious idea that GBS metadata could be fixed by coupling the

Google graphics with the catalog record of the respective institution—*thank you for sharing*. There is clear evidence of links to World Cat, there is also evidence that books are grouped by OCLC numbers, so we can assume there is a coherent base of authentic library data at the center. There are even catalog entries listed in GBS without the corresponding scans, leading me to suspect that catalog data co-exists with PDF-files like some gigantic party where everyone has lost their partner. Besides, all this is online, and there is no more mystery once a book has been found.

One should consider that Google has people drive around the streets of the world with an eight lens mega-camera on a pole fastened to the roof of their cars, taking panoramic pictures of street corners (and bedroom windows) and automatically linking in the GPS location data to Google maps. So we could assume that they could link a silly MARC record to a book scan by showing the Elphel 323 the call number on the outside of the book for 0.2 seconds, if someone had thought that important. Not a year from now, but let us be hopeful. So we must wonder and ponder. I just hope the girls and boys with the little latex finger covers are scanning the spine, even if there seems to be no sign of call numbers on many scans, which is curious since catalogers write call numbers all over the place.

So let me jump right in: concerning the quality of the scans, it is possible to pick out some shocking examples and regale an audience with the seeming incompetence of mighty Google. [See Paul Duguid, *Searching for Shandy*, Society for Scholarly Publishers, San Francisco, 2007.] We know better, we know what these people can do. Most scans are clearly perfect, considering the age of the material and the pace of the work. Terrible scans are not a fatal flaw that invalidates the project, but are errors to be corrected. Scholars in all fields will have to collect bibliographies of the Google entries in their area of expertise, evaluate the scans and plan and implement corrections, or start over if need be. I believe it will be worth the trouble for each field of humanistic studies, and during this exercise, much of older work that has been relegated to obscurity by the arrogance of various modernisms will be rediscovered.

Hand in hand with poor scans go the unspeakably, but not unexpectedly, poor optical-character-recognition results for the older scans. Here we are in fact teetering on the cusp of a fatal flaw because poor OCR of titles results in poor metadata and calls into question even the link up with the OPAC records of the libraries that supply the books scanned, should someone have heard the blogging in the wilderness. Poor OCR of the text of the books—in some cases the OCR approaches 0 percent recognizable text—invalidates the whole page ranking system. We will have more to say about this below.

The metadata problems, as they are presented for all to see in the beta, are the most troublesome, at least in the short term. This problem has a trivial side and a substantive side. The trivial side has been explored by Jeanneney; he relates the widespread mirth that he, le directeur, shared with his staff as they typed "Cervantes" into the GBS in 2005 and discovered the first Spanish edition of *Don Quixote* came up in ninth place. Before succumbing to the giggles, he might also have considered if Cervantes is not read more in English than in Spanish, world-wide, or if more people are looking for English translations on the Web. Stranger things have happened. Jeanneney betrays a rather inflexible sense of order and thus finds Google anathema. Also querying "Cervantes" is actually silly given the fact of page ranking, but one cannot expect that to have been understood in 2005. He might have looked for the Google holdings on the Enlightenment, or Dogmatism, or Voltaire, or some other field where he has expertise and let serendipity surprise him.

Yet we should not be entirely insensitive to the plight of a small language group; let's say six million Danes living next to eighty-two million Germans, growing up watching movies on television in English because there is no market for dubbing into Danish or even for Danish subtitles. The Scandinavians simply learn English, and Swedish and Danish and some Norwegian, enough Finnish to order a drink, and some German—a sensible and profitable attitude. Unfortunately, there is no getting around the idea of English as a shared language that facilitates communication. There was a time when French served that function in Europe. And the British would never have sold New Orleans.

Volume Sets vs. Pages

On the more serious side there are problems with the presentation of hits from GBS. The most serious, which can serve as paradigm, is that multivolume sets present a problem to a ranking engine. On one hand, from the library perspective, sets belong together, end of story. On the other hand, a ten-volume set is hardly a specific, monadal piece of information, as a single book, with a stretch, can be a monadal bit of information, just for arguments sake. The BNF and the Internet Archive and others in this field all display electronic holding records as they would appear in a library catalog, except that one can click on the record and download the file. Thus, all ten volumes are listed in the same place.

To date it still takes some virtuosity to find specific things, especially entire volume sets on GBS. But let us consider the possibilities; those of us who have been largely priced out of the book collecting business can now have PDFs of books we could never have dreamed of owning, sitting on our laptops. This is especially piquant in my case since I have spent considerable time creating electronic versions of the few sixteenth-century folios I do own. The fact is that rare books prefer to slumber in darkness, in well-padded boxes, away from harmful environmental influences. In addition, they are difficult to work with, bulky, stiff, and brittle as they are. All this has been obviated by page images on my laptops. Now I can work on several folios at the same time without a room-size treadle, which was the PDF-reader of the late Middle Ages.

In Google, the list of hits comes in an ordering that defies rational explanation, at least with my faculties; familiarity with the texts does not help at present. With Google proper, the search engine, we can say that the information market is determining the ranking. With hits on "Geschichte des Osmanischen Reiches" as a title search the results are a mish-mash. On the surface list of hits we get the fourth volume of Zinkeisen and the fourth and tenth volume of Hammer-Purgstall and a grab bag of other things. On the "book reader" page, under an unassuming *other editions* button, one can get other volumes, sometimes actually the same volume, scanned multiple times: one from Michigan, one from Oxford, one from Harvard. For a ten volume set that can be up to forty entries, showing just how far we have come in this field. At present, it may be that multivolume sets are being bundled behind the scenes with one volume swimming on the surface, and the rest and the duplicates not participating in the page ranking. We await a comprehensive solution with bated breath.

We have to try to understand Google's solution to get back to the problem. What would the Web look like if Google only presented its hits in either alphabetical or chronological listing? What if it presented only the titles of Web pages? Clearly the notion is absurd; we want indexing and we want sensible ranking, which is what we get. The index program had to look at the words on every page of a Web site. By the same token the index program has to look at every page of every book and present the right page of the appropriate book.

The basic idea is that a chronological or alphabetical ordering of data chunks of two hundred to eight hundred pages (books) is not sufficient. B&P have proven to themselves and to the world that it is possible to rank information more optimally than was fashion before. Google may want to recreate the sensation that occurred when their founders "downloaded" the Web in the late nineties. That, we assume, allowed the indexing algorithms to be improved in dramatic fashion compared to what AltaVista was doing at the time. Downloading the sum totality of books printed since 1500 for the purpose of improving the indexing algorithms is a problem of another order of difficulty not yet calculable—but still absolutely worth doing.

The fixes here are not simply correcting errors; they go to the very root of the page rank idea. Clearly the analogy of *indexed* Web *page to book* is cracking up. Books are not simple data items, there are anthologies, collections of every imaginable text brought together under one cover. The further back we go, the more strange things were bound together. Often libraries were rebound, the old wooden covers of folios were removed; the pages were trimmed and rebound, sometimes erroneously, sometimes deliberately bringing disparate things together. So the long term solution is to improve the metadata dramatically, including going to where even the OPACs rarely dare to tread, which is to analyze multivolume sets and give the titles of individual volumes. Google is attempting to cut the Gordian knot by simply delivering pages. It will breathe some fresh air in the halls of epistemology. Can you understand the Google indexing in your field of knowledge, and can you formulate queries so that you can scoop out valuable results? A first encounter with a book might be the open page to a quote, not the bibliographical entry. I can already see the convoy of the extremely learned heading for the hills.

In the short term, it means that one cannot find any one book without laboriously querying each title and having to get lucky at that. General queries of authors which we have become accustomed to through several decades of OPAC use yield patent weirdness. It is as though we are back two hundred years ago before the "lookup list of names" was first considered a good idea.

To give you an idea of the dimensions of the problem, somewhat of a worst case scenario, consider a list of all the dozens of various spellings of the name of Leunclavius, a German humanist, listed in VD17, the catalog of German books published in the seventeenth century. There is also a VD16. These materials are online. In addition, the German catalogs have high resolution images of select books available for downloading, including Leunclavius' chronicles.

Granted, Google weirdness is not without moments of serendipity, and is akin to finding some rare volumes for two dollars apiece at a yard sale; but remember, we have all been using ZVAB, Abe and others for years now, and we are no longer accustomed to base research on serendipity. But serendipity is still welcomed, especially if it happens every twenty seconds.

I think it will be important to keep the page rank idea from becoming the pervasive and exclusive ideology in presenting the older scans, that is, until we have a perfect electronic record of much of our textual heritage, or a perfect subset of an isolated field where we can experiment with algorithms that dig through data and throw up hits of previously unsuspected significance; a considerable number are, in fact, working on this. Until that time, it would be nice to be able to find things along the model of the OPACs and other finding aids of the research libraries. This is possible to a degree using the advanced search option, but the control of the output lags far behind the current standards for electronic catalogs. Some person hours should be thrown at alphabetical ordering and ordering by date, no matter how distastefully twentieth-century that might appear in Mountain View.

Once the records are complete, when the metadata is flawless and the electronic text representation behind the page scans has been proofread to exhaustion, let us unleash the algorithms and darned be he who first cries *hold*. In that brave new world, the Google relevance algorithm as presently conceived and the one-line query window may well play a diminished role in favor of more flexible selection and display programs that may start, dare we hope, with the semantic inventory of the text.

On the other hand, we may have to avoid the pitfall of seeking a comfortable order—in this case, in the study of the humanities. It could be argued that around the time of finishing a dissertation and preparing first lectures as a newly hired instructor, one can achieve a sense that the profession is progressing in an orderly fashion. One does have to pretend at least that the teaching and research has a goal that is not completely shrouded in the mists of evolving humanity.

One could also argue that as time passes, the inevitable fraying of that order as the new hire matures will lead to a conserving stance, as old values are asserted in competition with new values. There are innumerable examples of this phenomenon in the history of thought. It has been codified in the concept of paradigm shift which we will not elucidate further. I will also avoid getting into the history of philosophy except to say it is one thing to see this recurring drama played out in nicely edited texts, for example, Hegel-Schopenhauer, Dilthey-Husserl, Husserl-Heidegger; it is something else to live through it today as we are confronted with the Internet. As Hegel was writing on the *Phenomenology* to the sound of artillery fire during the Battle of Jena, 1806, if we can believe the story, he must no doubt have been driven by the thought of sweeping away the old teleological order of his teachers with a new vision of humankind and the course of history. It must have been painful to learn sitting in the afterworld after an unfortunate encounter with typhus, that he, Hegel, is accused of being apologist for State authority a few decades later.

In the face of the Internet challenge today we must avoid becoming an apologist of the values of progressive academics in the second half of the twentieth century. Granted, that time was marked by fantastic consolidation and systematic expansion of knowledge, and the process is by no means slowing. But does it make sense to yearn for the order imposed after WWII by publications like *The Year's Work* that were able to give a sense of order to a few cohorts of literature graduate students? The question arises: can we impose that brief episode of order, an order that was fraying even as it was being taught, on the effort of Google and the digitization of old books?

The question is: can the new generation be interested in the project of editing the OCR and perfecting the metadata on the millions of books scanned in the last five years? It will be a monumental task that will require more than hourly labor, it will require some conviction that the task is worth it. The task, to be clear, is to make sure the electronic text used for building the indexes for scanned antiquarian books approaches 99.9 percent perfection with procedures in place to improve the accuracy by 0.009 percent a year. In an ideal world, JSTOR would incorporate the errata lists of individual journal issues in its electronic text, thus achieving 100.001 percent perfection.

At least in the short run, we will have to accept perfection in the 60 to 70 percent range, although that estimate may be off. If it turns out that it will not be cost effective to clean the OCR, can we jettison the venerable humanistic values that prize the perfectly edited, perfectly represented text? What about all the effort to come up with a computer representation (mark-up) of every jot and tittle in old printing? There was considerable energy behind that thought some years ago; action continued into the present, as humanists could not imagine life without their trivia. Are we now at a point that we can imagine indexing 60 percent of a particular page and accepting a partial solution? If it can be shown that statistically, as far as information content is concerned, the 40 percent does not matter, can we live with that?

I am not answering the question—I am merely suggesting we do not dismiss it out of hand. I am intrigued by the thought that a reading of a particular page by a set of moderately competent eyeballs may get only less that 25 percent of the information. In a continuous reading of several pages in a row, the data for a page in the middle may be considerably less. But let me turn to old texts where inconsistent printing practices and a language in flux have presented acute problems for editors.

Rethinking Editorial Practice

Let me bring forth an example. The Chronicle of the Ottoman Sultans and the accompanying notes by Leunclavius is available in Latin and German and Czech in several editions published around 1590. For Leunclavius this was an ongoing project; he published pieces as the opportunity arose but died at the siege of

Gran before he could complete the project. His books, sources, and notes were lost. Leunclavius was the first to use Ottoman chronicles as the source of his work, thus it can be seen as the first systematic, even scientific treatment of the history of the early rulers of the Ottomans. To date no historical-critical edition of his work on the Turks exist. As a source of our understanding of the Turks, Leunclavius was at the very beginning, and his chronology has not really been brought into question. A high quality scan from the Bavarian State Library in PDF format has recently come on-line.

Unfortunately, we do not know which Ottoman chronicle he used as a source; we only have a vituperative letter from t he Chief Librarian of the Hapsburg Court Library against Leunclavius, but no mention of specific lost Turkish manuscripts, so I have been told.

So the question arises, *how should Leunclavius be edited in the age of Google?* In his German editions the printer uses all the common abbreviations of endings and the ligatures standard at the time. It is possible to render the text into modern German and ignore the contemporary typesetting conventions. This has been done with several texts from that period to make the texts more accessible. On one hand, there can be no discussion, else you will be paraded before the entire academic community and your mortarboard will be shredded and any epaulets ripped from your shoulders. Of course, the only path is to do a traditional edition with every variant, every ligature carefully noted. The fact that this has not been done yet, makes it unlikely that somewhere there is an expert in sixteenth-century German and Latin to undertake this task. Even if such a person could be found, we still need a six-year stipend to do the work and thousands of euros to publish the resulting volume.

But let us say, one downloads the pages from the BSB. Let us also say one does a straight transcription of the pages, which can be done at about an hour per page: five hundred pages equaling five hundred hours is about a summer's work for a nonspecialist; at seven euros per hour, the wages total four thousand euros.

Presto! We have a quick and dirty edition, and not that dirty at all.

With an investment of another several thousand euros, or, the labor of love for about a summer, the transcribed text can be modernized and a good bit of *information* on Leunclavius can be put into electronic space. The high-resolution photographs would obviate detailed markup of the text since the lines could be enlarged and disambiguated as needed. The reader can decide on the spot if the ambiguity contributes to the sense of the sentence or if the typesetter had run out of a particular piece. Dates and names could be culled out automatically, presented graphically and thus illustrate one of the structural organization of the work. In the case of the Leunclavius chronicle, the notes in the "Pandect" could be linked to the text of the chronicle, thus obviating the difficult back and forth—almost physically impossible either with microfilm or with the original pages.

Let us return to the question: Are we tied to the method-ologies of the past that made a fetish out of exact editorial practice? Of course, with the extant text fragments of the *Nibelungenlied* or the *Chevalier de la Charrette*, such detailed editorial practice is important in finding clues to the lost original from which the extant texts were copied. With works of literature, as in the Chansons of the Troubadours or the German medieval epics, there has been no dearth of scholars willing to spend a lifetime analyzing the texts. Of course, this work was done at a time when the canon of interesting or valuable texts was greatly restricted.

This focus on the foundations of European national literatures meant that some other texts were of less interest. Thus a chronicle of Ottoman history received cursory treatment, since its insights would have been incorporated in the work of nineteenth-century historiography by von Hammer and Zinkeisen, et alia.

Can we imagine a relationship to our textual tradition that relies on statistical measures rather than exhaustive editorial work. Let me embroider: there are eight manuscripts of *Chevalier de la Charrette* (A, C, E, F, G, I, T, V). These have been edited over the years to give us a "normal text" and an apparatus of variants. Thus one could read the text and follow the variants in the footnotes. With the advent of computers, it became possible to fashion a detailed electronic edition of the text which allowed side-by-side comparison of the lines of each manuscript and a juxtaposition of high-resolution images and an exhaustive index of the dozen different types of poetic figures in the work. My own work on the project made me think that the level of detail that we were putting at the fingertips of the users of the *interface* was far above what scholars would want to process or could process. There is not a routine practice of research that would require reading the actual transcribed and annotated manuscripts of a tradition, beyond setting up the normal text. The profession is more comfortable with the normalized, useful, readable text.

Perhaps if a digital Charrette Project had been around during the nineteenth century, when the discussion about Chrétien's origins was most active, it would have been a boon for the profession. In the early twenty-first century, lacking similar projects for other text traditions, the Charrette Project is little more than a prototype, an expedition to a far away planet in a part of the universe that will not be settled anytime soon. As such it is a valuable step in the direction of improving access to part of Chrétien's work. Yet one has to ask, does this level of detail add scholarly insight? If we pursue a policy of editing every manuscript of every tradition and presenting them side by side, will we add to the confusion, or will we finally unearth previously hidden features? One might consider the notion that revisiting the normalized editions and putting the individual MSS into tables may become a modern imperative and could have a pedagogic value for students doing the work.

One final example from a manuscript tradition that does not involve treasures of national literature is the Documentary Geniza. Here we have non-literary documents from over a thousand years ago that were preserved in the Geniza of the Ben Ezra Synagogue in Fustat, an ancient part of Cairo. The "Documentary" part of the Fustat collection contains secular documents, everything from contracts to bills and invoices to court documents and personal letters. They are primarily in Arabic written with the Hebrew alphabet. In the case of this document collection, the primary interest is: how can we gain insight into the daily life of the Jews of Fustat, their commercial activity, their relationship to the government, their conflicts, and their private communications? I should add that the Documentary Geniza is but a small part of the items preserved in the Geniza and also the least studied; the majority is religious documents, books of the Old Testament, that came to the end of their useful life and were ritually discarded.

In studying the Documentary Geniza there are special problems. There is a mix of Hebrew and Arabic. The texts are small genre, often letters with lines continued around the margins or additions scribbled in any empty space. Again, the wordlist of the corpus should be the starting point. From there one should go to the transcription which should be inspected side by side with images of the original document, recto and verso, at high magnification. When the last machine that makes Bromide prints in Cambridge finally breaks beyond repair, perhaps digital images will become the stock in trade. Then perhaps the entire corpus can be combined in a database of transcriptions and images from around the world. Perhaps the images could also be downloaded to enable work with local graphics programs. I suspect there may be thorny theological problems with the handling of electronic copies of Documentary Geniza documents and certainly with indiscriminate printing, although precisely the Documentary part should be treated with different rules than the religious documents. Much of this work has not moved beyond prototypes, although the prototypes are now over a decade old.

So clearly, in the humanistic tradition, we have privileged the artistic expression and have lavished fantastic resources on discovering sources and provenance. Much of what is considered non-artistic has received less attention. As we contemplate a global information system in which Asians and Africans and Indians and Europeans learn from each other's cultures, we may have to ask, how much will a user in Shanghai want to know about *Chevalier de la Charrette*? How much about Leunclavius' chronicle? In both cases, prose summaries may well be all that is required.

If we can get past the notion of trying to divine from which part of Provence the scribes of the eight extant manuscripts of *Chevalier de la Charrette* have come by examining their dialectal peculiarities, we could rediscover the story and the narrative power that made the text worthy of being preserved in the first place.

The same is true of Leunclavius. It may be possible to divine that there were actually several printing assistants setting the pages by classifying their use of ligatures and abbreviations. Yet, we might be missing the point. The important thing is to fix the concrete items of information that Leunclavius excerpted from his sources—be they Turkish chronicles or Latin translations—and try to compare them in both directions.

If such a strategy is used on both the Turkish side as well as the European side, computational techniques may well be able to separate fact from fiction in the history that Ottoman Turkey has shared with European states from the fall of the Seljuks to the contemporary Turkish Republic.

To return to the original question: if the electronic text that is used to index pages of antiquarian books is only 50 or 60 percent correct, can the algorithms still rank and deliver pages in a meaningful manner? If Google presents page 343 of the third volume of von Hammer's History of the Ottoman Empire, should I try to run with it or should I back off, wary of committing dilettantish acts.

When the Chinese write histories of the Ottoman Empire, will they have drawn on the bibliography Western universities have prepared? Will they worry about the transmission from Leunclavius to Pöckh to Hammer to Shaw? Will they accept translations of Western works or Turkish works—or will they be able to data mine our textual traditions to come up with their own view that finds a common denominator between

Austrian, Hungarian, Czech, Slovak, Slovenian, Croatian, Serbian, Romanian, Bulgarian, Russian, Greek, Italian, Spanish, and French perspectives? Who is not on the list?

I feel that the humanities face a methodological crisis in the establishment of global information resources. It may be possible to fence in national interest and write history that contradicts the version the neighbor is writing behind a similar fence. It may be possible to leave scholarly monuments and current practice unreflected. In the time after the Second World War, American scholars have been able to work in contentious areas of European history and create an impression of objectivity. Going back just fifty years earlier, we can see history being used primarily for national ends. This work continues to this day, as a glorious empire to some is just the frustration of glory denied to others. All the nations of Europe are still licking various wounds and indicting their neighbors to this day. It is certain that several million antiquarian books in all manner of fields will certainly enliven the discussion.

Reprise and Theory: The Field of Play

Allow me to repeat lest anyone skipped to this section. The field of play, in summary, is a contentious wrangle, a rugby scrum, about rights and permissions with very little concern for the fantastic opportunities this application of technology could have on the transmission of texts and scholarly agenda. To date, treatments in the print media concentrate on the controversy of competing rights, so that no acceptable consensus can emerge on the viability, usefulness, or promise of the project. At present, the main bone of contention seems to be out-of-print books that are within the generous copyright period, but for which no owner of rights can be found. Arguments are put forth that it would be better that these "orphan books" should not be made available than the right of possession for electronic copies go to Google. I continue to believe that Google is not planning to get rich off antiquarian books. One could imagine a similar field of play, had someone invented the lending library in the current age and owners of the rights to books were to dispute the right of library patrons to read a book without paying them for the privilege. Of course, an analysis of the usefulness and promise of lending books to all comers free of charge would be ignored in favor of the substantial grievances of the publishing industry. Fortunately, lawmakers of previous generations have had a grasp of the big picture, and it will take some time for the current legal trends to reverse the privileged place which education has held in the marketplace of ideas. Let us not be panicked by the sound of self-interest drums emanating from the media—Title 17 exemptions will hold. The perspective on scanning books should try to be academic, even scholarly, and reflect intellectual interests.

In this essay on Google Books, the legal issues, the issues of empire building, of information monopoly and privacy violation and all the attendant paranoia rushing in the direction of righteous indignation for grievances real and imagined, will have receded to the background. There is plenty of that elsewhere. This is an attempt to say, in a nice way, that we shall ignore the blogorama, and its global manifestations, most specifically its reductio ad absurdum: twitter. We shall also ignore the "news" journalism which likes to pander to those potentially aggrieved by any or all aspects of the copyright issue in the vast masses of the chronically aggrieved and thus finds in Google a convenient villain.

This sort of "news" flares up around the international book trade shows; alas journalists write about what they know sells. We shall seek other readers, the few, the proud, the minds at work. We shall also ignore most of the corporate celebrity journalism, as distinct from garden variety celebrity journalism. Corporate groupies explore all the deplorable possibilities in modern business life and have their teeth in Google to the gums. I emphatically choose to ignore this perspective, not because these possibilities don't exist, but because I don't want to waste the precious commodity of attention span there. Although the attention span about deplorable possibilities seems to be an infinite resource by itself, it makes attention to other things insurmountably difficult and hence unaffordable.

Google and Google Books are quite recent phenomena that are having a heretofore unimagined effect on our view of information—not just our view of information, but how we get from information to knowledge. We shall just assume a path from information to knowledge. I am thinking casually along the line of synthesizing information into something we can call knowledge, without attaching great philosophical baggage, at present, or looking too closely at what passes for knowledge. Given what has passed for information and for knowledge in the past, can we feel really good about our current efforts? No! The point is: getting information to the eyeballs is a first step in any subsequent assimilation, however haphazardly random, which in turn is a prerequisite to any conceptual processing, however jellotronically shaky, by the higher brain functions.

We have arrived, most certainly, in a new age for the delivery of information. The timely, elegant, consistent, and universally accessible delivery of information has become the trademark of Google and the cause of its astonishing meteoric rise. In the previous generations, getting information was an exclusive, esoteric, and difficult field requiring a long apprenticeship in academies and libraries and yielding unpredictable results. Should high-brow eyebrows arch at this inclusion of Google in the academic knowledge guild, we can only point out that Google did not reach that position through rhetorical persuasion or corporate clout or clever advertising, but rather through millions of users typing queries into its screens. This acceptance by the bottom rungs of the pyramid of seekers for answers to questions is often viewed with alarm by upper rungs, the initiated elite knowledge seekers. The secret is out however; reference librarians use Google more than most! It is all happening too fast, too many people are involved, and who will vouch for all this information? What conclusions will be drawn? Whither imprimatur? Whither our monopoly?

One way of dealing with meteoric phenomena is to demonize them; a less drastic measure is simply to ignore them, or better to compartmentalize them as too new, too trendy, too commercial, too unserious. This is the head-in-the-sand approach, very effective, but it leaves you with the head in the sand, not the most universal perspective. We cannot ignore that Google is in constant use and thus a gargantuan, ongoing cybernetic event. For better or for worse, if Google does not get it for you, you won't get it. So we need to talk.

One should add that there is a division of labor between the search engine Google and the user of the search engine Google. The search engine will present likely answers and exclude unlikely answers, the user has to recognize the answers as likely, find confirmation elsewhere, and know when the answer is not there. We are, after all, talking about assimilating information, not eating donuts; there is a minimum level of responsibility in processing information. Those not willing to rise to this low standard should not ask questions and just follow the twitter panoply or head straight to Krispy Kreme. Searching the Web carries no guarantee in individual cases; the overall track record, however, statistically speaking, is impressive.

The notion that Google has trapped and evaluated, if not actually stored, all queries typed into its query window as well as the subsequent browse behavior and the location of the query, and has done so for the last ten years, is so mindboggling in its implication, that I, personally, will immediately retreat into the conceptually much safer space of books, old books, preferably unread. The notion that the world's blog traffic which has its own blog-specific search engines, is plotted daily, in perpetuity, as some sort of global weather pattern with models to chart blog storms initiated by anything from a pop star photo-op to riots in France, also causes me to curl into fetal position and pull up the covers. I greet Google's and other's data gathering not with outrage or fear, but rather with amazement at the quantities of data that are collected and evaluated routinely, today, and I am convinced that collecting such data is important, if, not for historical purposes, then so that our queries bring ever better results. Certainly the bloggers have an interest in publicizing the accessing of their blogs by those who query and browse their blogs and preserve that information as a testament to the usefulness of their blogs. Surely, the user of information pays a small price for browsing information by having browse behavior documented anonymously.

My knee-jerk interest in knowledge is acute enough that I find it a pity that search queries are deleted after a time—just as it was a pity the library at Alexandria was burned down and looted periodically. One wonders what grievance is assuaged and what damage is repaired by deleting query data older than nine months or three months or whatever period of time will be judged safe by defenders of the public weal. And this against a backdrop of EU statutes where ISPs in Europe have to make six months of logins and browsing, including wireless connections in hotel lobbies, available to justice ministries for criminal investigations. I understand the need to keep ever-encroaching courts out of perceived private spheres, but I wonder if the washed should be thrown out with the bathwater. I understand that the gist of Web usage can be statistically described, that the variables, their clusters and their correlations can be accurately fixed in a multimonth cycle. One can only hope that future generations will not miss the full record of the curiosity of inquiring minds from around the globe at the beginning of the twenty-first century, and will be satisfied by the correlations of cosines of the square roots of standard deviations of various independent variables as they were calculated during successive nine month cohorts in the age of vociferous consumer protection. In the knee-jerk knowledge versus knee-jerk privacy struggle, I would like to err on the side of passing on more information to the future.

There are certain things that the consumers of information may not want to know about themselves; they want to reap the fruits of the insight into collective behavior, but they do not want to contribute their own behavior, no doubt out of modesty, not Kafkaesque guilt, reflexive nay-saying, or straight paranoia. It may be easy to correct statistically for this typically human behavior. I am sure Aristotle imagined the human drive toward knowledge differently than what goes on at Google query windows everywhere in the world or in the databases that process the records of that activity.

Nor do I completely trust the statistical science and its application outside very narrow parameters and clearly defined fields of work, such as stocking supermarket shelves when the Fourth of July falls on a Monday. Statistics can find an answer to any question asked, and one can optimize questions for certain statistical results. Of all conceptual tools, statistics has a great record for serving self-interest in the guise of objectivity. Thus the only somewhat clean sphere for statistics is where the only "interest" or "bias" is to solve a technical problem with an unpredicted result. I prefer to have statistics used to solve technical problems and to use continuous fine tuning to improve solutions; here Google rules the roost and has provided much steady wind in the sails of data mining. Google's work with information extractions from the Web has made this field seem attractive to a new generation of students. There is now so much exponentially growing information, all in electronic form, that academic departments see the need to mobilize response in order to find, test, and teach procedures to handle it.

Even formerly marginal areas such as text mining are coming into the spotlight given that most of the data on the Web to be mined is text. The application of mathematical methods to text research is generally underway. The question is, at what stage of development is this effort? I would say the question is open, indicating strongly that we are only in the effort's earliest developmental stages.

So despite the fact that we have a robust set of empirical, mathematized academic enterprises dealing with everything from computational linguistics, corpus linguistics, machine learning, translation to text mining, we have no way of applying these efforts to discover one solitary thing that is both interesting and true about just one text of millions. Text is all around us, and it is difficult to find an environment without the presence of text; indeed, the bulk of our knowledge is passed from generation to generation via text.

In the last three hundred years, we have created an amazing published record of texts, some with origins going back several thousand years. Yet this record is in a form of exponentially growing commentary that is outstripping our ability to decode it.

We have a tradition of sciences that grow from observation to mathematized representation and confirming observation. We have a tradition of excluding empirical research, not to mention of mathematical techniques from large areas of humanistic knowledge generated each generation. That exclusion has its source in part in the lack of familiarity with mathematical principles and their application by the students of texts. It seems that the enthusiasm for textual transmission dampens the enthusiasm for formal abstract representation. The practice of the division of knowledge into knowledge of the physical and knowledge of the moral has been perpetuated into modernity mostly by the inertial drag of the stewards of moral knowledge.

One could think of a fierce turf war between dogmatists and empiricists. The empiricists ceded all claims to anything dogma, mostly to escape the torture chamber. The empiricists then followed their visions where they would lead while the dogmatists continued to exercise power far beyond the intrinsic interest of their ideas.

The stewards of physical knowledge have not let the grass grow in their spheres of activity. Without going into a history of science, we can summarily state in summary that mathematization has greatly facilitated the transmission of insights from generation to generation. In the area of moral knowledge, improved conceptual tools have also produced efficiencies in the transfer of knowledge. So let us try to get to a bottom line: what stands at the bottom line of the mathematization of the physical universe? Let us just pick out some examples at random: space travel, global communications, computers, weapons of mass destruction, biochemistry, laser surgery, modern pharmacology.

Knowledge of the physical has undergone many stock splits and the shares have gained in value only to be split again until we have littered the earth and the universe with the artifacts of mathematization.

The bottom line of the stewards of moral knowledge is not as clearly defined. The physical artifacts, structurally sound buildings, extended human life-spans, efficient communication technologies, although they are universally present, do not count on the *moral* side. The only real artifact that can be placed on the side of moral knowledge is an outgrowth of the humanists' methodologies, the text, and it resides in the modern research library. Yet even here, most of the indexing technology, the catalogs, and the subject lists receives more impetus from the physical than the moral.

In German studies it is common to name Albrecht Haller (1708-1777) as the last person who had assimilated all current knowledge in sciences and in literature. It helped that his bibliography extends to fifty-thousand items produced, so one can assume that Haller dominated the discussion. Yet, he was the last one.

So we are really left with only one class of items to place on the moral side, several million texts, generally printed on paper. A mandarin culture has grown around these texts. Novices are taught to read and are subsequently initiated into the subtleties of various text traditions. All this was still somewhat manageable circa 1800, before multiple editions of Kant, before Hegel, and before textual studies began aping the organizational and exploratory drive of the physical sciences. In relatively short order, all extant fashionable texts were collected, described, classified, edited, and published.

Of course, the production of new texts in all fields did not abate, nor did the discussion about the texts in the accumulated record.

The plain fact is that the record has grown to such enormity that it can only be studied through judicious selection. By digging deeply into one statistically infinitesimal part of the record, we can perpetuate the illusion of living in an intellectually coherent world.

Statistics must obviously get a new wardrobe. Statistics do not make things better or clearer by themselves. The trick is always in the questions and the motivation, experience and perspective of the asker. In data mining the function of statistics is not so much rhetorical, i.e. gathering support for a particular position, but rather getting help to make some sense of overwhelming amounts of data. By *data* I mean the pages that find their way to the Web every day and not the data Google gathers on users (although the two should be inextricably linked in our thinking about the Web). Data provided by scholars is given imprimatur through use—the citation indexes in the sciences have demonstrated the principle. Unused information can be allowed to atrophy out of the system.

I have no confidence that the discussion about Google data-gathering has reached a level of seriousness for a meaningful discussion of the actual problems and the concomitant opportunities for science and understanding of antiquarian books.

The reaction of some seriously concerned Web users to build an "iron browser" that will not allow data gathering is not an encouraging sign. Personally, I would have loved to see what the ancient Greeks would have googled: booking two weeks at the beach in Argos, ordering peacock feathers from Alexandria, consulting the e-oracle at olympus.gk ….

The work done with the text units that are Web pages, recognizing content, evaluating, classifying, ranking and delivering has application far beyond Web pages. One does not have to go too far into the realm of future technology to see the similarity between text on a Web page and text on a book page. We are still in process of figuring out just what the specifics of that relation could be. One could posit that if it is possible to find likely pages out of the millions of Web pages, it will be possible to find likely pages from books. Any romanticism about the glory of traditional reading methods can be called into question by the vast quantities of texts and the recognition that even the most celebrated scholar must sample only a statistically tiny part of the record.

Computers are an indispensable tool in the field of textual studies, but I am not ready to sign over my personal power of attorney to multivariate algorithms. I shall, through necessity, leave much of the actual statistical science behind the Google search engine to the side; this has become an extremely technical, far ranging discussion. As far as the indexing of the surface Web is concerned, I want sausages cooked on the plate, not being competent to advise on the making of sausages.

The door, however, will be open wide for the statistical perspective on text, forced by the clearly inescapable understanding of the limits of human perception and specifically the human limits in absorbing texts through the eyeballs only. It makes eminent sense to seek help from automatic word counting, pattern recognition, variable correlation, and memory more powerful and reliable than our own. This will provide a sufficient grist for the mill.

From the GBS beta, it is hard to tell what selection criteria Google will apply to its scanned antiquarian books. So we will start with the notion that Google's first step is just bringing the whole area into motion by scanning pages and delivering PDFs. The second step is Google's utilization of OCR and thereby offering basic searching. We can assume that these first two steps are designed to provide sufficient quantity of user data to work towards improving indexing techniques. Finally, Google is throwing whatever else it has into the book browsing interface to encourage use (to improve indexing); at present that seems to be linking texts to maps, an extremely interesting approach for humanists since it promises to give the current maps a historical dimension. I can just hear Ted Nelson a few years from now: "Google now owns all of historical geography." Google also provides a virtual bookshelf and keyword searching of texts— again, no doubt to get a sense of patterns of use. Given that the Google people are basically, mathematicians, we can assume that somewhere in the blue-sky engineering plan for the next ten years, some considerable work with statistics and antiquarian texts is scheduled.

Information, Then and Now and To Come

In the past of humanities studies and continuing unabated into the present, information [read: books], having been somewhat vetted by the publishing industry and the appropriate academic peers, grows into the existing storage and indexing structures in libraries. As the published information grows, libraries adapt to absorb the material. Until very recently, if information did not make it into the library, it was lost, with rare exceptions. Teams of discipline-specific scholars and librarians are in charge of keeping the indexes current and remembering the various nuances of the literature of specific fields. The indexes are detailed subject lists, liberally supplemented by the personal experience of scholars in the field, which includes many librarians. Of that personal experience much is lost each year as valuable scholars leave their money, their house, family and car behind, but take much of their knowledge with them, off into the better world beyond.

It is true that in most technical fields, this process has been automated into a citation index and that most work is done in online environments. Research results are also presented in thematically discrete chunks, making not only indexing more effective, but also showing a greater systematic approach to the research agenda. In the humanities, which is our interest here, the pace is not quite as frantic and the need to base new research on specific, quantifiable previous work is limited. We still live in a world of rhetoric, wild gesticulation, ego projection, and pathos. Yet it is not entirely arbitrary: information in the form of books and articles, some in electronic form, is reviewed, evaluated and, if found congenial, quoted extensively. This information forms itself into a sort of contemporary dogma of the fashionable in the best sense of the word. One should say that truth or validity or factuality or self-evidence or even reasonableness does not determine this process completely, neither in the past, nor today. The most awful ideologies and most absurd drivel, on many occasions made it onto the academic charts; however, the process does advance; vast quantities of materials are produced and some major avenues of systematic progress and regress are kept open.

The development of the Dewey Decimal System in the late nineteenth century and the parallel development of the Library of Congress System are examples of responses to the dramatic increase in the number of texts to be stored, while keeping viable the American tradition of open access stacks and shelving by subject. While subject based cataloging presents a great increase in the workload of librarians, it is a great aid to the efficiency of a researcher in finding and evaluating sources, and it improves the logistics of book retrieval from the shelf, and information retrieval in general. It is a great convenience to have all the books on a subject in the same place.

The older tradition of sequential numbering of acquisitions and the shelving according to volume size, which continues into the present time in Europe, is not an optimal solution to the information/knowledge problem and seems to err on the side of the custodial. It might increase the storage efficiency from the perspective of space by obviating unexpected storage require-ments of certain subjects and periodic expensive reordering, but it inhibits research by making the physical retrieval path for items of the same subject longer. However, one should keep in mind that subject shelving and subject groupings developed as practical devices to deal with physical items and were not conceived as a universal map of knowledge. Modern electronic indexing schemes may not be this modest. Through the dramatic improve-ment in electronic catalogues in the last decade, and the ability to cast both wider and more precise electronic nets through searching, many of the deficiencies in the physical layout of library storage is mitigated. The efficiency deficit in sequential shelving has been largely resolved, and the subject indexes have taken airs of a universal epistemology.

But what about the Web, what about information growing up outside publishing channels that does not want or need a place in the library structures? To be fair, from the modest beginning with CD-ROM databases, libraries have not been inactive in embracing electronic sources. Of course, that was still a time (the 1990s) when you had to go to a place made of bricks to get at the CD-ROMS. Today, although one can do everything from home or office or Wi-Fi spot, libraries are still very much sorting and sifting Web materials as part of their own presence on the Web. Yet, the Web is dynamic, items come and go, items go out of date and are forgotten and there is no Internet police that will come to some server and remove all the rotten links. This also impacts the work of reference librarians in the electronic age, who struggle to keep various Web study guides and finding aids up to date. In the past, finding aids were also out of date, but we didn't mind as long as some aid was provided. Out of date or incomplete Web resources seem to damage the general credibility of the Web for serious work, an unfair assessment.

Everyone realizes that the Web is a vast accumulation of information, both savory and unsavory, current and out of date, true and patently false, serious and patently silly. The Web reflects the world with its savory and unsavory elements.

As a portal into the Web in general, Google does heavy lifting to get users to the right place in this accumulation of ever shifting electronic stuff. Yet, there is an important side to Google, a side not involved with searching the surface Web. Google has taken on roles having to do with culture, education, and the progress from information to knowledge that should not simply be lumped with all the flotsam and jetsam spilling out from the Web onto Google result lists. It is true that Google is supplanting the role of the library as a source of information. Who was the last person on the planet to say: "Oh, let me run to the library right quick to get xyz bit of information." Google did not make the Web, it is trying to make some sense of the Web. Making sense of the Web is neither limited to putting things in alphabetical or numerical order, nor is it limited to reflecting traditional subject headings. It becomes a matter of assigning an order to things that appear chaotic.

Data mining is an advanced science; in the case of Google, we can speak of planet-wide strip-mining in the best sense of that word. It has its roots in the algebra extension of the late nineteenth century, and it is evolving to application of mathematical techniques in ways that are reaching deep into the fabric of day-to-day life from supermarkets to life-insurance to weather forecasting.

There was a time, not so long ago, when data mining was scorned, certainly in humanities circles. It was seen as a testament to the impotence of researchers who would let automatic processes do their work. There is still an existential component in wrestling with the texts of our tradition that does not tolerate short-cuts. It is a given that the between-the-ears wetware is what is to be trained in the humanities. The goal is to create cohorts of hairless, featherless, bipedal organisms who would work on the accumulation of cultural artifacts. That such attitudes were still rife in the eighties and nineties of the previous century, despite decades of knowledge explosion, demonstrates the myopia of the humanities collective. I do think the Web snuck up on the humanists. Many of us were working on digital humanities projects, barely tolerated by the mainstream, thinking ourselves nevertheless at the very forefront of the delivery of information—and we were, for about two seconds, till the Web took off and made the university experiments seem extremely underfunded and tentative.

As things stand now, Web users are the recipients of information selected by algorithms; decisions are made behind the scenes and automatic processes operate to select for us what we cannot do ourselves without virtuosity with search terms. Of course the lack of transparency in searching is much less opaque than the *editorial* or institutional criteria for the selection of information to publish in books and articles in the past, going on to this day. However, it is nevertheless disconcerting to consider that the results of a specific search will change from month to month.

This is not a problem as long as the Web is an adjunct to traditional methodologies. As a set of eyeballs, my only interest is to submit a query, not to have a personal overview of the Web—much of the new material that shows up in queries is of minor interest. The serious academic sites do not change any more quickly than the standard works in the field or the holdings in a library. My interest in submitting a query is to get at particular information, often outside my field. It is the task of the algorithms and the girls and boys in the back room at Google to dig through the Web gunk and bring forth hits on my query.

From there, the automatic processes have no more impact on my research. The automatic programs have brought information to my eyes. The things brought forth were not made automatically, but represent traditional human writing and organizing. So, on one hand, the influence of the automatic processes is extensive—on the other hand, the influence on my work is negligible. The convenience of getting multiple media types at the first string query from diverse Web sources far outweighs the inconvenience of wading through irrelevant hits. I would rather discard the hits myself than use a system of fixed subject categories where some person or committee has selected materials approved for display. The reason is simple: I will never know what I am missing in a selected hierarchical system. The dynamic calculations of Google do give a strong guarantee that some new star or some new maverick on the information horizon will find its way quickly into the mainstream.

Given this dynamic information space, it is possible to blame Google for all sorts of phenomena. If one wants to be anti-Google, one can lay the cause for self-medication with non-prescription pills of both the ill and the hypochondriacs and the resulting potential catastrophic consequences at the door of Google, since it is through Google that these types of queries are submitted, and with Google's calculation snake-oil vendors are ranked and thus given imprimatur in the minds of the weak-minded. Journalists like to ridicule Dr. Google when they should be ridiculing patients seeking myriad Dr. Quacks. To be fair, one should only condemn the sites on the Web that actually provide the information on spurious remedies; after all, it is possible to find quacks in the phone book and to buy phony supplements at the mall.

A more reasoned approach is to evaluate the queries themselves. Indications are that Google is starting an epidemiology project since it seems to be able to predict outbreaks of specific infectious diseases by the queries it receives from specific locations in the world. It is clear that we have vast numbers of users and vast numbers of information servers. The electronic information servers outnumber traditional depositories of physical information items by a large factor. There is really no alternative in this global electronic environment than to design clever statistical measures for what to pull out for any given query. Given the nature of the beast, our own tolerance and flexibility and ability to evaluate what we see will have to supplement the first step taken by Google in presenting a list of hits. We shall have to develop the same flexibility when we ask Google to show us books when we query. We really have no choice, we will be shown books; all we have to do is to begin to like it.

Contemporary habits of thought automatically associate Google with trendy mass-market culture and its various squabbles caused by greed and simple human nature. Nevertheless, people will use Google to find something on the Web and be happy to have found it, all the while complaining about Google's hegemony or commercialism; this is analogous to complaining about the Church, but still wanting a child baptized and the grandfather buried under its aegis.

More troublesome is the critique of Google, or rather the dismissal of everything Google, that concentrates on the very mass of things that Google brings forth. Essentially it is the confusion that Google is not a content provider but a search engine. It does take a few nanoseconds of thought to appreciate the difference. The latest victim to fall prey to this confusion is the European Commissioner of This, That and the Other proudly announcing the launch of "Europeana," a portal funded by the EU into some millions of cultural artifacts. At present the collection is mostly from France, but it is scheduled to grow to ten million items to be contributed by all EU member states.

Commissioner Reading is careful to emphasize the difference between *Europeana* and Google for the benefit of the readers of the *International Herald Tribune* [Oct 2008; Google: europeana herald]. Her main point seems to be that "Europeana" is an archive of cultural artifacts, growing steadily, systematically, arranged thematically, and authenticated and neat, while Google presents only chaos. It would have been better to say that Google is a path through chaos. It is, however, a fair and obvious point; the Commissioner goes on to say that a Google query of "Chopin" yields several hundred thousand hits and that it is difficult to sort through the information, to separate the wheat from the chaff (my paraphrase). This old biblical chestnut in its various permutations is usually a safe metaphor to use on occasion in public when one has not spent the time in private to consider the issues. In this case, however, it is entirely inappropriate.

The Commissioner fails to appreciate two points: first and most important, one uses Google to get to *Europeana*, unless one can intuit the url: www.europeana.eu. It is not fair railing against the taxi that is taking you to the Louvre for not being the Louvre itself. It is a valuable service after all to be taken to a site even if one does not know how to spell it; it is hard to know how widely familiar the –eana suffix is in a world of multiple non-European, non-Latin-alphabet cultures.

Second, about the Chopin query: trying several national Google portals, the string "chopin" yielded the Chopin societies, the Grove entry, the Wiki entry, links to CD sets, et cetera. Given that each of the first five hits provide myriad links, including the Europeana, that delve deep into Chopineana, it is hard to see the chaos among all the clean and neat orderings of information.

Google has in fact dipped into the chaos and brought forth, brilliantly, Chopin. The feat is all the more remarkable in that Chopin is a common name in parts of the world and the name of any number of commercial products including liquor made from the potato.

It is shocking to see bureaucrats in charge of multimillion euro information projects parade their lack of awareness of even basic information industry concepts. That could also explain why the site crashed, burned, and disappeared for weeks, mere hours after its launch. Fortunately this does not happen to Google, which understands the global information weather. This does not mean that Europeana is not a fantastic site; its organization of various media about Chopin and others, with attractive thumbnails, is impressive. But it will still not replace Wikipedia or Google; why would it want to? Why frame the discussion in antagonistic terms, let's be happy with Europeana—welcome to the Web—or welcome back to the bigs, and let's pull in the claws.

The Europeans have not invented the library with *Europeana*, they have merely stocked a virtual library with artifacts of different media types. Its conventional ordering techniques, its bookmarking facilities, and its liberal downloading policies will be a great boon to education. Europeana is concentrating on the high points of Western cultural heritage and thus lives in a world that has been well-ordered for some time. Essentially, the universal histories of the nineteenth century, the contemporary handbooks of many disciplines and the ever *neo* contemporary cultural discussions are presented in a nice friendly interface. This is a whole world, hermetically sealed, a pretty place, a politically correct place, a sensitively diverse place, an appropriately chagrined place at humanity's inhumanity to humanity; there is no need to rake through thousands of sites on pornography, extremism, dangerous ideologies or simple idiocies, or simply out of date junk, personal vanities, or product information to find the crucial bits of Chopin nestled among the high culture Web sites. There is no vodka manufacturer with the name of Chopin in the *Europeana*, but there is one on the Web. *Europeana* is not rocket science and is not data mining, its only current goal is to contribute convenience of access and perhaps to spin history a bit more pro-European while poking the Americans in the eye with all the stuff they have that is older than the Mayflower. It is curious that the gentry, surrounded by its culture and art and history, should scorn the miners, be they gritty Yorkshiremen a hundred years ago or the mathematicians from Silicon Valley.

We may have to consider strange and radical ideas to get beyond limiting ourselves simply to achieving more convenient access to things we already know. It may be possible to find ways of ordering information beyond that of the alphabetical or chronological listing. As European culture (i.e. Western culture from the Urals to the Rockies) comes in close contact with cultures with radically different sets of assumptions in California and Asia, and as new generations of information specialists without a background in classics work through the mass of materials generated every day and the materials having been deposited in the past, other paradigms may emerge, paradigms still only faintly visible.

There is no reason, statistically speaking, to expect the general public of whatever political persuasion or ministerial rank to be logically consistent or aware of the source of their judgments. Defense against the new, defense against the appearance of chaos everywhere, naturally leads to a cautious ambivalence—a healthy attitude. Google has harvested much of this ambivalence due to its high visibility at the gates to chaos. Yet it is still possible to pursue serious non-destructive analysis without journalistic fear mongering or celebrity pandering. Problems arise when we move outside the realm of the shared horizons of the general public and the tumults of pros and cons to a specific academic horizon where the general commonplaces are not helpful and must be removed before certain avenues of thought can open up. It is not helpful to perpetuate misunderstandings. Although one could make the argument that misunderstanding is the chief stock in trade of scholars in the humanities.

In summary then: the field of play is academic. Thus we can afford to ignore much of the current discussion since it is not concerned with academic issues. Our interest looks towards a horizon where all texts known to humanity are digitized, perfectly OCR'd, indexed, semantically and syntactically analyzed. The question we would like to consider is how do we get from here to there and what role will Google want to play in that journey. Since we are not there yet, we should concentrate on equipping the expedition to get us there. That will include persuading people that it is worth making the trip and defeating the people who maintain there is no there where we would like to explore. Let us remember, the "here" is rampant subjectivity, unreliable memory, overwhelming masses of material, and completely inadequate strategies for compensation for these deficiencies, leading to rhetorical strategies culminating in wild gesticulation and shouting. While it is possible to make a good and comfortable career with the tools of the "here," the material requires we launch expeditions to "there," and the Google digitization has left Goshen a good while ago.

Just remember: "Google is the best and Google is the worst," let's work in the space between the two Googles. And that goes for all of you all in Brussels too.

Books, Read and Unread

We shall concentrate on the problems and opportunities for the functionality of Google Book Search (GBS) with antiquarian books, in full confidence of the validity of the idea of scanning old books. Much has changed in the field of text scanning in the last decade, and we have no reason to doubt the integrity of the academic institutions doing the work or the value of the raw materials they are bringing to the light-table or, above all, the importance of creating a wider distribution for antiquarian textual material. Arguments about the integrity of the project or about the legitimacy of the effort should be done now, before we start, not when we get to specific examples. I don't want the response to an example of text searching to be: "Yes, but they are just after dollars" or "Yes, but that is just American cultural hegemony."

To some degree we all share the historical and cultural legacy of the entire world, even if every grouping has its own perspective. Graduate studies at American research universities try not to restrict study to Americana, although a good bit of that does go on. All Americans, north and south and in Brooklyn, have languages they share with Europe, and the field of studies in the humanities generally divides up the larger field of Western Civilization (widely despised and widely practiced) into departments based on specific European cultures and languages. A decade or two of multicultural agenda supplemented by last-gasp neo-Marxism has not really changed the lineup of main-stream humanities departments; it only has added significant areas on the periphery and slightly skewed the output of various departments in faint atavistic echoes of class-warfare agendas. However, the European bureaucrats trying to hype their Europe project while emphasizing national uniqueness of the member states are getting it wrong when they start applying political agendas in academics. Each European country has always had academies to study the other cultures. The United States has always been a refuge for European academics seeking to escape to greener pastures, from the naked persecution of the 1930s or the underfunded shambles that higher education has become in many parts of Europe today. American universities have always been able to sport an air of universality, or at least impartiality, when dealing with academic disciplines based on national languages. The call to a chair at an American university is still quite welcome, and doubtless the wires to the Europeana will run hot under the Atlantic (or over the satellites), not even to consider all the Europeana that has been carted across the ocean by wealthy Yankee collectors and by Europeans fed up with Europe.

Not every cultural group has made it an important target to study its textual heritage in exhaustive detail. In addition, a close look at the unedited texts published in the nineteenth century and now available in PDF, will make it painfully obvious how wide and deep the chasms between cultural groupings, even those with a common political history, had become. The unedited antiquarian materials of that time will have to be approached with some care and much professionalism, lest modern-day book burnings—or rather book deletions—are inspired among the legion of *correct thinkers* of all stripes.

Yet the textual utterances of the world are finite; only so many surviving books were published in each preceding century. We can see the beginning of an age where we no longer find it sufficient to have made exhaustive lists of these texts on the computer, but we will want the texts themselves on the computers. It is not just a matter of a convenient distribution channel, but also an opportunity to apply electronic search methodologies that will increase the ability of scholars to work with this material.

These developments are going on in a climate of technological revolution in working with texts both ancient and contemporary. One word only to reiterate the developments in the contemporary book trade: the limited preview items in Google and Amazon are quite astonishing. Especially the scans of the most recent scholarly offerings are extremely helpful in evaluating the usefulness of recent publications for one's own work. Gone are the days of casting longing glances at the shelf reserved for new arrivals next to the circulation desk. Simply find the book in question online, open the table of contents, read a few paragraphs, and submit several searches of specific lexical items that can give you a good idea of the author's slant. Of course, what I would really like to do is to download the recent publication to my laptop and have the publisher charge my credit card a reasonable price, ideally, based on production costs minus printing and shipping costs. To date this service is available only for about 300,000 items, not all, of course, first line publications.

Selling books is a business. We have seen the disappearance of small, locally-owned bookstores in the last quarter century and their consolidation into large chains. Bookstores have become bigger than supermarkets in floor space. You no longer go to a bookstore just to buy a book; you go to hang out, have a latte, check your e-mail on your laptop, eat lunch, and perhaps buy something on impulse on your way out. Many more people go to bookstores today that ever in the past. That is good.

One also browsed bookstores twenty-five years ago, but generally only as a form of intellectual exercise, a subtle form of foreplay on Saturday night in university towns. Today large bookstores are part of the mall experience across the nation. So we can dispense with the nostalgia for the locally-owned bookstores, they were a bottleneck to text access. Books, music CDs, and films on DVD are mass market items that are sold at malls. We can also dispense with the elitism that casts a jaundiced eye at mall-goers in mega-bookstores. Everyone approaches texts at their own level. There are preschoolers romping on the floor in the kids section; there is a retired postal worker turned history buff reading Churchill in a stuffed chair; there is a non-traditional learner working through a study guide at a long table looking very much like a graduate student in the ivory-covered halls of learning.

Books are a good business only if it is possible to lure people to the texts. The corollary is: education in the humanities is successful only if one can lure students to texts. What may have started as a romp on the carpet of the children's section, may well lead to an oak-paneled reading room.

So we have jettisoned nostalgia for small bookstores and their narrow aisles of books, and we have abandoned sneering at the non-privileged tentatively approaching texts at malls. It is time to consider the *topos* of the graduate student or the world renowned scholar sitting in the oak-paneled reading rooms surrounded by dusty tomes working on something obscure.

We must start by updating the image of the bookstore made of faux bricks, non-flammable foam and aluminum studs. For every mallgoer who finds the path into the brick veneer bookstore, there are three people at home, mouse in hand, browsing the Internet bookstores.

But what about the academics in their ivory towers? (If we can still apply that metaphor to today's research universities.) Clearly the ivory tower has been remodeled; wire has been pulled into every room from the porter's lodge to the scholar's chambers. The first things to go were the card catalogs—the venerable *Zettelkästen*—the methodological foundation on which much of knowledge growth was based. The early adopters created extensive combined databases of both the new and old holdings; the laggards scanned cards and delivered the images. The next to go were the encyclopedias, now online or out of business. Encyclopedias were considered low-brow research and not greatly missed, but they were closely followed by all sorts of national biographical dictionaries, often the only source of information, reliable or semi-reliable, on dead white men. Close behind were the major reference works.

Many journals are electronic into the nineteenth century. Recent issues are all digital. Any texts of the canon are on *Gutenberg*, and the real classics are on Perseus. Today the practice of copying manually a series of paragraphs for purposes of citation is rare. In the past, many errors crept in when copying first from the book into notes, then from the notes into the manuscript, and then from the manuscript into the typescript. Other artifacts from just one generation of scholarship past have not survived into the digital age: remember retyping pages? Remember text preparation as character building?

So, for example, today, I want to quote a paragraph from *Anna Karenina* about philosophy. I have asked myself the question, *does Tolstoy mention philosophy?* I vaguely remember that there was some passage about Levin and philosophy. I simply log onto *Project Gutenberg*, bring the novel up on the screen, search for a phrase, and mark, copy, and paste the paragraph:

"Of late in Moscow and in the country, since
he had become convinced that he would find no
solution in the materialists, he had read and
re-read thoroughly Plato, Spinoza, Kant,
Schelling, Hegel, and Schopenhauer, the
philosophers who gave a non-materialistic
explanation of life.

Their ideas seemed to him fruitful when
he was reading or was himself seeking arguments
to refute other theories, especially those of the
materialists; but ..." [*Anna Karenina*, part 8,
chapter 9]

I will not complete the quote, since it can be brought up with
a few mouseclicks from anywhere in the world, within reason.
Tolstoy and the consolations of philosophy, not a pretty picture,
not terribly discriminating and not overwhelming in detail, but
Levin did not kill himself, just because philosophy "read and re-
read thoroughly" was no antidote to the existential angst of
Russian land barons. Alas, there is no correlation between talent
as a philosopher and talent as a novelist until the 20th century.
But I digress.

The process of putting the quote into this text took a few
seconds. I challenge anyone to find these paragraphs in a printed
edition as quickly—or at all—even if the text is familiar from a
recent reading. We cannot do a search of lived experience and cut
and paste the results, here lies the bedrock of the epistemological
problems with texts. That means, essentially, if you have read
something and would like to find a passage two weeks later, you
will be able to find it only with difficulty. Memory taken from
texts by reading cannot be recalled with precision, the
photographic memory phenomenon notwithstanding. By means
of a *text search* feature, the keywords or phrases that can be re-

called from the reading experience can lead to the correct entry point into the text quickly.

So it is never the first experience of a text that can lead to anything approaching knowledge. The most one can hope for is a memorable experience. Only subsequent visits to the text can cement the experience of the text sufficiently to create some lasting, written explanation, some careful descriptive analysis. I don't mean to undercut enthusiasm and inspired rhetoric, and I am willing to be swept along; however, there is a sober side to the study of texts, all sorts of texts, studied over a long period. Memories of lunch will compete with memories of part 8, chapter 9 of *Anna Karenina.* This is not a bit of philistinism, merely an admission of the limits of the human perceptual processes and the glad acceptance of help from the computer. I am prepared to give a ten-minute head start to find a passage, printed book versus text file; go get the book, let's rumble.

So what is left in libraries that is not in electronic form? Well, quite a bit actually, but the argument stands; most research volumes that used to stand proudly in the architecturally impressive *Reading Rooms* can now be googled from home.

The market has been active in enabling technological innovation. It is easier to maintain a database than a card catalog. Drawers with paper rectangles do not scale up very well into the millions. Electronic encyclopedias became commercially feasible when Internet connections reached a certain level. Myriad other electronic sources are funded either by subscription or with public money. There are not vast amounts of money to be made in this area, but existing publishing obligations can be made more efficient, and costs can be covered with enough left over for the occasional luxury automobile and palatial country estate.

But let us remember, marketing cannot be an argument for scanning old books. In the realm of new books, it helps the sellers and the buyers, by informing the market and, very peripherally, keeping the eyeballs close to the Google logo. The market has to become efficient, and distribution has to be liberal, attractive, and welcoming. Rules that inhibit information about a product are in no one's interest. The argument that the market of uninformed buyers, buying things they don't need, is abridged, will, let us be hopeful, not sway the U.S. District Court.

Old Books

That said, the ground prepared, the field of investigation circumscribed, potential misunderstandings identified, potential false starts avoided, approaching the end, we can finally begin for real. In this discussion I would like to focus exclusively on those items scanned by Google (and, incidentally, by others) that are clearly out of copyright. The only "owners," the only legitimate claimants to residual benefits are those with the training and the ability to read, absorb and internalize them. This does not remove the topic from contention, on the contrary, but it does remove the naked self-interest that informs the copyright discussion. A considerable number of the ten million plus Google scans fall in that category. As European libraries are scanned and Europeans can be persuaded to let us download their PDFs, books of the 18th century and earlier will also become available; For them rare begins with the 17th century. Here the implications are tremendous for a small group of stakeholders: research libraries, used book sellers, photocopy providers, and scholars interested in texts older than one hundred years. The only potential losers are the used book sellers and the copier people. Perhaps there should be a law against providing free PDFs of expensive, rare, or hard-to-get books of the nineteenth century; I think not.

Booksellers will still have the purses of collectors to dip into, and working scholars will find other uses for their money. Let the shabby truth come out: old books are considered investments, to be bought cheap and sold dear, and working scholars not married to an heir/heiress were priced out of that market decades ago, and incidentally, Google had nothing to do with that. The photocopy business will undergo some changes as more and more electronic versions of journals and books come online. While this deprives libraries of considerable amounts of mad money, copying vast numbers of books and articles wastes money, paper, toner, and electricity, not to speak of time.

This leaves two potential winners: libraries and scholars. And winners they are, unless they fall into one of the many black holes that the Google universe contains, like searching for something with a famous namesake. Pity the person working on John Jones or Johann Johannson or the Bill Clintons not from Arkansas.

Libraries win because they can deliver their stock in trade more efficiently, thus overriding the losses in the copier revenue stream. [That is an attempt at a joke.] It is inevitable that the scholars, also clear winners, will eventually rather work with PDFs (or some even more elegant delivery system yet to be designed) on their laptop, than with brittle, often badly printed texts—although not all of them realize that yet. [That is not a joke.] Whoever says that one cannot read books on the computer has not done any serious text work with old books lately, and they are legion.

There is no magic in the printed book, just as there was no magic in the legal pad versus the keyboard. All the arguments about the importance of the hand and pen moving over the paper (manuscript preparation) have been exposed as bogus, not by logic or rhetoric, but by universal computer use for wpscript production. Similarly, the notion that information can be excerpted or assimilated from the handheld printed page better than from the laptop screen, will be shown to be unfounded. In fact, similar productivity gains are possible in the assimilation of old texts via laptop, as have been achieved via word processing in the production of new texts. It is merely a question of developing some virtuosity and reengineering old habits.

Not only can one keep several instances of the PDF reader open at the same time, even multiple instances of the same book can be open at the same time, with a little creativity. Pages can be enlarged at will to read small print, or broken print, or smudged sections, or tiny footnotes. It is easy to go from one part of the book to many others and back with a mouse click, and, for the paper junkies, any page can be printed out. For that matter, the entire book can be printed out.

I have been convinced of this by the experience of working with primary texts in PDF form from GBS and in working with electronic texts in general. In transcriptions it is possible to keep eye-skip to a minimum since the line to be copied is directly over/under the line to be written. Eye-skip still occurs, but is generally discovered while working on the next line, annoying, but unlike the medieval monks, we have the destructive backspace. PDFs are superior to microfilm for ease of use by a factor of ten. I can also work on texts that the library will not let out of the building. I don't have to be online to do my work. And, above all, I can work away from my desk, on the train, in the cafe, at the beach.

So let us recapitulate, just in case the reader missed the previous instances of this list. Repetition in my favorite rhetorical device. The topic is Google Books of the nineteenth century:

1. No copyright discussion, we concentrate on scanned books that are clearly out of copyright, books older than one hundred years.
2. Scanning recently published books (since 1923) is a completely different matter, with completely different implications, than scanning old books.
3. Google Book Search (and other book scanning projects) are big and getting bigger by the day.
4. The number of old books, scanned and available for free download and text searching, in many humanities fields is substantial.
5. Working with PDFs is better than with Gutenberg media pressed on dead trees.
6. Finding entry points into a text via searching key words is a great aid to interpretation of a text and the subsequent descriptive analysis.

Having recapitulated the ground rules of this discussion, let me sketch out the landscape from a different angle: there are problems with Google, for all its wonderful achievement. I don't want to minimize all the laudable activities of Google and Google's magnificent ongoing contributions to Web-life, from searching to epidemiology. I remain a fan. The problems I want to address have nothing to do with evil empiric world domination, privacy rights violation, or the disenfranchisement of authors.

The problems arise from the fundamental idea behind Google's phenomenal success. We should not forget that the Google founders are mathematicians first and billionaires second. They have a business manager who takes care of making money so they can do what they do best: crunch data. Their phenomenal success is not due to luck or chance, but due to the ability to spot trends in large amounts of data. Data mining is not done with picks and shovels but with mathematical formulas. The only luck involved in the success of the Google founders was being born into academic families and being at Stanford at an important phase of the development of the Web. The rest was an obsessive tendency to crunch data that no one else considered worth crunching. There's gold in them there Web pages.

The underlying philosophy can be stated relatively simply: Google will calculate and recalculate the significance of specific items of information, or Web pages for short, periodically, based partially on user demand, partially on references (links) to the page. That means there is no real permanent significance and no real permanent order. Market conditions (i.e., the interest of users as expressed by their queries and subsequent page viewing and linking) modified by tweakings of various motivations and legitimacy, determine the significance and the ordering. Since we, the eyeballs, are statistically like sheep, we will only use the first few hits Google presents, thus giving Google power effectively to decide what information we see, statistically speaking, and thus creating interest among advertisers.

While this simple thought has been found to be amazingly effective in dealing with the terabytes of information that have found their way to the Web in the last decade, problems arise when Google finds and ranks things on the Web that already have a fixed place assigned in the research libraries and of course in the humanities publishing and teaching enterprises. In the academic world, picking the first three hits will only get a *D-*. The good grades are given to those who can work through the whole list of hits, which is called bibliography in that world. Bibliographies also cannot be infinitely long, at some point, items of low relevance have to be excluded. The mention of an especially fetching leather chair and matching ottoman in a novel should not be shown as a low priority item in a query of the "history empire ottoman," no matter how low.

Before the people who should have stopped reading this long ago, arch a skeptical eyebrow, let me explain. Allow me to strengthen my argument for the skeptics by more precisely defining what I mean by *humanities* and *humanists*.

By humanities, generously understood, I mean the collective work in literature, philosophy, theology, art, history that has been going on for well over two millennia. This heritage of text operates under the assumption that the world makes sense and we can try to understand it. Though some may disagree with that proposition, had generations upon generations of scholars following Aristotle not tried to categorize and describe nature— an enterprise then known as philosophy—you would not have a cell-phone, for there would be no electricity except when lightning strikes your thatched hut.

The realm of humanists starts (narrowly defined) with what is preserved of the texts of the Greek thinkers before Socrates; it progresses through Aristotle, to the post-Roman church, to the establishment of European universities in the Middle Ages, to the humanists of the renaissance (when the enterprise really picked up steam), and finally, to the modern international research universities that have trained enough programmers and engineers and academics of all stripes to conceive the Web and write Google and build all the things that make modern life, for better or for worse.

Conclusion: Humanists and their predecessors have been studying masses of information for well over a thousand years.

So let's take a closer look:

humanists: 1,000 years, double that and add 500 if you go back to the Greeks (2500);

Google and Googlesque: 10 years, add 5 if you count Gopher and AltaVista (15).

This is not to devalue Google, to the contrary: humanists are helpless when it comes to modern marketing. No scholar of English literature will be able to calculate a hierarchy of information items concerning "digital cameras" or "bed and breakfast in Colorado" or "Shakespeare plays." And one cannot forget that millions of queries per day are sent over the Web and, for better or for worse, answers need to be provided for people all over the world on all subjects imaginable and not.

However, humanists do know their way into the past; they have organized information about myriad cultures, languages, and beliefs. They have worked on structuring information so that each generation can be trained to take up the work of the previous one. For all the internal critique of this system and all its shortcomings, we have filled out, if not fulfilled, some of the dreams and speculation of the great Greek thinkers who first dared to figure out their world.

So for Google, as something new in the intellectual landscape, it is an extraordinary achievement that some recalculated order arises from each query to meet the growing volume of ever shifting interests. In general, the users of Google are satisfied. Their satisfaction with Google is in fact reflected and passed on to the next user. Brilliant. The system works, money is being made, information is being delivered, and questions are being answered.

However, the recalculated ordering of a specific *market*, in the case of Google proper, a World Wide Web of Web pages, is not the only game in town, nor is it the only game that Google plays. Google does not recalculate the location of the Cross-Bronx Expressway in Google Maps, just because of the interest expressed by people in Connecticut wanting to get to New Jersey and vice versa. Google did not come upon the location of the Cross-Bronx by collecting mouse-clicks from users.

Some considerable number of people went to the trouble of putting the GPS coordinates of the Cross-Bronx along with every other street and alley in the Bronx and in the rest of the world into a database. Maps with street names were extant long before the Web. High-resolution satellite pictures of the world have come online in the last decades. Overlay the two, write all that is written on the map into a database, and don't forget the house numbers for each block, and every gas station, bank, dry-cleaner, and establishment of fine continental dining—and voila. The functionality of the GPS system and the Google extensions on the Web reflect centuries of work in cartography and uncounted thousands of hours of database work in recent years.

By the same token, humanists have spent considerable energy in organizing their domain. Each piece of text has its place in a modern research library; when that piece is not there, an error has occurred and must be fixed. Google map queries are actually similar to certain academic queries where quite precise information is requested and required. One looks at a map, generally to find a specific place. I would go to "Google the search engine" to find lakes in Northern Italy, but I would go to "Google maps" to look at the roads around Lago di Como or the address of a specific hotel. It is a matter of expectations. I may be looking for a long weekend at some lake, or I may be trying to figure out the route to a specific lake. Any serious delivery of scans of our textual heritage will have to reflect the order of our research libraries. At least in the realm of the older scans. Picking the top of the list is acceptable only for some situations; generally, the whole list has to be examined. This does not invalidate the fact that in the wisdom of Google, reflecting the interests of its mouse-clickers, *Romeo and Juliet* is number one on the Shakespeare hit-parade. This could change if Brad Pitt and Angelina Jolie were to do *Coriolanus*.

I don't really remember when I first used Google; I was using Alta-Vista, probably in the late nineties, having worked extensively with Gopher before, and I was pretty happy and fairly amazed at what I was getting. Then someone said: "Have you tried Google?" There was no going back. Google was just better, there were fewer redundancies, the screens were neater and somehow it always found what you were searching.

Initially there was some discussion of how they did it; at the time they did not have a large staff, and the final theory was that they were extremely clever and should keep on doing what they were doing. Who worried about the underlying philosophy?

Today, however, it would be irresponsible if the underlying idea of Google were not questioned, its implications examined, and suggestions for its extension offered. The comparison of Google and humanists above is an attempt to show how young Google is, in a world that has been organizing information for over two centuries. The Web burst upon us enabled by technical possibilities. Google burst upon us to meet the need to retrieve information from the Web. The structure of the Web contributes significantly to the methodologies of Google. Here lies the genius of Google—as well as the source of problems.

There is one more thing to be said of Google: it seems to be an organization operating outside inertia. In that regard it is in contrast to humanists and libraries which have lots of it. Inertia is the tendency of a moving body to stay in motion and a body at rest to stay at rest. In actual practice, it means that things tend to slow down and stop, and once stopped, it is hard to get them moving again. Google, without inertia or with unvarying inertia, seems to stay in motion, countering the laws that limit the rest of us. Someone at Google says, "...let's scan all books," starting at Harvard, Stanford, Michigan and whoever else wants to sign up, and no one says: "Are you nuts? That's more than ten million books." Instead they organize the work of libraries around the world, and they are doing it, at thousands of books a day. As one who understands inertia both personal and institutional, I am filled with admiration and wonder at all the projects Google is undertaking. Hey, I got an idea, lets do genomes! Lets do international epidemiology of infectious disease.

Since Google has shown us that it is possible to operate without inertia, we can assume that other information delivery organizations will spring up with similar powers. This will not stop until there is not a scrap of paper, or canvas, or clay tablet, or DNA strand on this planet that is not in electronic form and accessible with two mouse clicks. Google is expanding its scope to include more and more types of information.

So we must consider a typology of information. Let us keep it simple and do a clean division in two: the Web versus humanistic genres.

For the purposes of argument let us assume two kinds of information:

1. Loosely structured and thematically diverse
2. Tightly structured and thematically coherent.

Web information behind the Google one-line search screen is unstructured and diverse. The text of a novel published before 1923, exceptions notwithstanding, is tightly structured and thematically coherent. Let us not distract ourselves with technical definitions out of the realm of databases; novels were here first.

For the purpose of this argument let us also assume two contrasting types of questions:

1. Questions that help us get on with daily life. (e.g., How the heck do I get to Duluth? What is the boiling point of iron? Who was Grover Cleveland? What is the phone number of my best friend in high school? How many eggs in an omelet?)
2. Questions that deal with academic issues and that have to do with discovering complex relationships often obscured by time and prejudice and ignorance.

The purpose here is not to devalue one set of questions in favor of the other.

The irony is that both sets of questions require a search engine; a greater irony is that Google's one-line query screen, invaluable in the day-to-day, is equally invaluable in academic research, for many academic questions are of the first type. However, the academic needs search tools that have to be programmed differently from how they are in Google in its present incarnation. An interesting question is whether Google, as it expands into fields of thematically structured information, will adapt or whether some other engine will be more appropriate.

My first experience with network search engines that calculate (i.e., rank the significance of hits) was with Glimpse in the nineties. At the time, my goal was to put English and German novels on the net with a search and display interface that would expand students' interpretive abilities. The thought was that if you suspected some metaphor was significant, for example, "mother-of-pearl spread over the open shell of heaven" (Herman Broch's *Death of Virgil*, 1954), you simply enter the query string "mother-of-pearl" and get a nicely formatted list of all instances of the string in the text, surrounded by some lines of context.

In the Broch example, a query will yield some thirty hits that in turn yield a neat, convincing, thematic analysis of a novel that no one really understands. The mother-of-pearl theme trace is convincing, especially when coupled with some other queries that lay open the thematic structure of the text.

Glimpse was designed to search through large quantities of text, broken into arbitrarily large subdivisions, (e-mails, patient records, technical documentation, questionnaires, etc.) and bring out hits ranked in order of significance. A typical small application for Glimpse was to index the last eight years of e-mail. A query of "European parliament" will bring forth all the e-mails on that subject. The ranking was rather simple and depended on how often the term would appear in a particular mail. The mail with the highest count would be privileged.

Thus it would be easy to find relevant pieces of mail from the past and get up to speed on the discussion at the time. Since Glimpse was the only public domain, UNIX network search engine available at the time, I concluded it was worth a shot to try it with literary texts. Texts had to be marked up in a minimal form (i.e., split into individual files and passed to an indexing module.). The resulting files could be arranged on Web pages. Query windows could be opened, and simple or complex Boolean queries could be sent to Glimpse. The resulting output would be a neatly formatted list of hits with the key-word hit surrounded by a line of context and a link to the file, cursor postponed at the hit.

Since the system was intended as an interpretive aid for literature students, the queries were generally simple—crude but effective. For example, it was possible to discern that "money" in the sense of coins for purchase was limited primarily to Shakespeare's Comedies while the Histories used more generic terms like gold. While this insight is modest, it nonetheless can lead to fruitful speculation about the respective social classes in Shakespeare's plays and their relationship to wealth. The speculation is especially valuable since it could be buttressed by a definitive set of quotes from the plays. Dissertations have been written with less.

For all its modest success, the Glimpse system showed that it was adapted for humanistic purposes and that it was designed for other agenda. Initially, the page ranking was the main problem and attempts by our UNIX gurus to bypass the ranking feature proved difficult, or my attempts to be taken seriously by the UNIX system people on this point were seen as quixotic. Why would some moron want to disable the ranking feature? This alone speaks volumes since it indicates that ranking, not hum-drum boring searching, was the chief design criterion.

While I don't mind an algorithm trying to rank the hits from my e-mail archive, I have no use for an algorithm to rank the hits for "silver" and "gold" in *Henry V*. In unstructured information, some preliminary automatic ranking is acceptable; in structured data (in the humanistic sense of beginning, middle, and end), the ranking of hits is done by the user after careful and detailed inspection of the results. The great sensation, I used to say to whoever would listen, is that it is possible to upgrade your brain with some nifty computer peripherals. With Glimpse, as long as the hits per query were under fifteen, there was no problem, since it was possible to inspect the hits and see the location in the text although they were not chronological. With hits over one hundred, interpretation became almost impossible because the pattern of occurrence could not be perceived, forcing post-processing of the output list, as such, no real problem. In time the problem was solved—the right switch was set by the systems people, and Glimpse has ranked sequentially for the last decade.

For the humanist, a hit in the first paragraph is generally more significant than six hits somewhere in chapter five. A hit in the first paragraph of chapter five is generally more significant than five hits somewhere in the middle of chapter five, exceptions notwithstanding. In any case, it is the task of the user to determine the significance of a hit based on its place in the text and the surrounding context. The computer's job, in this rudimentary example, is to present the hits so the human user can spot the patterns of use. A possible corollary that extends the range of the computer would be: the computer presents patterns that escape the perceptual faculties of the reader and lets the reader evaluate their usefulness in analysis. Until ranking programs get much more sophisticated, and well they might, humanists will prefer well-formatted chronological lists, possibly supplemented by graphs or other spatial representation. Nix on ranking by the proverbial black box.

For me, the Glimpse experience was an example of the problems of adapting software designed for business and engineering to the demands of text scholarship. The lesson I drew from the experience was that humanists needed to write their own tools to meet the very specific needs of a specific text corpus. I learned the lesson and started programming my own algorithms with substantial modifications depending on whether the Minor Works of Dante, Judeo/Arabic texts from the Cairo Geniza,

Husserl, or a Romance by Chrétien were the target. So theoretically, the story could end here: humanist retires to the ivory tower, programs text search algorithms, and lives happily ever after. And he may yet. But the world does intrude; the omnivorous appetite of Google blurs once more the distinctions between the humanist and the rest of the users. By not limiting its scope to Web pages but including books of scholarly interest, the old discussion of the needs of humanist versus the needs of the rest has opened again.

Let me add one more example of this general problem of requirements before we return to the consideration of Google books in the present. If a corpus has unsystematic spelling, a mix of languages, or transcriptions from other alphabets, the one line query window will not work. In that case, queries can only be formulated after a close and detailed examination of a list of the extant strings in the text (i.e., a word list). A one line query window assumes two things: first, there is a common language between the user and the information; second, a complete and exhaustive list of results is *not* required.

To restate the point, when I query, "bed and breakfast in Colorado," I don't want all of the above, just a selection of about twenty. When I query "gold" in Henry V, I will not be successful until I have formulated a query based on the total semantic content of the play to include all synonyms, metaphors, and anything else that belongs to the semantic category of wealth. In my experience, the variant spellings in older texts make automatic semantic processors not reliable when compared to a complete semantic inventory of a specific corpus coupled with a patient humanist to sift through the data, regardless of volume. This may change with time.

So it is clear that the assumptions that Google makes when it presents the one line query window and the page rank processor, for all their effectiveness with everyday queries of unstructured data, is not sufficient for specific humanistic research. Nor should they be. Given the humanists' need to work with data structured in subtle ways and the need to receive complete and definitive results, the question arises: how can the two systems be brought into harmony?

Philosophy texts present a special problem. In contrast to mimetic texts, which can be compared to the world, philosophy texts describe an interior world of perceptions and relationships that can find no easy correlation in the visible world.

Clearly there is a conflict of the "statistical view" of things, all things including texts, and the humanistic view, or specifically, the philological view of texts.

Computational linguistics, marginally a humanities discipline, more properly a natural science or engineering discipline, as is linguistics proper, has no problem working with relatively small samples of texts and coming up with analyses based on these samples. The questions they ask and the answers they get (for example: text *xyz* was written by a high school graduate from Maine) do not improve by increasing the sample size. Alas, nor will ours, so let us return to the humanists.

There is an antiquarian side to the work of humanists that has resisted the introduction of sampling. There are, of course, exceptions of all sorts including epistemological radicals and militant skeptics, but the general ideology of most literature as well as philosophy people and the historians is that texts have a beginning, middle, and end; they can be read, they can be understood, and one must consider the whole thing, lest grievous error creep into analysis. Any analysis that misses an important point made in any one of hundreds of paragraphs will hear from some member of the profession who has not missed that important point.

It would be easy to assume an opposite position and counter that an empirical statistical sampling would be ever more reliable than the memory of individuals under the influence of hormones, perceptual dysfunctions, age-induced cognitive disabilities, and the whole range of idiosyncratic intentionalities rampant in universities. Even more radical positions are common.

Of course, there are statistical systems that are not dependent on sampling, but it is not easy to separate and keep grasp of various methodologies in the tumult of the marketplace of ideas.

Thus, it is possible to do a stylistic analysis of Virginia Wolf, based on various assumptions and techniques. The statistical view can look for recognizable features in a range of models. The philologist looks for themes, metaphors and a range of literary devices as well as patterns of occurrence, regular and anomalous, that hang in memory during reading. But it may take a power search through the whole text looking for repeating phrases to find two identical paragraphs in a novel. Granted, as I explained above, it is the strangest thing I have ever found.

Once the identical paragraphs are in front of the eyeballs, the statistical samplers are gone, as is the program that finds repeating patterns of words, what remains is the scholar rummaging through a text, often reread, to explain a strange feature in the narrative. Of course, the programs may be reactivated should new questions have to be asked of the text.

Clearly, the "thematically structured data" argument requires clean, proofread electronic files—files that can be created with off-the-shelf tools in a relatively short time. For a motivated operator, it is possible to do a scan every 15 seconds, yielding 240 scans per hour. Given that double pages will be scanned that gives us close to 500 pages per hour. The greater the care with scanning, the greater the accuracy of the OCR, and the translation of the images into actual electronic text. It is however possible to achieve raw, unprooofread, unpaginated text at a rate of 500 pages per hour. The subsequent cleanup of the text to make it useful in an indexing environment can vary with the quality of the images scanned. The quality of the images depends to a great degree on the quality of the source. Well-printed books generally can be processed quickly; given some virtuosity with text editors and the liberal use of clever macros, another hour will yield 500 pages of clean, unhyphenated, paginated text. Another hour to check all the footnotes, another hour to read through the wordlists and find errors. Fortunately, the errors an OCR program makes are different of the kinds of transposition errors humans make while writing and thus are easier to spot. Typical errors for OCR are m = rn, e=c, h=li; in other words, the inconsistent application of ink on paper causes the computer to fail to recognize letters in fairly predictable patterns.

This sort of work is quite useful and can pay off in big dividends as an aid to reading and all the post-reading extraction of information. It certainly is not possible to read 500 pages in an hour, trained speed-readers excepted. Yet the experience of reading, whatever the fidelity or randomness of the resulting memory, is essential to all analysis, expert or sophomoric. After reading and notes, working with a text revolves around tracking certain themes through the text. Of course, reading, the experience of letting each sentence of a text interact with the brain to produce a sort of lived experience initiated by the author and completed by the reader, can yield wildly different results. This is a well guarded secret of professional pedagogues concerned with texts. Their main technique is to tell students that if they just read well enough, they will understand what they read. At the same time, the pedagogues become the measure of whether something is understood correctly. The whole system is based on bluff and bluster, and it is really only some years after the PhD that you realize that reading is more problematical and that the transmission channel from author to reader is full of noise and that other aspects, other than understanding what you read, really fill the gaps created by the noise. Everything from the charisma of the teacher to a shared ideology to the will to have it be a certain way, are much more important than what some author years ago might have actually said—not even considering what the author might have actually meant.

One way to clean out the transmission noise and to hold back the ideologies or rhetorical enthusiasms is to do a thorough semantic inventory of the text. This involves creating a word-list, establishing the main semantic categories and their members, and looking for repeating phrases and doing the theme-trace.

The theme-trace is a technique that can be done with clean files and depends on the notion that in thematically structured data, elements must be introduced systematically. Thus, the integrity of the subject requires that no random elements are added to the discussion well into the discussion. If we are talking about pepperoni pizza, it is not permitted to consider the joys of mountain climbing in the sixty-seventh paragraph of the pizza treatise. If such digressions occur, they will be unearthed by a theme trace and can be evaluated.

The theme trace starts with the first paragraph and proceeds chronologically through the book. The themes in the first paragraph are identified and plotted in the rest of the text. Each paragraph is examined for new themes or old themes. Texts can be typed by their fidelity to the opening sentences or by their introduction of new things in the middle. Tentatively it is possible to identify a type of exploratory text that is used by the author to meander to some destination unknown at the beginning. This is different from a text that states its purpose and progresses towards its stated goal, which is neatly wrapped up at the end.

This sort of careful text work is not widely practiced. Various ideas about computers and texts assign the computer some sort of automatic processing role. Since that would abridge the autonomy of the reader, it is easy to reject such a role. In actual fact, after the computer is finished with some query or algorithmic process, it is the task of the reader, the one who gave the computer its task, to evaluate the results. The results must be examined critically and many queries yield no worthwhile insight. Yet the results of computer processes are generally not random since they represent some systematic examination of the text (all and-pairs, all time references, all adverbs and their verbs, all prepositional phrases with "in"). Such list and rereading at the entry points to the text of the items on the list can help in focusing the reading. At the same time, most readers do not know that they need help with their texts, and if they do feel they need help, they look in the wrong places, in ideology or in rhetoric, to get at certainty. That computers can lead the reader deep into a text by providing entry points for systematic rereading has not yet hit the charts.

And it is high time. Clean files are available from *Project Gutenberg* and uncounted other archival projects working on electronic editions of texts.

One could say that the canon is generally done, except for important texts of the twentieth century that are still cash cows for the descendents; as I have said before: one should really create a fund to buy these deserving heirs off so we can use electronic tools on these texts. The Google scans of library books produce OCR (i.e. non-image files of text that can be processed word by word) of variable quality. Modern editions or well printed older editions can be scanned and OCR'd with near perfect accuracy. The older the books that are scanned, the more problematical the print, the tighter the binding, the more uneven the paper, the worse will be the image scanned. And most important, the more careless the operator, the worse will be the text for searching.

The fact is that Google has scanned millions of books with bad OCR. So we can either reject the work, or try to read the images as an alternative to reading the original, which is not much better, but at least they can be magnified on the screen. Cleaning up the OCR of a million books is a work of pharaonic dimensions that makes doing the image scanning seem like a picnic by the lake. It is a project that should be started, even if it is finished only after the sun goes red giant.

So the temptation will be to work with faulty data, jettisoning the philological ideals of completeness and ignoring any standards demanded by the idea of thematically structured data. Let us mine what data there is. Clearly, the people doing the work have no allegiance to methodologies developed over the last two hundred years without computers. Computers are not there to augment existing methodologies; data is data and we can build OCR error rates of 50 to 80 percent into statistical analysis. So we may have the choice to insist on antiquated standards appropriate for an early phase of the analysis of texts, or go with the future and let the math whizzes at Google drag us off to horizons where we would never have gotten with reading, sloppy or careful.

So would it be possible to imagine a scenario where an algorithm could go through books, identifying features that could yield a satisfying ranking system? In other words, what is a real piece of "quality data" from Aristotle? Let's assume an unstructured collection of structured data: primary texts and secondary texts (books and articles), descriptive analyses and commentary of the primary texts and commentary of other secondary texts. To deal with this mass of unstructured data, scholars impose order. In annotated bibliographies, fields of research are summarized to allow students or scholars outside the field to come up to speed. However, it is not uncommon for there to be four annotated bibliographies on the same subject, covering different time periods or not.

At some point, dealing with this mix of commentary and counter-commentary becomes messy. There are, however, threads that run through all these texts, a system of citations unraveling in chronological order. Thus it is possible, at least in the rough, to define the parentage of ideas. Actually, it could even be phrased as a popularity algorithm. Texts in the past are ranked by the frequency in which they are quoted through the ages. What parts of Hegel are quoted by Marx himself or by generations of neo-Marxists to the present. What parts of the Greek tradition are quoted by Hegel and could have been passed on to unsuspecting Marxists or neo-Marxists? At present, such work is being done only haphazardly. Everyone has some idea what ideology some particular commentary presents, especially for things written in the thirties and forties. Should that be part of a field, students are generally trained to be aware of pitfalls.

Less well researched are traditions of specific quotes that are passed from generation to generation without awareness where the chain starts. Even misquotes or out of context quotes are sometimes passed on blithely. By mapping these threads, a comprehensive system could discover many bogus analyses and also discover the true innovators.

In another area it would be possible to renew the links between the retelling of history, which has to be done by each generation, and the sources of that retelling. By matching up citations to original sources [a chronicle written at the time of a specific Sultan of the Ottoman Empire] and the sentences of retelling, one can compare the sentences of retelling and discover examples of fidelity to sources or attempts to spin history for some identifiable agenda.

Such scenarios, however, demand perfect scans and perfect OCR of not just the text, but also the notes. Once that is done, it would be an easy database problem to fill up a specific sentence of Aristotle with a chronological list of all those who cited that sentence. For example, the first sentence of the *Metaphysics* and all translations of that sentence and all citations through the ages of that sentence. Clearly, much is done with translation; each age and each linguistic group spins Aristotle for their agenda. Thus Greek sentences of two and a half centuries ago can be loaded with the metaphoric *mouse clicks* of writers through the ages who have logged a citation.

Of course a look at that record would be revealing for the history of Aristotelians and various neo-Aristotelians.

It would also be interesting to see what other *-isms* have enlisted this sentence for their cause. It would be possible to find an *-ism* which finds its ideas from some other *-ism* but is not aware that there is some Aristotle DNA lurking in the past.

By starting Google Books, Google has opened a front where this question can be played out in detail. By scanning vast numbers of books and putting them behind its query interface, Google has entered an arena where the library catalog in its electronic incarnation (the OPAC) rules.

Google Books, in its present beta general search screen, does not differentiate between the title of an actual book, a bibliographical reference to that book, a phrase from any book, and a comment about that book. While this may seem horrific on its face, it does lead to some amazingly serendipitous discoveries that would be difficult and time-consuming to duplicate with traditional library tools and would require extensive training.

The OPAC, the card catalog, will present all instances of the work of an author in the collection nicely arranged in chronological order and subdivided according to the specifics of the case. It is, of course, also possible to query other OPAC fields that are in the underlying data structure called the MARC record. If the collection has a book by or about Shakespeare, for example, which does not show up on the results of the OPAC query string "Shakespeare", there is an error in the data, and a librarian needs to go and fix the MARC record. Human error aside, the OPAC is expected to yield definitive results. Theft of material items aside, the books on the shelf are expected to reflect the order in the OPAC.

So, what is the score in a hypothetical Google versus OPAC match. Please remember that our category for this round is "Books of the Nineteenth Century." Let us compare the outputs and analyze the results.

The Match

Ladies and Gentlemen! For the Undisputed Championship of the World of Information, tonight's title card. In the magenta, crimson, or maroon corner, representing generations of librarians selflessly ordering knowledge since 1636, the fourth largest library system in the world, ten million volumes and counting, from across the river from the great city of Boston, the catalog of the combined Harvard libraries, let's hear it for *HHHHHoooolllisssss.*

And in the blue, red, yellow, and green corner, barely ten years old and in the book game only since 2004, representing millions of unwashed and unkempt eyeballs on the screen who have no idea what a Harvard is, or a HOLLIS, but keep asking millions of questions anyway, and growing by thousands of books per working day, at present more than ten million entries, and adding more than a million books per year. From the Valley of Silicon, we have *GGGGGGGoooooogle Booooook Search.*

Okay, no low blows, and no medium-high blows either; break when I say *break*, let's make it a fair fight. Go to your corners and come out swinging at the mouse-click.

And here comes the first query, typed into the opening search box: "History Ottoman Empire." And they're off. And HOLLIS has reached its "search limit" and will only display the first 1,000 records; clearly miffed at such imprecision, HOLLIS surmises we would be advised to modify our search. And Google comes in with a whopping 13,900 hits, and HOLLIS' head is just bobbing from the whirlwind blows. And the referee shouts "Break! Break! Human perceptual limit for information exceeded." Google is restricted to "Full text view only." And Google presents 1920 hits, limited to "Full View" only.

Google's first hit is Edward Upham's *History of the Ottoman Empire, from Its Establishment, till the Year 1828.* Edinburgh, 1829.

If I were in a used book store, I would think I had scored a great coup. I have just shoplifted—I should say—been given at no charge, a rather rare volume. But, unfortunately, only the first volume of two. This is still the great mystery that puzzles this presentation, where is the second volume of this set and of every other multivolume set in GBS? I have arrived at the Twilight Zone Used Book Store where of all the multivolume sets only one volume is on the shelf. Still, things were really getting exciting for the Ottomans in the first decades of the nineteenth century, and besides, I like to be given complete sets.

In any case, we have landed Upham as the first hit. A little poking around in Google Books in a new window yields an obituary and several short biographical entries.

Hit 9 on the Google list is a review of Upham's *Ottoman History* in the *Edinburgh Literary Journal*, 1829. It is hard to know what to make of either the first volume or the review, without the bibliography which may be in the second volume. With the review, the obituary and the biographical entries we have enough to write an adequate Wikipedia entry—if we were to incline in such directions; I could imagine an enterprising undergraduate could weave a nice little paper on the British attitudes towards Turkey in the age of Byron and of Greek independence. Upham was a bookseller in Bath, and it is quite comical to hear his outrage at the end of the first volume, as he laments the loss of Corvinus's library of some thirty thousand items during the capture of Buda after the Battle of Mohacs, 1526. So we will put the book aside for further study, later, when the second volume appears out of the mists of Google. In any case, Upham would not be a proper beginning to a study of the Ottoman Empire. [Subsequent queries much later located volume two but no bibliography, a common practice at the time.]

The next three entries (GBS) come under the heading of pure serendipity: an 1835 catalog of the Library Company of Philadelphia, another 1835 catalog from London, and an 1826 catalog from Charleston. I actually have no idea where such books are actually stored in the library, nor would I want to take the time to find out. While this is also not something to be given to novices without lengthy contextualization, these three catalogs reflect fairly the state of knowledge about the Ottomans from serious historical works in the first quarter of the nineteenth century.

Cantemir, Knolles, and Ricaut were the main works before Hammer and Zinkeisen, in the nineteenth century and Iorgas later. For a historian it must be curious to imagine living at a time when working with a mere twenty books could give you the sum of what is generally known about the Turks in your time, a few exceptional contemporaries and several million Turks notwith-standing.

The third hit on the Google list is a Universal History, in twenty-five volumes, published in the midst of the Napoleonic times. *Universal History*, William Mavor, London, 1807. We happen to have the good luck to get at vol. 12 (and only vol. 12) - which contains the history of Korea, India, Japan, Hokkaido, and the Ottoman Empire in that order. From just a cursory glance at the contents it seems to be a history of the commerce to what was known at the time as the "East Indies." As such it should be extremely interesting, not so much about what is says about its historical subject but about the turn of the 19th century, and the early attitudes toward "East India" and the subsequent company of that name.

We could go on, [I hope the reader will initiate the query to accompany this reading] but let us summarize.

The "Full View" hits on "History Ottoman Empire" clearly yielded "high quality information," even in such a cursory examination. However, it yielded nothing that would not require extensive contextualization; as such, not really a problem. For general consumption, limiting the match with HOLLIS to the "Full View" is not workable. In its present state, GBS presents only a strange, albeit fascinating, grab bag of things that are available for downloading.

From the perspective of today, we have seen where the untrammeled nationalism rampant in all parts of Europe in the nineteenth century can lead. We can no longer read and believe histories from that time written from the perspective of Great Britain or France or Germany, for example, no matter how stylistically polished. So is Upham about to be discovered and take his place with Gibbon? This is where contextualization is required if the dormant are to be dug up again. This is not at all to say that they should not be dug up, quite to the contrary. We have made some progress in our understanding—or at least we know where some grievous errors were made.

Of course, if we were to query, "Geschichte Osmanischen Reiches," we would get one volume each of Hammer and Zinkeisen, who actually brought limited systematic methodologies to European Ottoman studies, but that would require more than passable German.

This brings up again the question of how the GBS is to be used. If it is to be analogous to the surface Web search engine with users typing any old thing to get some smattering of information to solve some peripheral question, that is not so hard to achieve. If GBS is to provide a relatively small number of experts and dilettantes with graphics files of rare books, it can exist securely in its niche, a sort of refuse heap of ideas and tendentious formulations of bygone times with a query and browse function.

However, since we do have clearly "high-brow" items represented in the antiquarian books, it would be a shame not to deliver "high-brow" information, information in great need of contextualization, information that can lead to some synthesis of understanding, an area commonly called higher education, taking 10 to 15 years of concentrated work with little reward. Bit by bit, this presentation is being herded into an area where tools already exist, having been built over centuries, and it will become a matter of adding value to the tools, unless by some stroke of algorithmic brilliance these tools can be transmogrified.

There is some validity in the argument that the Web and the electronic representation of text and images have really renewed education. The university buildings are still the same as they were one hundred years ago, but what goes on in them has changed dramatically under the impact of computers. The computer has brought profound methodological changes.

Information existed before the Web. Every scholar or hobby-ist had a drawer full of projects waiting for someone to come through the door and express interest. With the advent of the Web and personal Web pages, these projects as well as many publishing projects could develop an electronic existence separate from the paper publishing channels and all the closed doors and overhead of that world. Thus, information could be piped directly from the desk of a scholar to the eyeballs of many users, cutting out the middle persons. It became a brand new world with liberalized rules, with fewer gatekeepers, with Cerberuses wagging their tail, and with new opportunities. This development coincided with any number of standard reference works going online so that it became legitimate for reference librarians to suggest googling to seekers queuing at their counter. Thus we started to mix the vetted and the unvetted and many who could easily get vetted and printed chose not to for convenience sake.

Antiquarian books are potentially a similar phenomenon. Many are of no real interest. Any interest that is generated from a book not in the larger canon will not seriously upset existing scholarship in the short run. However, each set of antiquarian books that have become dormant also has a set of texts in close proximity that are active and are part of a field of study. Ideally, queries to Google books should lead into one of these fields of study and not exhaust itself with arguably bad books. The problem is that this is not the surface Web, nor the deep Web, but rather the realm of academic wizards and pedantic dragons that are suspicious of dilettantes and have only several years of hard training in store for aspiring novices. Their caves are littered with the blanched bones of those found unworthy.

However, let us stop daydreaming and focus on the match. Let us stay with the English works related to the string "history ottoman empire." This is, after all, a fight. If we include the "limited pre-view," which includes the snippet and the no preview, we get a more interesting landscape. The output of the query "History Ottoman Empire" is described below.

The first item on the "All Books" listing is Shaw and Shaw, 1976. We should say that modern history writing is pretty much a minefield especially in the Middle East. The Shaws produced a history that emphasized the national idea of Turkey and are widely celebrated for that. Stanford Shaw spent the years after becoming emeritus at UCLA as an honored professor in Turkey and was widely mourned at his death in 2007. The book is pretty safe for novices, lots of facts, uncomplicated conceptual schemes trying to extend the past into the present with all the attendant problems of such a project.

Fortunately, we can see only the first volume, so we don't get to the really contentious bits.

The title page is thoroughly ordinary, but the Table of Contents is hot, which means links take you to the chapter clicked. One click, and Google takes us to the first paragraphs of chapter 3 on Mehmet I (1413–1421), an unusual case among Ottoman Sultans who was attempting to restore some semblance of authority after the ravages of Tamerlane and married a Byzantine princess. The point is the text can be read—although some pages will be omitted—which is really the only thing at issue here.

There are double maps for downloading: "The Decline of the Ottoman Empire" and another, "The Rise of the Ottoman Empire."

And Google is not done yet, here comes Google map, ladies and gentlemen; this is a tag-team match. Google Maps shows us quotes from the book that mention place names and the corresponding spot marked on a map from Google Maps. This is actually a very promising feature, especially in Middle Eastern history where place names are a serious problem. Many sources, recent or ancient, treat place names cavalierly, under the assumption that everyone knows where these places are. Often there is no real attempt to make things clear to scholars trying to figure out who did what to whom and where. Adding to this problem is that each troupe that came through and conquered called these places something else—and early scribes often made mistakes. Place names are a real problem. It would be extremely interesting if Google maps were to acquire a historical dimension. There are cities that exist today that go back to before the ancient Greeks that have six names. What if Google maps could disambiguate all that?

Oh, oh, here we have a mistake. GBS was not able to close the hyphenation of "Germi-yan" in the OCR. So Germiyan (today Kirkuk) cannot be linked by Google Maps. We don't know how many points the judges will subtract for that one. But Google is not through.

In poking through the reviews on the automatic WorldCat link, one gets the impression that Shaw & Shaw has created some intense discussion, some outside of academic circles, including the delivery of an explosive device to the couple's residence in LA that remained harmless. Nonetheless, it is mentioned as the first comprehensive book on Ottoman history since Iorgas, whose 5 volume work was finished in 1913.

So this was quite a performance by Google. Clearly high quality information was delivered, and we are just on the first hit. Clearly we have been lucky.

HOLLIS is also an amazing tool. If I am trying to get a complete bibliographical record of something, my first click is HOLLIS.

By looking at the HOLLIS listings one can get a good impression of the dimensions of a field. The reordering of items by author, title, and year make it easy to find things quickly— even if being able to actually get the books in question is a remote dream.

On the HOLLIS query "History Ottoman Empire," the first twenty hits with the oldest first go all the way back to 1454—a manuscript and microfilm of ten manuscript pages with four different handwritings. I'll leave it at a *Wow!*

HOLLIS can obviously do alphabetically by author. Wow! [I hope the reader is initiating the query in another window.]

Below is a MARC record, the librarian's magic potion. When librarians are a little depressed and are given sufficient quantities of alcohol, they will admit that a percentage of MARC records contain errors. The percentage rises with the degree of depression and has topped at 78 percent. Nevertheless, the MARC record is an extremely valuable tool. It has a seemingly infinite number of fields that are infinitely extensible and can be parsed by computers, hence its usefulness—but more importantly, librarians have been filling in the electronic records for several decades in libraries all over the country.

Anything HOLLIS can do stems from this file. Much depends how busy the librarians have been. Much of the problems surround field 651, the subject field. All possible subject areas have been analyzed and potential entries created.

FMT BK
 LDR cam 22003494a 4500

001 011428839-9
005 20080506093811.0
008 071105s2008 njuab b 001 0 eng
010 |a 2007061028
015 |a GBA819776 |2 bnb
0167 |a 014524551 |2 Uk
020 |a 9780691134529 (alk. paper)
020 |a 0691134529 (alk. paper)
0350 |a ocn181142088
040 |a DLC |c DLC |d BTCTA |d BAKER |d YDXCP |d UKM |d C#P
043 |a a-tu---
05000 |a DR557 |b .H36 2008
08200 |a 956/.015 |2 22
1001 |a Hanioglu, M. Skr.
24512 |a A brief history of the late Ottoman empire / |c M. Skr Hanioglu.
260 |a Princeton : |b Princeton University Press, |c c2008.
300 |a xii, 241 p. : |b ill., maps ; |c 25 cm.
504 |a Includes bibliographical references (p. [217]-230) and index.
651 0 |a Turkey |x History |y 19th century.
651 0 |a Turkey |x History |y Ottoman Empire, 1288-1918.
049 |a HLSS
SYS 011428839

But the Marc Record is not a big deal, I think we get a better view with the Full view, which is more user friendly.

With HOLLIS, as with the Internet Archive, we have entered a realm of order. Chaos is not tolerated. Things are ordered alphabetically or numerically—that is it: author alphabetical, title alphabetical, date of publication: ascending—date of publication: descending. The user has a sense of control. Given the resources that have been poured into the libraries that HOLLIS represents, one can get a good idea of what books are out there in just about any field. The holdings go well into the Middle Ages, at least on film, and the contemporary publications seem all present and accounted for. However, HOLLIS eschews placing some items ahead of others. HOLLIS has no clue what is important and what is not. We have other listings in various fields that order and annotate resources. as well as reserve reading rooms to privilege sources. Given the inertia in libraries, it is not surprising that no one is thinking about adding features to the local OPAC to take into account recommendations from the faculty. So one could ask: *is the present OPAC sorting system sufficient and not to be extended?* One should ask: *is it sufficient to rank by alpha-numerics?*

Let us consider the notion that much of library use is really haphazard. There are twenty thousand students at a medium-sized public university. Half of them take some English literature course. There is an undergraduate library and a research library. Reading and research has to be spread out, given that for most monographs there is generally only one copy in the research library and possibly three in the undergraduate library, if it is a potential source in one of the large enrollment courses. One could imagine a world where some department would check circulation statistics, gather reshelving statistics, and integrate that infor-mation into a collection development strategy, beyond fielding requests from faculty. I can see the rolling eyes of librarians. Would we even be asking this question were it not for what Google offers in that direction?

One would wish one had the same HOLLIS type control with Google output. But here we are flat slam up against the idea of Google, an idea worth billions. A variation of the idea, a corollary to the original theorem is: we have each made several billion dollars with page rank, so please step off. We, B&P, rank things, and when *you* have made several billion dollars, you can write a program that lists things alphabetically or in descending order by date. Still, Google users will not be satisfied with the first page of hits. Some grouping by date, genre, and subject (information taken from the MARC record) would be desirable. Also, the back link phenomenon is missing, as opposed to linked

Web pages to indicate significance. I doubt that downloading statistics and the incorporation into the personal accounts will serve as reliable metrics for significance—although the idea is intriguing.

We have never considered libraries that had an infinite number of copies of each book. We have never considered a library where each text is indexed and searchable. Bibliographic searches can be done, and the equivalent of a stack carrel for a particular graduate student can be created. The professor might say: "You are now a graduate student in Medieval English History; here is your 240 GB external hard drive with all the books you will ever have to read." Even the reading patterns could be collected. When the computer decides that all pages have been turned, and the eye-tracking device is satisfied, the degree is awarded.

Given the problem of intentionality in human knowledge and the general unreliability of activity between the ears of humanists, I say let them rank, and perhaps they will come up with things that we cannot pick out of HOLLIS' well-ordered world.

And most amazingly, HOLLIS knows its limitations as Google does not. HOLLIS will never be more than an electronic card catalog. Or is this true? Google did blow into libraries and turned the operative inertia there to movement. Why should HOLLIS be immune?

But we are coming to the end of the Google-HOLLIS match, ladies and gentlemen, and it has been a bruiser. Both fighters are showing the strain.

[NB: Alas, for reasons not entirely clear, the HOLLIS links to Google Books now require a Harvard password. Perhaps this has to do with some policy of openness. Other institutions have passed the delivery of e-resources to third parties who also require institutional logins. I suspect some considerable fees are changing hands. This requires opening a separate window for Google queries. At first blush it does not reflect well on the technical competence in research libraries if computer work is farmed out. I dread the day when a login will be required for HOLLIS because the catalog is overwhelmed by outside queries.]

There you have it, a direct quote cut and pasted from a HOLLIS Full Record in 2009:

Discover more in Google Books

[full text available]

Discover more about this book

Pressing the button on Prof. Hanioglu's HOLLIS record takes you to a set of pages similar to that of the Shaws', this time done by Princeton instead of Cambridge. So really, with the exception of the neuralgic reaction of some defenders of the old order and some briefs by some very well-dressed lawyers defending their careers, there is no real problem with a conflict of traditional academics and wildly extravagant Google projects. Saner heads have prevailed. Function triumphs over form, and productivity is on the rise.

So there is no winner of the Information Smackdown except the users. GBS has performed extremely well, but I cannot give full marks. Again, we have an example of Google as the best of search engines and the worst of search engines. Shaw and Shaw comes in two volumes. HOLLIS clearly shows two volumes. Google, for all its ancillary dazzle, has no mention of volume two. Curiously, if you go to the Amazon site, it is quite possible to search through the second volume in an interface considerably different from GBS, imitating the Kindle. The table of contents, the index, and random pages are there. So the question persists, *why is GBS a single volume outfit?* (2009) But let us not obsess.

We are between the devil and the deep blue sea. Modern Books are commercial items to be bartered in the marketplace, MasterCard on the barrelhead. In an amazing concession, publishers, kicking and screaming, allowed snippet preview, which is basically useless. However, were I to order Shaw and Shaw, for example, I would get several pounds of dead tree. And were I able to buy an e-book, chances are I would not be able to integrate it into my electronic work environment except as a PDF file. But what I really need is an authoritative electronic text of the book so I can integrate it into my personal electronic workbench. And that goes counter to the current idea of *bartered item*.

Perhaps with Google Books, B&P are trying to create a test bed where we can get away from alphanumeric sorting, away from the scholar's hubris of knowing where everything is, and finally toward a page ranking that will find the pages that we are looking for and present a more comprehensively helpful group of bibliographical items for further study. In any case, GBS is not the end for libraries, scholarship, or brilliant reading and writing. To the contrary, it is a tentative beginning that may be due for a growth spurt that will create a gangly and awkward youngster who will continue to grow. The match is over; everyone please retire to their study to contemplate the electronic future and what they are doing to impede or further progress.

Where is Google Taking Antiquarian Books?

Since we have restricted our view to antiquarian books at times, we were able to concentrate in conclusion on the relationship of OPAC and GBS. The idea was to present a contest. We have determined that OPACs can sort alphanumerically with Booleans on any combination of fields in the MARC record. Thus, a definitive list in different subjects can be created. That list can be presented in any number of ways; however, as it is conceived presently, it will never be more than a simple-minded warehouse inventory program, as opposed to a sophisticated warehouse inventory program.

GBS really does two things: *rank* and *search*. Most of the outrage by the Europeans and by those who long for the good old Eurocentric days, has centered on Google's ranking. The suspicion is that it is possible to buy a high ranking, or that a particular demographic (e.g., American undergraduates studying the French Revolution) could skew ranking in a particular direction by clicking only their bibliography. That ranking could be insensitive to non-dominant cultures is also a concern.

Some people are going to a lot of trouble to create an adversarial relationship between an imagined use of sources that is commercially disinterested and not influenced by dominant demographics (e.g. the practices of European Ministries of Education), and a use of sources that is not arbitrary or indifferent to local mores (e.g. user based ranking). The notion that current French educational practice is culturally disinterested is too absurd to consider. To be afraid of the clicking power of American undergraduates privileging their reading lists over time seems plausible, but it can be feared only by European academics who may be drawn into the global information age.

One posits some Euro citizen scholar, untouched by modernity, happy in a social hierarchy derived from rigid class distinctions and not tempted to accept a teaching position in the United States. The legion who have fled to the US and are writing syllabi for undergraduates merely strengthen the sycophantic characteristics of those who stay. The library does not get involved in the messy business of privileging one book over the other. Every citizen scholar is a link between a mentor and information. The Ordinarius determines what is good and what is bad; the library provides, and librarians help find what is needed; the citizen scholar assimilates correctly structured information and writes appropriate monographs. The state under-finances education, sets the rules for employment and is pleased. Nobody switches jobs and nobody is ever fired. There is no hope to escape the progressive dumbing down of the cohorts of students which is embraced as socially just anti-elitism. In the race to the lowest common denominator there are not enough students from Asia to make everyone look bad except in the Conservatories.

So what alternatives exist to this scholarly utopia? At first the fear of information megaliths that have the technological expertise and the motivation to execute extraordinary projects around information must be overcome. The assumption is that the citizen scholar is too stupid to look through fifty antiquarian books. Citizen scholar will take the first three hits from a GBS query on the history of the French Revolution and will write the definitive history based on the Google sources, ruin the students in his or her charge, get thrown out of the profession (rather unlikely), and spend the rest of a wretched life living on a steam grate near the loading dock of the Pompidou Center.

What if the analogy to the surface Web is wrong? What if the people using GBS are not harried surface Web users who click only the first hit and then run on to the next thing that pops into their mind? What if GBS users are in fact browsing the used book store? They have walked up to the desk and ask the proprietor: "Got anything on Ottoman history?" The proprietor smiles and says: "Here are 1,500 items, but please don't write a definitive history based on the first three I hand you and eat out of a dumpster behind the Pompidou Center for the rest of your life." You smile back: "Thanks for the warning, not to worry." And then you start digging through the greatest trove of antiquarian books on the Ottoman Empire you have ever seen, and ideas for essays proliferate. You don't act stupidly but professionally, with circumspection. Let us hope citizen scholar will sense the empowerment of the prospect of a very large library of free sources.

So, perhaps the ranking is overrated as the driving force for users. What could be the driving force for Google to rank? Let's say that "limited preview" and "Full View" are used. Is Google trying to steer readers to a particular set of books? Is Shaw and Shaw a defensible first choice for a modern history of the Ottoman Empire? Or is Cambridge University Press paying off Google to sell its two-volume histories? Or is the *History of the Ottoman Empire* just one of many loss leaders for other lucrative placements of bestsellers. Let's be generous and grant Google some objective metric in picking Shaw & Shaw as first. Google has saved people a lot of time and wondering which history of the Ottoman Empire to read. The worst fears of academics are realized; the unanointed are empowered to find their own way.

So one could ask, if Google is selling rankings, is anyone paying for rank 10? Probably not. Perhaps we could ask, given that the Cambridge University Press sells books, is there some conflict between selling books and disseminating information or knowledge? No? If a CUP book shows up as a rank 1, is that bad?

If there is no real reason to fear ranking, especially among circumspect users, then what is there to fear about searching? The answer is: not a thing, nothing. Searching is good. Seek in electronic text and you will find.

Let us leave the discussion here, at a rhetorical low point. I have repeated the crucial points throughout, but I will be content to strike the summary that illuminates all since the future will come into view soon enough, at the earliest, with a ruling in the US District Court expected sometime in 2010, at the latest, gradually over the next decade. In the meantime I declare a Happy End.

e-BIBLIOGRAPHY WITH COMMENTS:

Links to the Darnton Essays:

The frequent, sometimes biannual, contributions to the *New York Review of Books* by Prof. Darnton go back to 1973. I have chosen three that deal with the same set of questions that Prof. Grafton wrestles to the ground, the position of "printed text" in the age of "electronic text" with the spectre of Google lurking everywhere.

I was somewhat disappointed not to be able to find Prof. Darnton's speech at the 2009 Frankfurt Book Fair online; I was puzzled really, until I discovered the collection of essays, published concurrently with the Book Fair. I am sure they were not hawked at the fair. His publishers probably have a clear idea that the book will sell modestly in the current climate. Of course, everyone has a right to make money; it is the American way, and Prof. Darnton should enjoy his monopoly over his own essays. One could argue that it is not a real monopoly since most of the essays are available online, gratis. However, it is curious that the MIT Press search of the *Daedalus* issues does not seem to recall "What is the History of the Book?" from Summer 1982. Inquiring minds want to read. I suspect restraint of trade, an attempt to lure us back into the stacks. However that may be (just having a bit of fun), given his starring role in the Google debate, his track record as a public intellectual, it would have been a splendid piece of statesmanship to have collected his essays into a Web site for the perusal of *les citoyens*. The e-book is available from Amazon for twelve dollars, the same price as one *Daedalus* article would cost.

The little volume is a disappointment on one level. The cover, which is intended to be clever, is in fact a gaffe that will insult every technologist with eyes to see and a heart to feel. The title, *A Case for Books*, is actually printed on the picture of a book with wires sticking out. If you look closely at the wires, it is clear that neither the Photoshop operator, nor the editors, nor Prof. Darnton noticed that the wires are total nonsense and an affront to all of us who own e-readers. It shows insensitivity to the delicate and fragile details of technology that should no longer be tolerated in the twenty-first century. First of all, book readers use mini USB connectors. Second, wires no longer just disappear into devices, they have connectors. Third, pasting a PC power cord connector next to a label clearly indicating a USB connection is the very height of contempt for the very ordered and rational community of technologists. Small wonder that Prof. Darnton longs for the reading rooms of the fifties; that book reader of his will never boot.

1. "The New Age of the Book," by Robert Darnton, *New York Review of Books*, March 18, 1999. [Darnton, 1999] http://www.nybooks.com/articles/546

2. "The Library in the New Age," by Robert Darnton, NYRB, June 12, 2008. [Darnton, 2008] http://www.nybooks.com/articles/21514

3. "Google & the Future of Books," by Robert Darnton, NYRB, February 12, 2009. [Darnton, 2009] http://www.nybooks.com/articles/22281

4. "The Future of Libraries," by Robert Darnton, Frankfurt Book Fair, October 2009. In: *The Case for Books*, Public Affairs, New York, 2009, available as e-book. [CB]

5. "Google and the New Digital Future," by Robert Darnton, NYRB, December 17, 2009. http://www.nybooks.com/articles/23518

Links to the Grafton Essays:

There are several texts to be mentioned in chronicling Prof. Grafton's engagement with Google Books and digital humanities. The list may grow, as it has grown since I innocently started writing a review of "Future Reading" over a year ago. Google Books formally ambushed me in 2007 and caused me to drop all sorts of projects to devote time and writing to understanding this phenomenon. A review of the literature is a convenient starting point and a help to many who simply do not know how to evaluate extremely recent trends. The pages Prof. Grafton has produced are substantial enough that they can serve as a basis of forming an opinion. Yet before we can accept the judgment of one of the authorities of our time on books and scholarship, we must make sure he has as firm a grasp of the present as he has of the past. All the texts save one are available for inspection on the Web; the *Daedalus* piece can be purchased for twelve dollars from MIT Press.

1. "Future Reading," by Anthony Grafton, *New Yorker*, November 5, 2007. [Grafton, 2007-1] http://www.newyorker.com/reporting/2007/11/05/071105 fa_fact_grafton?currentPage=all

2. "Adventures in Wonderland," by Anthony Grafton, *New Yorker* (online), November 5, 2007. [Grafton, 2007-2] http://www.newyorker.com/online/2007/11/05/071105on _onlineonly_grafton?currentPage=all

3. "Codex in Crisis," by Anthony Grafton, Harvard University Press, 2009. in *World Made by Words,* Harvard University Press, 2009, pp. 288–324. Limited edition published by Crumpled Press, New York, 2008. Not available electronically. [WMW]

4. *Authors@Google*, Anthony Grafton, hour lecture, February 12, 2009. http://www.youtube.com/watch?v=2tUCbClRPXg

5. "Google and the Judge," *New Yorker*, September 2009. [Grafton, 2009-1] http://www.newyorker.com/online/blogs/books/2009/09/ google-books-and-the-judge.html#entry-more

6. "Apocalypse in the Stacks? The Research Library in the Age of Google," by Anthony Grafton, *Daedalus*, Winter 2009. pp. 87–98. [Grafton, 2009-2] Available electronically from MIT Press, $12. Xerox at the library, $0.45]

Other Links:

"Libraries and Google," ed. Miller and Pellen, Hawforth Press, 2005, available online.

JN Jeanneney, "Google and the Myth of Universal Knowledge", University of Chicago Press, 2007 (Original French 2005). (For a serious review, of the original French, see or google David Berman, *D-Lib Magazine*, Dec. 2006).

"Scan This Book!" by Kevin Kelley, *New York Times Sunday Magazine*, May 14, 2006

> http://www.nytimes/2006/05/14/magazine/14publishing.html?_r=1&pagewanted=all

"Annals of Law. Google's Moon Shot: The Quest for the Universal Library," by J. Toobin, *New Yorker*, Feb. 5, 2007.

> http://www.newyorker.com/reporting/2007/02/05/070205fa_fact_toobin#ixzz0cVupagoa

The European Library, by Ioanna Mamali Mueller, 2007.

"A Library to Last Forever," by Sergei Brin, *New York Times* op-ed October 8, 2009.

> http://www.nytimes.com/2009/10/09/opinion/09brin.html

Charles W. Bailey, *Google Book Search Bibliography*.

> http://digital-scholarship.org/gbsb/gbsb.htm

www.ingramcontent.com/pod-product-compliance
Lightning Source LLC
Chambersburg PA
CBHW051045050326
40690CB00006B/606